MW00528134

MUSTANG

RECOGNITION GUIDE
1965 - 1973

BY: Larry Dobbs, Donald Farr, Jerry Heasley, Rick Kopec

A year-by-year, model-by-model, review of Ford's fabulous Mustang in pictorial detail.

MUSTANG RECOGNITION GUIDE
1965-1973

By Larry Dobbs, Donald Farr,
Jerry Heasley, Rick Kopec

PHOTOGRAPHY
Tom Corcoran, John Eaton, Donald Farr, Gary Hanson, Jerry Heasley, and Rick Kopec. A special thanks to Bill Buffa and the rest of the Ford PhotoMedia staff who produced the beautiful Ford photographs that are reproduced in this book.

Compiling a book of the technical complexity exhibited by this volume is a major task. These are a few of the people who helped make it possible: Bob Aliberto, Glenn Bornemann, Jim Bridges, Jay Brown, Eddie Caheely, Richard Conway, Paul Duprey, Ford Motor Company, David Fowler, Mickey Graphia, J.R. Gillespie, Jim Greenly, Tom Horne, Dr. Dan R. Jones, Paul McLaughlin, Brad Mobley, Ted Musial, Paul Newitt, Jim Osborne, Jerry Ostalecki, Bob Page, Danny Rockett, Bobby Spedale, Steve Strange, George Wahl, and Jim Wicks.

Library of Congress Catalog Card Number: 90-86322
ISBN 0-9624908-2-2
(PREVIOUSLY ISBN 0-941596-00-1)

Published by
CALIFORNIA MUSTANG
SALES AND PARTS, INC.

Printed and bound in the United States of America.

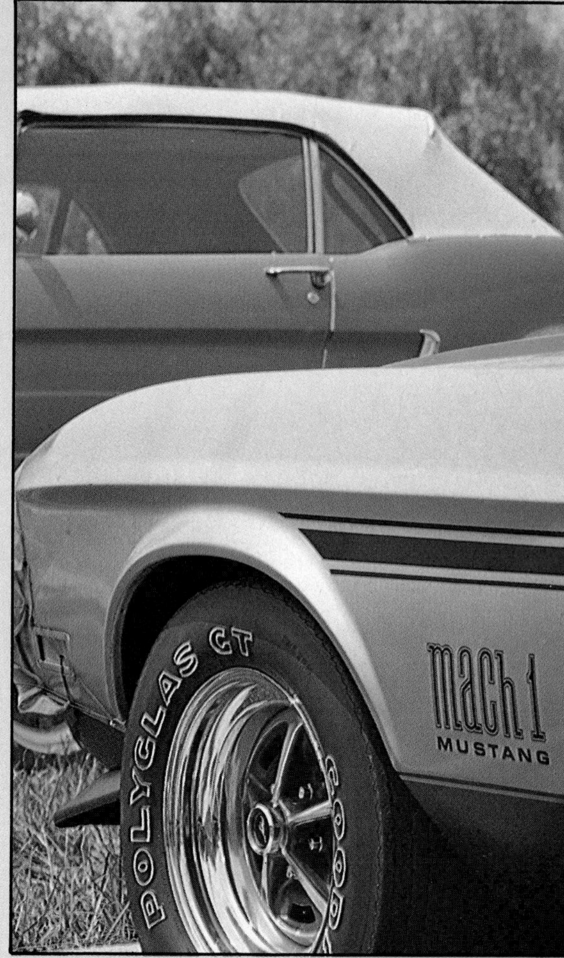

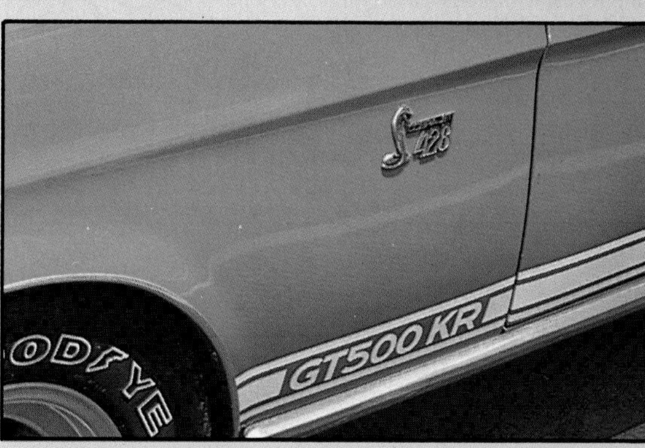

CONTENTS

MUSTANG
PUBLICATIONS, INC.
410 BRANNEN ROAD
MUSTANG MONTHLY
G.T. 500
GOODYEAR

FOREWORD

Donald Farr

Larry Dobbs

"1964" THE PREDICTION: "Expect to see the Ford Mustang going everywhere. . .doing everything. . .with just about everybody!". . .FORD MOTOR COMPANY.

"Americans will have to be deaf, dumb and blind to avoid the Mustang name.". . .Newsweek Magazine.

THE REACTION: Between April 17th, of 1964 and August of 1973, Ford Motor Company produced 3,000,000 first generation Mustangs. Buyers were anxious to prove the accuracy of the optimistic predictions.

THE RESULT: The Mustang became the most popular new car ever. Today, auto enthusiasts looking for a car with classic styling are selecting the Mustang; and those seeking transportation from a car with simplicity and dependability are rediscovering Ford's Mustang.

INTRODUCTION

by Jerry Heasley

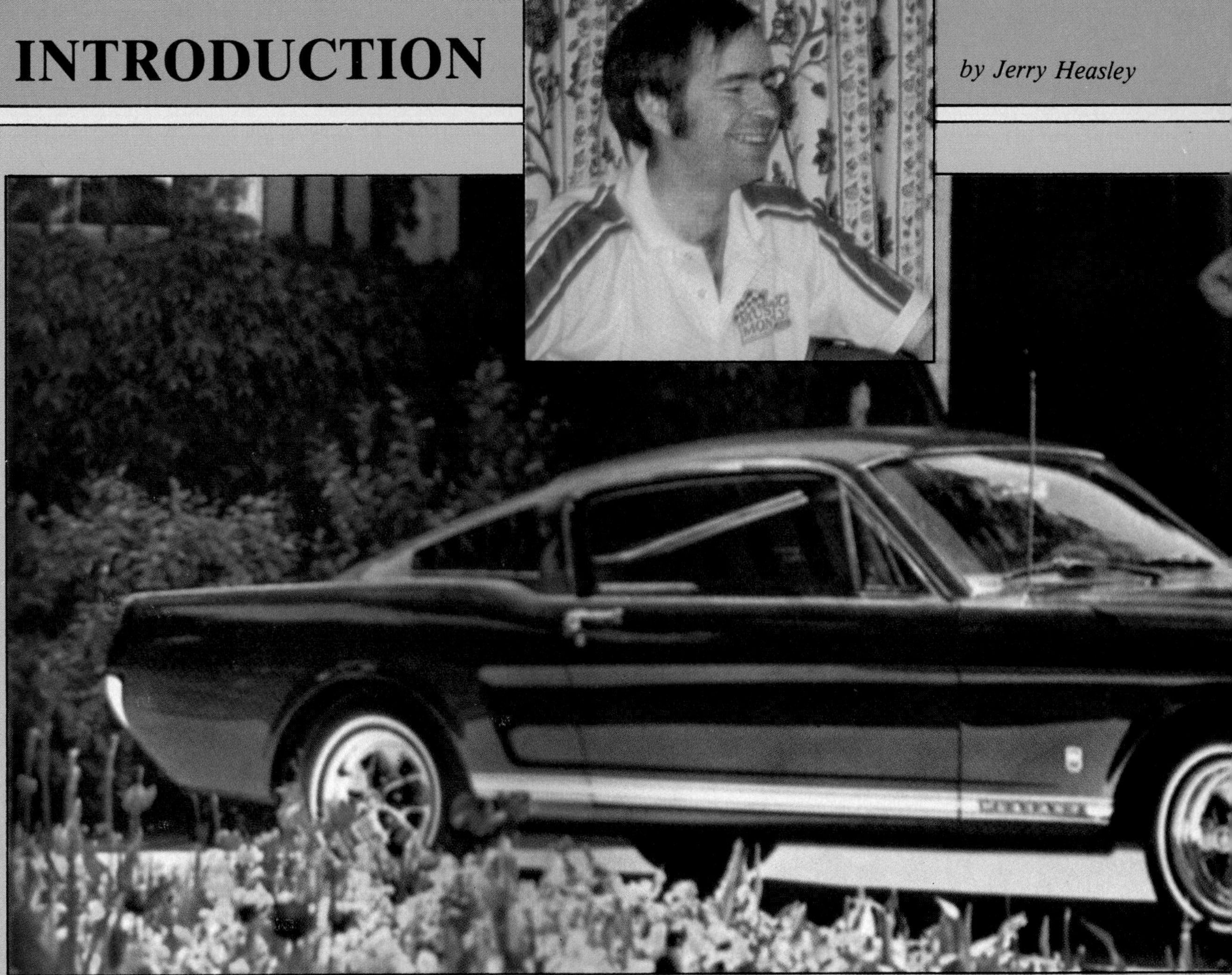

The 1965/1966 Mustang is easily the most recognized car of the entire post war era. It was "the" trendsetter of the 1960's, and it spawned a whole group of domestic ponycar competitors — the Chevrolet Camaro, Pontiac Firebird, Plymouth Barracuda, AMC Javelin, Mercury Cougar, Dodge Challenger.

After 1966, and through 1973, the look evolved (a restyling generally every two years), but the Mustang success formula remained the same: Build a sporty coupe with clean lines and a youthful image, but with the practical four-seater capacity of a compact, then load it with enough options and accessories to allow buyers to order-form whatever type of compact they desired — from luxury to economy, from sporty car to family car.

New car buyers went crazy with the Mustang back in 1965, and the fascination continued right through the entire first generation.

Likewise, today's driver is attracted to the 1965-1973 models — and for many of the same reasons that seduced new car buyers. Of course, the body style, model year, and specific options and accessories make for a large number of different Mustangs. Therefore, in this book we intend to "recognize" each of these cars, but first we'll condense and summarize many of the facts that created the Mustang. It's an important part of a recognition guide.

PRE-MUSTANG

As early as 1960 it was a hunch, an idea in the mind of Lee Iacocca that a market existed for a small and inexpensive personal car, one with the flashy good looks of the two seater Thunderbirds of 1955-1956-1957. But this time, the car would hold four people (instead of two), and it would retail for the price of an economy car (instead of a luxury car). Iacocca appropriately termed it, "a sports car for the masses."

No doubt, the first Thunderbirds had been great image builders for Ford Motor Company, even outselling the Chevrolet Corvette by about a ten to one margin. Everybody liked those old "T-Birds". And a major part of Iacocca's new "Total Performance" Ford image was to introduce some similar package to the then old-fashioned Ford line-up inherited from former Ford Division general manager Robert S. McNamara. In fact, for several months Iacocca toyed with the idea of a four place version of the old 1957 Thunderbird,

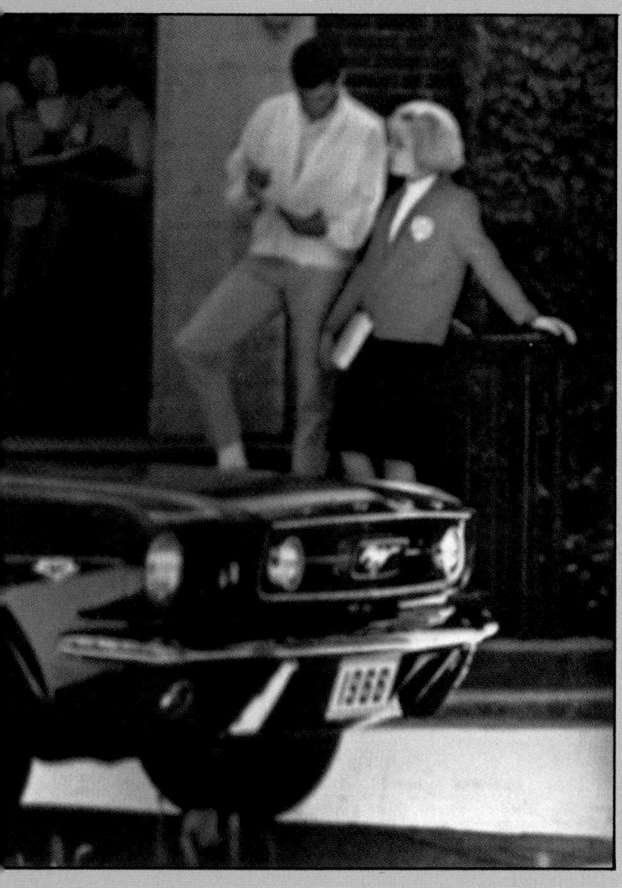

mated to a 1961 Ford Falcon chassis. That was the so-called "XT-Bird" that Iacocca finally flatly rejected because the finished prototype vehicle proved for practical purposes another two-seater itself, fitted with a pair of tiny child-size jump seats and a convertible top. Flashy and sporty? Yes. But a high volume seller? No.

By 1961, it was evident that a whole new car was needed, not a stretched version of the old Thunderbird. Iacocca and Ford executives wanted desperately to counter the success of the bucket-seated Corvair Monza, introduced early in 1961. Now Chevrolet had another sporty, youth-oriented model to go with their already smashing Corvette sports car. Even Studebaker had an exotic, sporty four-place coupe in their Avanti. Exciting cars they were, but from $500 to $1500 more than the car envisioned by Iacocca. His less expensive, sporty, personal car would have a much greater market. Yes, it would draw sales from a Corvair Monza, a Studebaker Avanti, perhaps even cutting into sales of the two-place Corvette. But it would not be a competitive counterpart to any of these sporty automobiles, nor would it compete with any other automobile in the world.

Still, before Ford Motor Company would invest perhaps fifty to one hundred million dollars into a totally new car, they wanted to make sure it would sell. The Edsel fiasco of 1958-1960 was a painful corporate reminder of a new concept car without the necessary market, red-inking Ford Company ledgers about a quarter billion dollars. And remember, it had been extensive market research that had helped to foster the Edsel!

Therefore, in the final analysis, it was the enthusiasm and promotional talents and power of Ford Division general manager Lee Iacocca, combined with positive feedback from market research that won the go-ahead from the corporation to productionalize a new sporty compact. In fact, that's why we call Lee Iacocca the "father of the Mustang."

MUSTANG DEVELOPMENT

The new sporty Ford was to fit somewhere between an all-out, two-place sports machine (such as the Mustang 1, a British sports car, and the XT-Bird), and the sporty versions of the more conventional compacts, which included the new Falcon.

Still, the new Ford had to have that right look, and the Median and Allegro series of clays (among others) fell short of Iacocca's approval. What Iacocca wanted to see was a sporty but classy little coupe, perhaps with the air of an early Thunderbird, or with the crisp, debonair lines of a Mark I or a Mark II Lincoln Continental. After more than a dozen renderings, the Median and Allegro series were finally scrapped, and a new series of clays were begun, with a fresh approach.

However, significant progress had already been made. In the Mustang I, you can see that characteristic side sculpturing and Mustang running horse (on the front fenders) that became a part of the first production car. Even more significant perhaps was the name — here was the first Ford to carry the Mustang logo. Originally conceived as a possible Ford production sports car for the domestic market, the Mustang I became more of an engineering show car. You've heard of its smashing acceptance by the public at Watkins Glen in 1963. With exotic features such as a tubular steel frame, V-4 Taunus/Cardinal engine mounted "amidships", transaxle, aluminum body, integral roll bar, magnesium wheels, and much more, this car showed the public the new performance look of Ford, helping to advance the youthful performance image of a new Ford called Mustang.

STARTING OVER

After more than a year of studying development and idea cars, four styling studios with FoMoCo were invited to build clay models — but this time in competi-

tion. Their new design was to produce a car to fit the following parameters:

1) A price less than $2500.
2) A length less than 180 inches overall.
3) Four passenger capacity.
4) Bucket seats in front, and bench seats in rear.
5) A floorshift.
6) A peppy six cylinder engine standard, with room for an optional V-8.
7) A distinctive sporty look employing the long hood, short deck styling theme.
8) A long option/accessory list.

The four studios involved were the following: 1) Ford Division, 2) Lincoln/Mercury, 3) Corporate Projects, and 4) Advanced Styling. From this point (August 2, 1962) development moved swiftly. In about two weeks (August 16, 1962), seven clay models were ready, and one was chosen. It was the "Cougar", submitted by Ford Division Studios (David Ash, executive designer; Gail Halderman, Ford car manager; and Joe Oros, head of Ford and Lincoln/Mercury design).

Of course, the name Cougar was later changed, first to Torino (or Turino in some renderings), then later to Mustang. For a time, "T-5" was also a likely choice, since "Project T-5" had been the early code name for the sporty car envisioned by Iacocca.

In September, the clay model "Cougar" of Ford Studios was approved, and engineering would soon begin the job of tooling for projection. Also, several running prototypes of the Cougar were built — one of which became the fabulous Mustang II show car.

The boys at engineering now entered the picture, their task to keep intact the style and clean lines of the "Cougar". Already Ford planned to use previously engineered components from the Falcon and Fairlane car lines — chassis, engine, transmission, suspension, even some dash and interior components. (It's what inspired one writer to call the new Mustang a "Falcobra".) Using the components produced through previous light car engineering held down geometrically on production costs, as well as shortening engineering time, allowing Ford to put the car in dealer showrooms in the short time of about eighteen months — from about September of 1962 to about April of 1964 — and at a base price under that magic $2500 mark. As the car took shape, it was obvious to automen that Ford had a winner, but it was the car-buying public who would make or break the new compact Mustang. Had market research and Iacocca guessed right?

DEBUT

Friday, April 17, 1964 was sales day one, and Ford dealer showrooms from coast-to-coast were crowded with people eager to see the new Mustang in person. Of course, by the 17th, the public had already been bombarded by sights and sounds of the new Ford Mustang via a major media blitz of publicity — in magazines, network television, and newspapers. As you know, TIME and NEWSWEEK carried simultaneous cover stories on the new Mustang in their April 17th editions. Plus, other national magazines carried major and minor articles — LIFE, LOOK, ROAD & TRACK, CAR LIFE, CAR AND DRIVER, SPORTS CAR, MOTOR TREND, POPULAR HOT RODDING, ESQUIRE, SERVICE STATION MANAGEMENT, SPORT ILLUSTRATED, SPEED AND CUSTOM, SPORTS CAR GRAPHIC. Plus, Ford bought-out the complete advertising in the 9:30 to 10:00 p.m. time slot on the television networks (ABC, NBC, & CBS). If you're curious, the three shows were "Hazel", "Jimmy Dean", and "Perry Mason". Ads also appeared in about 2600 newspapers, in approximately 2200 markets across the country, plus ads in 24 national magazines, contributing to more publicity than ever for a new model car.

Due partly to this positive exposure, and also to the real life market and need for this new type of car, the Mustang climbed to one of the top five selling models in the country. Perhaps Mustang could have been #1, in fact, had Ford been able to build the cars fast enough. Demand certainly outstripped supply in that first model year. A Ford Motor Company college resource paper, published in 1974, here gives some specifics of the frenzy of excitement caused by the arrival of the new Ford ponycar in dealer showrooms:

1) In Chicago: A Ford dealer felt he had to "lock the doors of the Mustangs in his showroom because so many people were crowding into the cars at once that they were in danger of hurting themselves."
2) In Pittsburgh: A Ford dealer could not get a Mustang off the wash rack, "because of the crowd of people pressing below."

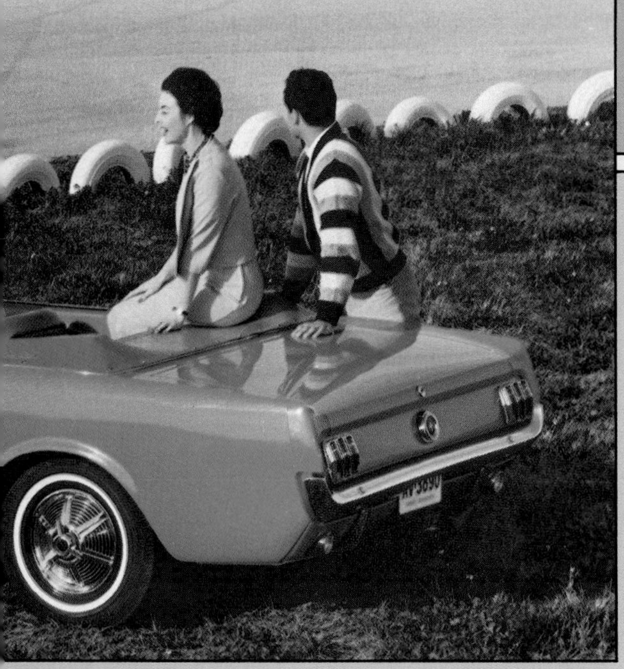

3) In San Francisco: A truck driver, "apparently thrown into a trance by the sight of the car, could not take his eyes away, and drove his truck straight through the showroom window."

4) In Garland, Texas: Fifteen eager buyers bid for the last Mustang in the show window, with the winning buyer sleeping in his new Mustang until his check cleared the bank in the morning.

MUSTANGS TODAY

Today, drivers are constantly discovering (or re-discovering) the Ford Mustang. That's why it might be unwise to park your sharp Mustang on a used car lot — unless you really want to sell it. You could be in for a dose of that same hysteria that afflicted new car buyers. Even the media coverage that engulfed each new model has returned. Witness "Mustang Monthly" magazine, and the very book that you are reading.

Of course, the original 1965 Mustang holds a special niche in automotive history, and it is a favorite to many thousands of enthusiasts today. But through 1973, the so-called "first generation" Mustang remained, evolving and changing with each model year but still every inch a Mustang, still exciting and gathering an enthusiastic following. Other automakers imitated Ford's original ponycar, but the Mustang stayed on top of the sales charts throughout that entire 1964½-1973 era.

It's the wide range of different types of Mustangs, coupled with the mega-production (almost three million!) that makes the marque so possible today to hundreds of thousands. In fact, here's where the Mustang gains such an edge in popularity over Corvettes, and hoardes of other hot collector cars of the post war era — in sheer numbers! So many more drivers can buy and drive a Mustang! Prices vary from very low (say three figures) to very high (say five figures).

It was the extremely long option/accessory list (through nine and one half model years) spread over three body styles, that created such a diverse mix of Mustangs for today. When new, you could order-form an economy car, a sporty car, a family car, a luxury car — or any combination the varied order-form would allow.

MUSTANG RECOGNITION

Therefore, what today's Mustang owner needs is a "recognition" guide, to chronicle each model year/body style combination, with complete details on options and accessories. No matter what Mustang you own, we intend to "recognize" it here.

Each chapter covers comprehensively a single model year, with chapter one taking-in 1964½ and 1965. However, even the so-called '64½'s are coded "5" on the VIN (Vehicle Identification Number), effectively making for an extended model year. But since many minor and some major differences exist between "early" (say '64½), and late (say '65) first year Mustangs, we have also recognized many of these details.

Each chapter will begin with a short lead-in, prefacing the model year with the purpose of its existence. Then complete details will follow on that model. These facts and figures are gathered from the extensive files of "Mustang Monthly" magazine, from a wide variety of sources — including original factory sales brochures, dealer brochures, showroom catalogs (dealer catalogs), Ford Car Facts Books, owners manuals, owners newsletters, shop manuals, soft trim books, Ford and Mustang related club and automotive publications, and more.

Complete details on body styles, exterior features, interior appointments, drivetrain and suspension details, etc are included. Even facts on the interior of the trunks and the type and style of the wheels are here — plus recognition of other important mechanical details, from the cooling system to the exhaust system.

Of course, the specialty models are detailed here too — the GT's, Boss 302's, Boss 429's, Boss 351's, Grande's, Mach I's, the California Special, and the fabulous Shelby's — plus more.

Each chapter and model year will contain options and accessories, dealer and factory installed. One important point to bring out here is that an option is defined as a component that replaces part of the standard equipment, while an accessory is defined as an extra component that is added to the car to improve its beauty or usefulness.

As you know, the Mustang was restyled in 1967, 1969, and 1971, making for four different groups of similarly styled cars within the first generation. These major groups are divided into the following years:

1965-1966 1967-1968 1969-1970 1971-1973

Still, this book devotes a complete chapter to each model year. We think this arrangement will better recognize each of the various Mustangs in more detail. As this recognition guide will so well reveal, the 1964½ to 1973 Mustangs are one complicated bunch of cars to describe comprehensively.

1965

The purpose of the original Ford Mustang is clear. It was built to capture a new market, which was emerging in America in the early 1960's — a market first realized by automen like Lee Iacocca (and DeLorean over at Pontiac) and later underlined by extensive market research. Primarily, this new market was thought to consist of the millions of young people who were entering car buying age — the young people from the often-called "post war baby boom". No doubt, the first Mustangs catered to this huge group.

However, as Iacocca well knew, and as market research reported, the growth of the multiple car family was also a big factor. As families became more affluent in the 1960's, there was a growing need for smaller, second cars, for carrying groceries,

or for shuttling kids to and from school.

Therefore, initially the Mustang was styled to appeal to as wide a base of buyers as possible — young and old. With three body styles and a lengthy and varied option/accessory list, the buyer could build his own sporty compact, right there on the order form. It definitely had a youthful image, for Ford automen knew well the adage: "You can sell a young man's car to an old man, but you can't sell an old man's car to a young man."

To further boost the performance image of the Mustang, Ford commissioned Carroll Shelby to produce a special two-seat, fastback Mustang, which was ready in early calendar year 1965. This "Mustang GT350", would answer the Corvette — on the street, and in SCCA (Sports Car Club of America) "B" production racing.

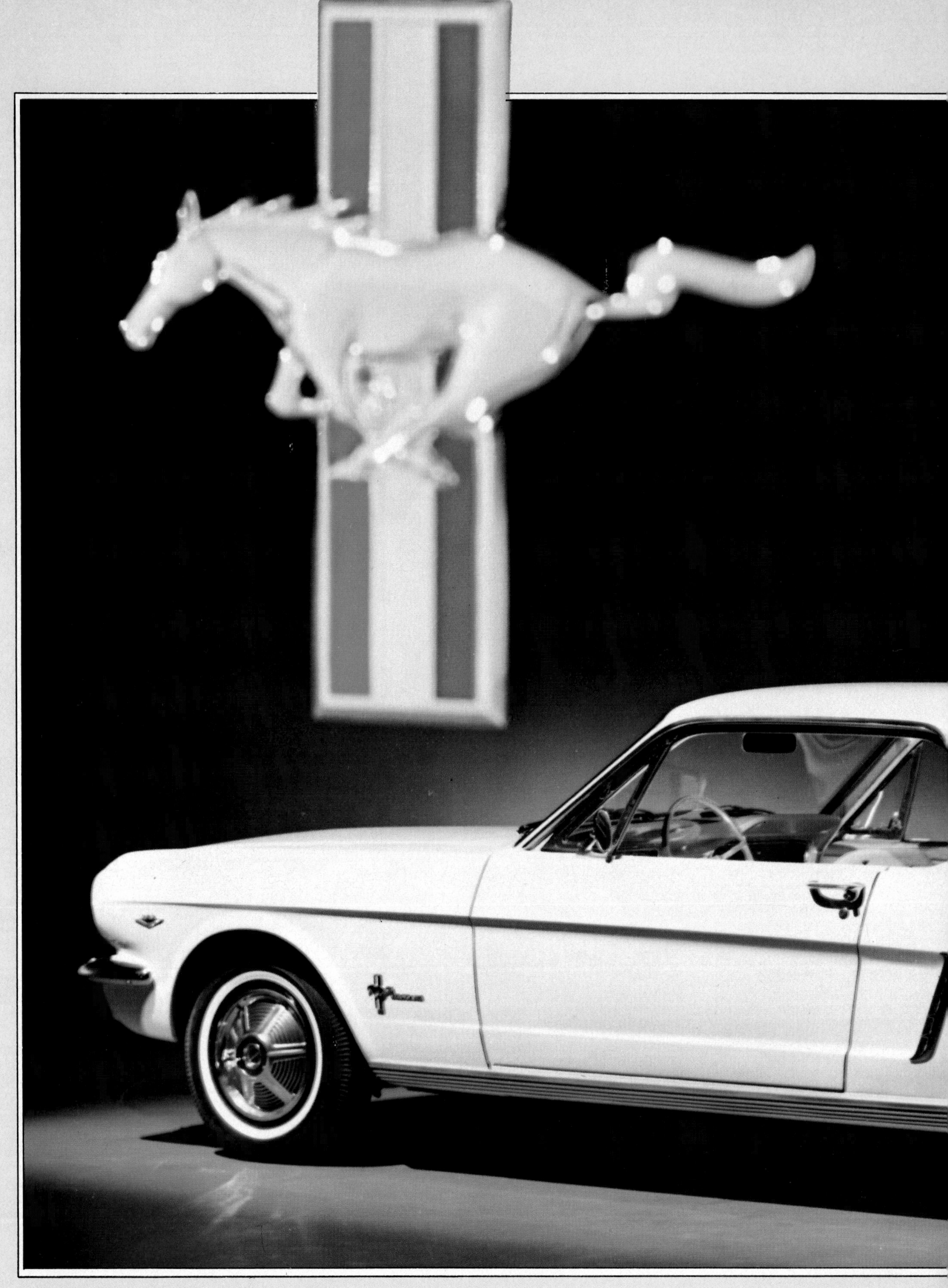

Did Ford Motor Company really manufacture a '64½ Mustang? Ask a Purist of early Mustangs that question and you'll be answered emphatically, "Yes"! Now, try to find a Mustang bearing a 1964 model year code, or one titled as a 1964, and you'll have a long search. But, there is something that is unique to the early 1965 Mustangs. They were produced on the same assembly lines, simultaneously with 1964 Fords. So, although sold and titled as '65s, these 1965 Mustangs are actually of the 1964 production era.

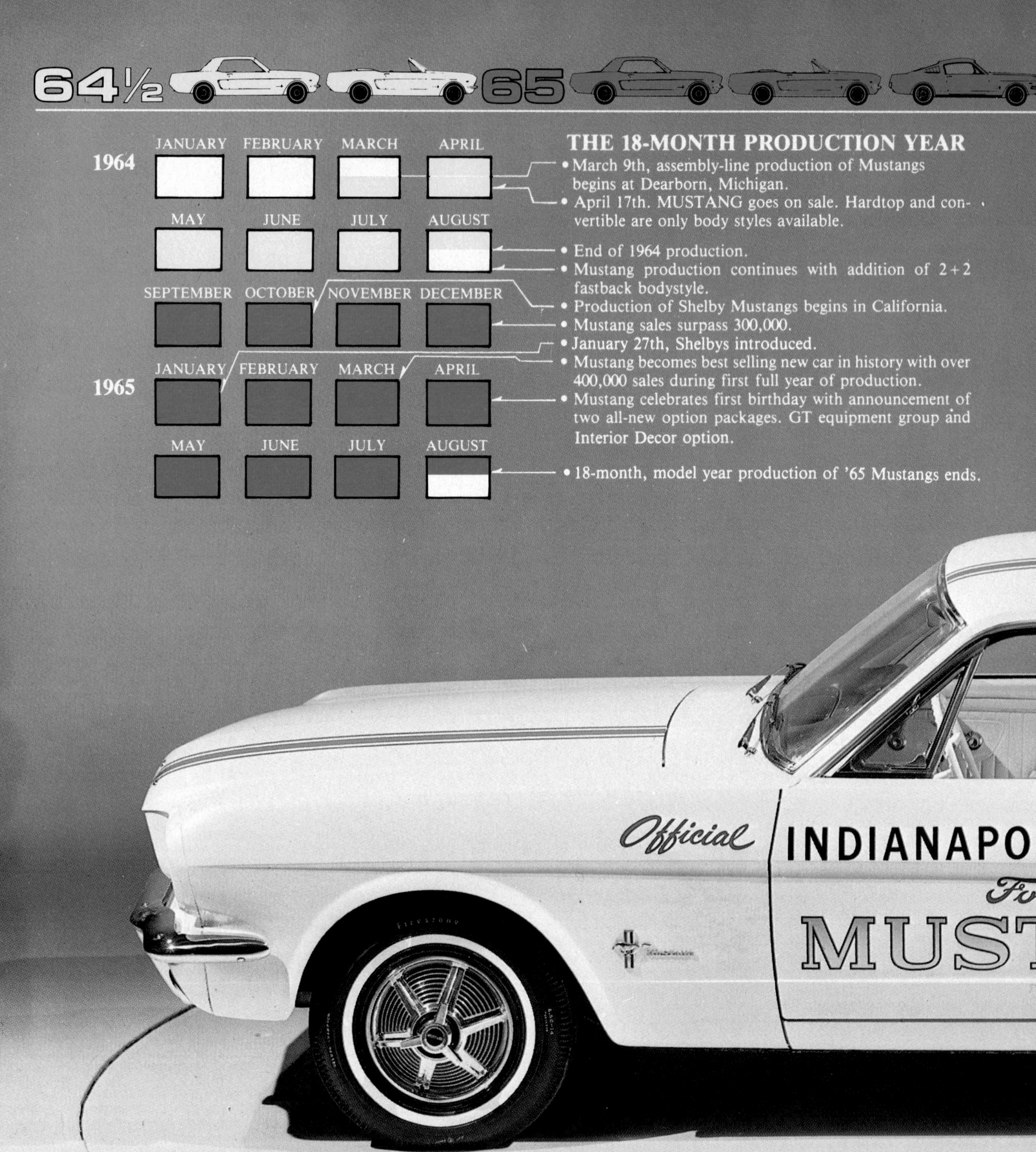

64½
65
1964
1965
JANUARY FEBRUARY MARCH APRIL
MAY JUNE JULY AUGUST
SEPTEMBER OCTOBER NOVEMBER DECEMBER
JANUARY FEBRUARY MARCH APRIL
MAY JUNE JULY AUGUST
THE 18-MONTH PRODUCTION YEAR
• March 9th, assembly-line production of Mustangs begins at Dearborn, Michigan.
• April 17th. MUSTANG goes on sale. Hardtop and convertible are only body styles available.
• End of 1964 production.
• Mustang production continues with addition of 2+2 fastback bodystyle.
• Production of Shelby Mustangs begins in California.
• Mustang sales surpass 300,000.
• January 27th, Shelbys introduced.
• Mustang becomes best selling new car in history with over 400,000 sales during first full year of production.
• Mustang celebrates first birthday with announcement of two all-new option packages. GT equipment group and Interior Decor option.
• 18-month, model year production of '65 Mustangs ends.
Official

"Drivers, start your engines!"

Beginning with the vehicle warranty plate, Mustangs produced between March 9th, and August 17th, 1964, have a letter of "C" through "H" stamped in the date code. Refer to the warranty plate decoding charts for complete warranty plate information. Aside from the warranty plate, quite a few deviations exist in the interior, luggage compartment, engine compartment, as well as the exterior, and drivetrain. The simple thing to do, would be to list every identifying difference. The problem with such an attempt, is in the vagueness of when and where changes occurred. For example, a running change implemented in the Dearborn assembly plant, might not have taken effect until several weeks, or even months later in, say, San Jose. In fact, changes, or production variances that occurred in one plant, may never have been incorporated at another.

Furthermore, some cars manufactured much later in the 18-month, 1965 model year are often found to be equipped with items supposedly of the '64½ production vintage. When dealing with a particular change or variance, an early-to-late production comparison is often a more accurate description than the normal '64½-'65 comparison.

Production changes are generally centered around model year transition, and thus identifying them by the manufacturer's changeover in dating is fairly easy. However, with the 1965 Mustang, there were more changes which took place *during* the 18-month production span, than occurred at the 1965 to 1966 model year changeover. There is therefore more production differences between early and late '65 Mustangs, than there are, between '65 and '66 Mustangs.

Mustang was the official Pace Car at the nation's most famous auto race in May, 1964. Only one month after introduction.

BODYSTYLES

Buyers of the first Mustangs had a choice of two body styles, hardtop or convertible. Then in September of 1964, the 2+2 fastback joined the Mustang lineup.

Fore and aft, the first Mustang represents the pinnacle of American automobile styling. In profile the smart sculptured sides are accentuated by the combination long hood and passenger compartment.

The kicked-up rear adds a sporty flair to the Mustang's attractive and uncluttered appearance in all body styles.

MUSTANG

Early production models have a beveled hood edge and grille side panel. The bevel is deleted later in the '65 production year.

EXTERIOR

GRILLE: The focal point of a 1965 Mustang front end is the running Mustang emblem. Instead of running in the traditional counterclockwise race track direction, production was already underway when stylist realized their Mustang emblem was bolting off in the wrong direction. The emblem is set inside a corral to match the grille's outline. Stubby vertical, chrome struts secure the grille ornament at the center. Two slender chrome arms jut outward from the ornament horizontally, almost to the outer edge of grille opening. The grille consists of hundreds of successively-linked, hexagonal openings forming a honeycomb appearance. It's a stamped, one-piece metal configuration and is painted bluish-gray. This provides a neutral background for the grille ornament, giving the horse a suspended or running free appearance.

The sides and bottom of the grille opening are accented by a 3-piece chrome and argent trim strip that runs along the grille outline. Three simulated air-gills flank either side of the grille opening.

HEADLIGHTS: The sculptured look of the 1965 Mustang front end is further accented with the single headlights having a faintly recessed appearance.

FRONT BUMPER & VALANCE PANEL: Protection from the early Mustang's front bumper is questionable, as it extends only slightly beyond the body components. However, the flush, contoured shape pleasingly highlights the car's sporty front.

The contoured theme of the 1965 Mustang's frontal appearance is carried through by the lower valance panel. Amber turn signal/parking lamps are fully recessed into the valance, directly beneath the headlights on either side. The parking lamp housings are chromed, as are the two bumper guards, which attach vertically beneath the Mustang's front bumper.

HOOD: The leading edge of the 1965 Mustang's hood completes the upper outline of its grille, and then swoops sharply aftward on either side to meet the curvature of the headlight assemblies. F-O-R-D is spelled out, in widely spaced block lettering at the leading edge of the hood, thus completing the symmetrical appearance of the car's front end.

Early production '65 Mustang hood bumpers have a recessed phillips screw to secure the rubber bumper to the stud.

Later production '65 Mustangs have a domed hood bumper molded onto the stud.

SIDE EXTERIOR: The sculptured styling of the 1965 Mustang's side exterior begins immediately at the leading edge of the long front fenders and becomes increasingly pronounced as it progresses aftward creating a scooped appearance just forward of the rear wheel opening. The front bumper wraps around, stopping only inches from the front wheel opening. V-8 equipped models are identified with the engine size cast in a 4½'' wide chrome emblem affixed to the front fender, approximately half way between the top of the fender and the trailing edge of the bumper.

The large, full-view wheel well openings, typical of sports cars of the sixties, are accentuated on the 1965 Mustang by slight wheel lip flairs, molded into the fenders. A smaller variation of the Mustang running horse appears a few inches behind the front wheel opening. In this instance the horse is running in the proper direction, forward. The emblem is a one piece chrome medallion cast atop a brightly trimmed, red, white and blue vertical bar. Affixed just behind the medallion and immediately beneath the horse's tail, M-U-S-T-A-N-G is spelled out in bright letters, die cast as one piece. *2+2* appears along with the Mustang lettering on fastback models.

A tri-colored fender emblem and name plate appear on the Mustang's front fender. Initially the lettering was 4 3/8'' long, but was lengthened to 5'' later in the '65 production year.

DOORS: 1965 Mustang doors are opened from the outside by a round pushbutton integrally set into the stationary, chrome door-pull. Once open, the doors operate on two strap type hinges. The lower hinge is equipped with a two-stage door check to allow either a partial, or full-open position. The latch is configured of two sturdy catches, that when closed, clutch the cylinder-type post affixed to door jamb. Ford referred to them as "Bear-Hug" design. The bright metal, lock cylinder is located just beneath the door handle, and is encased flush with the door's surface. The ignition key is required to lock or unlock the 1965 Mustang's door from the outside.

MIRRORS: An exterior, rear-view mirror is standard on all 1965 Mustangs. The circular, manually adjustable mirror is attached to the top leading edge of the driver's side door, far enough aft to allow clearance for opening the vent window. Ford designers made the vent window assembly an integral part of the 1965 Mustang door.

GLASS: 1965 Mustangs are equipped with tempered safety glass all around. The windshield is also laminated for greater shatter resistance. The windshield and rear window have stainless steel moldings around their outline on hardtop and 2+2 models. 1965 convertibles have a bright metal frame encasing the entire windshield, including the side post. These are painted on hardtop and 2+2 models. Convertibles have clear vinyl, zip-out rear windows. Side windows, on all body styles, are framed in stainless-steel.

Mustang doors are interchangable on all bodystyles in 1965 and 1966, however the side & rear windows vary between body styles.

Squared key operates ignition and door locks. Oval key operates luggage compartment locks.

Mustang's "Bear Hug" door lock & striker.

Standard left hand exterior mirror (optional right hand mirror is identical)

OPTIONAL MIRRORS

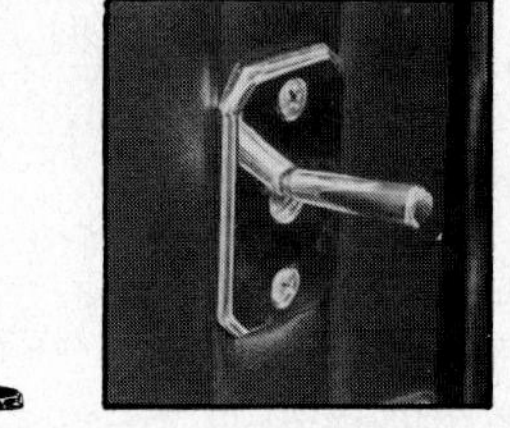

A. Mustang and Shelby racing mirror. B. Remote control left hand mirror is operated by control (at right) mounted on inside of driver's door panel. Matching right hand mirror is non-remote.

'65 Mustang convertibles have clear plastic, zip-out rear windows.

Vent windows latch from the inside, and are interchangeable between bodystyles.

Hardtop

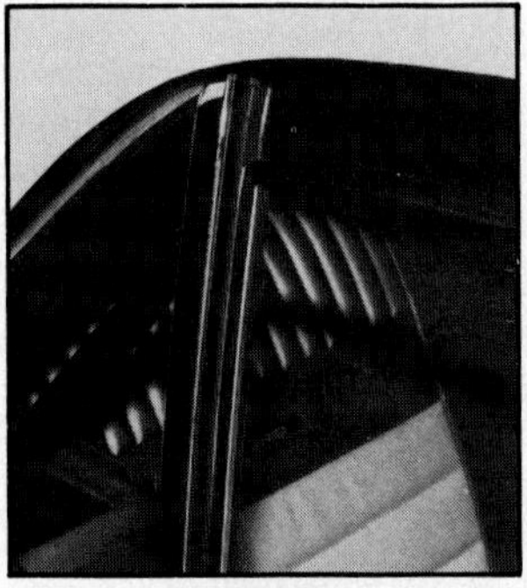

Convertible

Fastback

The side and rear windows are unique to each bodystyle, while '65-'67 Mustang windshields are interchangable between bodystyles.

Convertible windshield frames are bright metal.

Other models are painted the car's exterior color.

REAR QUARTER: The sculptured side scoop that begins at the front fender, terminates just forward of the rear wheel opening, giving the appearance of a scoop directing air to the rear brake. The simulated air-intake scoop is accented with a bright-metal trim. (Deleted on fastbacks and cars equipped with certain option packages.) A bright metal rocker-panel molding approximately 3'' wide runs from the front to rear wheel well opening on fastback models, but is optional on other '65 body styles.

Convertible tops were manually operated unless the power top option was ordered. Originally, color choices were black, white, or blue. As a running production change, tan replaced blue for subsequent '65 production.

'65 Mustang convertible, with optional rocker panel molding, back up lights, and simulated knock-off, spinner wheel covers.

Fastbacks are equipped with air extractors in the upper rear quarter panel.

ROOF: The 1965 Mustang hardtop roof has a sculptured concave indention that goes from either quarter panel's top edge, up and around the outline of the rear window. Fastback roofs are void of this sculptured outline and are fitted with an expansive, sloping rear window. The 2+2, and hardtop models are fitted with bright-metal drip moldings, running from the base of the front vent window along the roof outline to the rear quarter panel.

'65 hardtop with optional vinyl roof

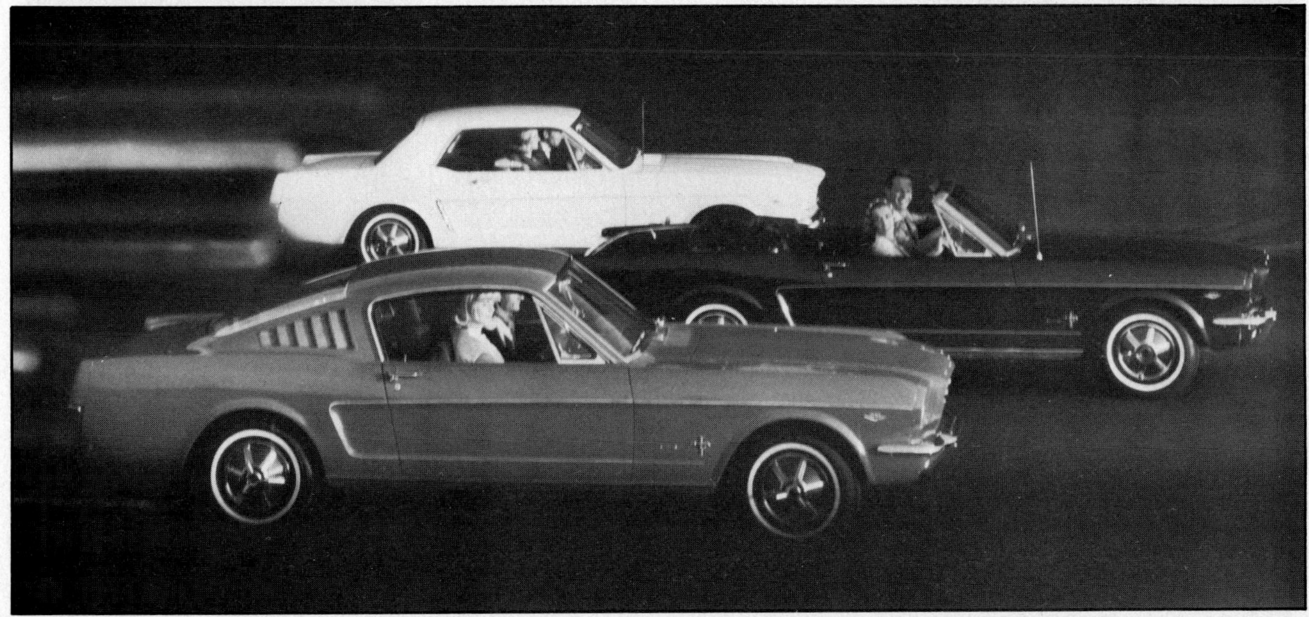

REAR EXTERIOR

The 1965 Mustang rear was the view Ford chose to leave simple and unclutted. Only the essential fixtures are visible, with every item having a function.

Triple tail light effect is created by tail light cover having three slender openings.

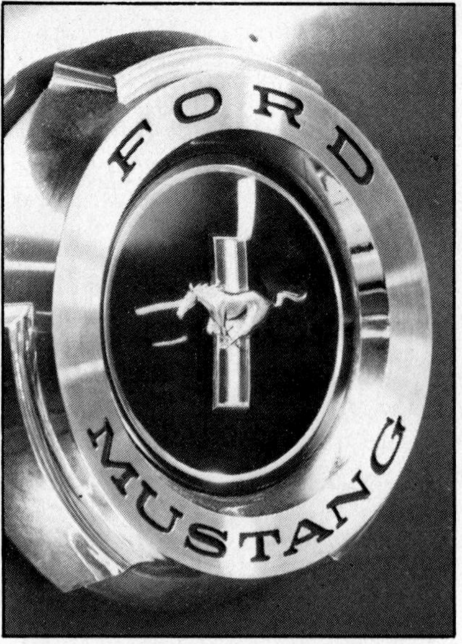

Thermal embossed Mustang insignia is encased in center of gas cap.

TAIL LIGHTS: The untrained eye will see three individual, slender vertical tail lights on either side, when looking at a 1965 Mustang. Actually, there's only one tail light assembly on either outboard side. The illusion of multiple lights is created by the bright metal tail light door or cover, being configured with three vertical openings. When mounted over the tail light lens, it appears as there are three separate lenses. The tail light housing assembly is mounted behind the trunk panel, inside the luggage compartment. There is only one, three-stage bulb in each assembly, that functions as tail light, brake light, and turn signal.

GAS CAP: The 1965 Mustang gas cap is die cast bright metal with a ceramic center. It is centered directly between the tail lights. The cap is of the twist-to-open design. The fuel filler neck is slotted to accept the ear-type, retaining clips on the reverse side of the cap. In addition, the filler neck is progressively beveled, so that, as the cap is twisted tight, increased pressure is applied to the retaining clips, thus holding the cap snug. Shortly after introduction, a retaining wire was added to the gas cap. The retaining wire allows removal of the gas cap, but retains it within the circular wire's grasp, thus preventing loss or theft. The words "FORD" "MUSTANG" are stamped into the gas cap's circular perimeter, FORD in black at the top, and MUSTANG in red at the bottom.

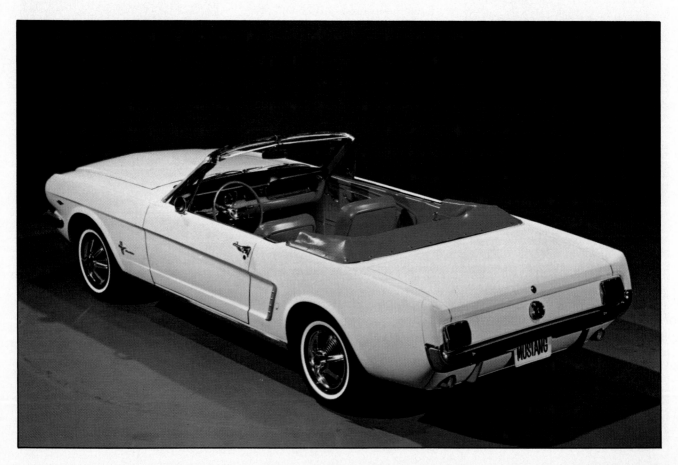

TRUNK

LUGGAGE COMPARTMENT

With the spare tire in place the 1965 Mustang has 9.0 cubic feet of usable luggage space in the hardtop and 7.7 cubic feet in the convertible. Although typical of sports cars, usable luggage space is only about 5 cubic feet in the 2+2.

At introduction, the trunk mat was made of a thick, heavy-duty gray burtex material in hardtop models and a gray speckled or gray plaid rubber (depending on assembly plant), in convertibles.

The 1965 Mustang spare tire is secured to the luggage compartment floor with tire's outside, facing up. An anchor bolt, passes through the wheel-center opening and is hooked to the trunk floor. A disc collar is placed over the anchor bolt and the entire assembly is then secured with a large wing-nut. A scissors type jack is stored beneath the spare tire. The jack is operated by a long bolt permanently threaded through the entire jack assembly.
The bolt head is the same size as the wheel lug nuts. Therefore, the socket-ratchet type lug wrench provided, operates the jack, as well as removing, or tightening the lug nuts.

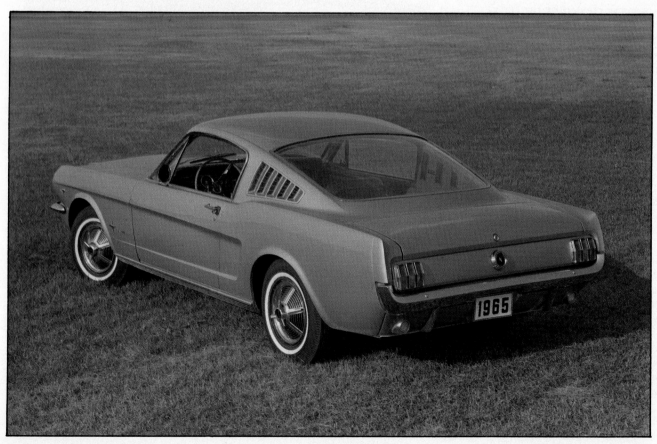

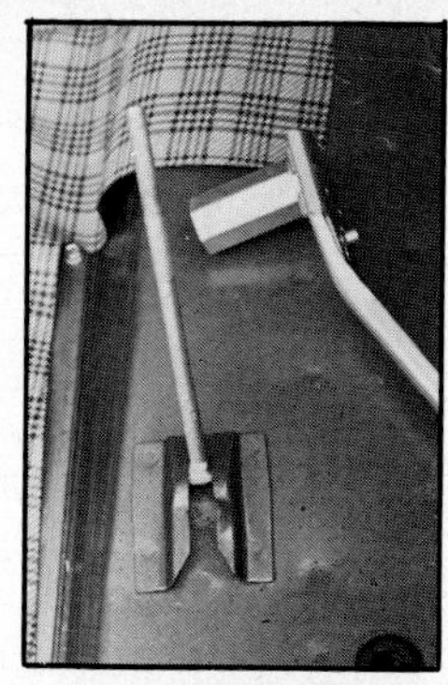

Early production 65 Mustangs have slotted anchor bolt & hold-down.

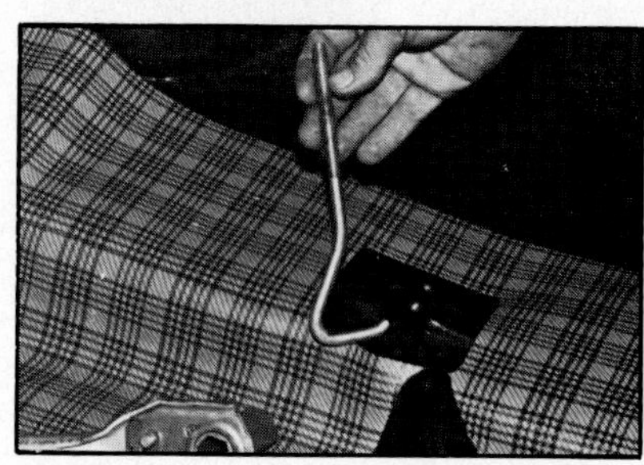

Later production models have a pass-through, hold-down and hook-type anchor bolt.

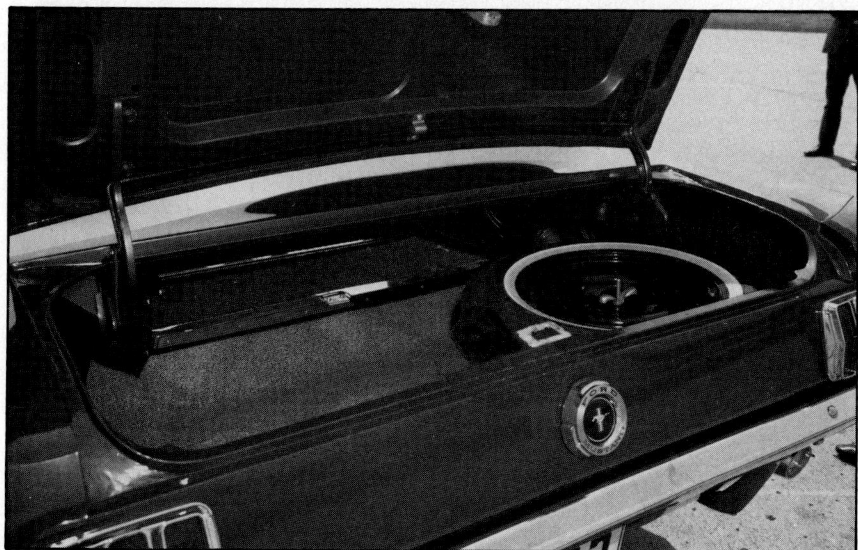

'65 Mustang luggage compartments have 9.0 cubic feet of space in hardtops; 7.7 cubic feet in convertibles and 5.0 cubic feet in fastback models.

REAR BUMPER: As with the front bumper, the 1965 Mustang's bright rear bumper is intended more as accent to the Mustang's overall appearance, than for protection. The Mustang's rear has an ever-so-slight bow in the center and the bumper contours to the faint curve created by the car's shape. At the outboard ends, the bumper curves sharply upward to meet the rear quarter panel's end caps. The sides of the bumper's upturned ends are then flush with the sides of the quarter panel's trailing ends.

LOWER VALANCE: The rolled under effect of the 1965 Mustang's rear is achieved by its' lower valance running the breadth of the rear, and then curving smoothly into the trailing profile of the lower rear quarter panels. The car's rear license plate is attached directly in the center of the rear valance, beneath the bumper. Below the rear bumper, and a few inches inboard of the tail lights, 1965 Mustangs received, as standard equipment, a bright vertical bumper guard on either side. A bracket fastens them beneath the bumper and to the base of the lower valance. Back up lights were optional on all 1965 Mustangs.

'65 Mustang standard interior.

'65 Mustang Decor Interior option.

'65 Mustang Bench Seat option.

INTERIOR

Several here-to-fore options in most American cars were standard equipment on Ford's new Mustang. This is especially true of the Mustang's interior. Most significant, are the bucket seats, and floor-mounted transmission shifter. The 1965 Mustang interior was offered in a choice of five, all-vinyl upholstery colors, as well as two color choices of cloth and vinyl in hardtops, all standard. All-vinyl interior colors were: black, white, red, blue, or palomino. The cloth and vinyl combination could be had in black or palomino. The latter were phased out by mid-summer of 1964.

A sixth color choice of "Ivy Gold" was added to other five all-vinyl standard colors in the fall of 1964. The palomino color was phased out in mid summer of 1965, and replaced with a lighter tan vinyl called "parchment."

SEATS: Bucket seats are standard in the 1965 Mustang with a bench seat optional in the hardtop and convertible. The standard front seats are the same on all three body styles, however both the upper and lower rear seats, all differ. Front, metal to metal seat belts are standard in 1965 Mustangs.

The Decor Interior Group, often called "pony interior" was optional on all body styles after March of 1965.

CRASH PAD: Another standard feature of the 1965 Mustang's interior was the padded crash pad atop the instrument panel. The crash pad is made of foam rubber, molded over with vinyl, and color keyed to the interior. The contour of the crash pad forms a hooded visor over either side of the instrument panel, dipping smoothly downward at the center. This adds continuity to the interior's two-front-passenger theme, plus adding a degree of sportiness to the Falcon-type instrument panel. The radio's speaker grille is mounted in the top of the crash pad directly in the center. It, too, is color keyed to the Mustang's interior trim scheme. At the pad's base, following the contour of the hooded visors are bright trim strips which secure the pad to the instrument panel.

'65 Mustang instrumentation with optional RALLY-PAC.

INSTRUMENTATION: The 1965 Mustang's complete instrumentation is contained in a longitudinal speedometer-instrument pod assembly inset in the metal dash. The overall assembly creates a wide bezel-type appearance. Except for the actual instruments, the assembly is constructed entirely of molded plastic. The front of the bezel is painted with a camera-case black finish and is abundantly trimmed in bright mylar around the warning lights and gauges, as well as the bezel's outline. The "HIGH BEAM" headlight indicator is immediately to the left of "O" MPH on the speedometer.

Only one indicator light is provided for the turn signals, and flashes, whenever a left or right turn is selected, or when the optional emergency flashers are on. This indicator light is immediately to the right of "120" on the speedometer, and is labeled aptly, TURN SIGNAL. The only gauges are FUEL and TEMP. Respectively, they flank the left and right side of the speedometer, appearing deeply inset, due to the instrument bezel's configuration. Set directly beneath the speedometer numbering, are three rectangular cutouts. The center cutout is slightly wider than the others and houses the odometer.

To the left of the odometer is the OIL warning light. To the right is the GEN or ALT warning light, (depending on which type electrical charging system the car has). In the center of the panel, directly beneath the dished out area of the crash pad, is the optional radio. If the radio has been omitted from the factory, a blanking plate is in this area, color keyed to the metal instrument panel. To the right of the radio, and exactly opposite the instrument panel, is the glove compartment. Unlike the instrument bezel, its' metal appearance is not betrayed, as it is solid cast metal with a bright outline trim and push-to-open button in the top center. The traditional Mustang cast atop tri-colored vertical bars is affixed to the glove box door's right side. The entire background area is camera case black to match the instrument bezel.

'65 Mustangs use Falcon-type instrumentation, but black and bright mylar (plastic chrome), instrument bezel is unique to Mustang.

An optional Parking Brake Warning Light is located on the lower left of the Mustang's instrument panel. Both rectangular and circular shaped lights were dealer installed items.

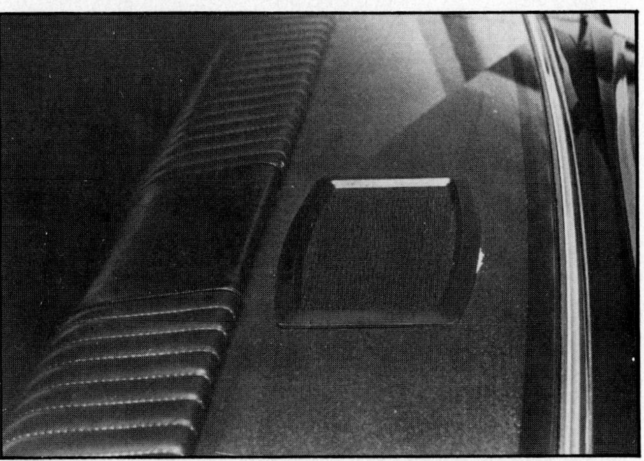

Rear seat speakers were optional in hardtop models. The same speaker grille is used on conventional as well as the reverb type speakers. Both were dealer installed.

SWITCHES & CONTROLS: The lower half of the instrument panel has a rolled-under effect and contains several knobs and switches. To the left of the steering column are the windshield wiper and head light knobs. The 1965 Mustang is equipped with a conventional 2-position parking lamp/head light switch. The dimmer switch is mounted on the upper left floor board area. To the right of the steering column is the ignition switch and cigar lighter.

Early production '65 Mustangs have an "A" (for Air), stamped onto the driver's fresh-air vent knob.

The "A" was deleted later in '65 production.

This dealer installed accessory carried Mustang p/n C5ZZ15313-A

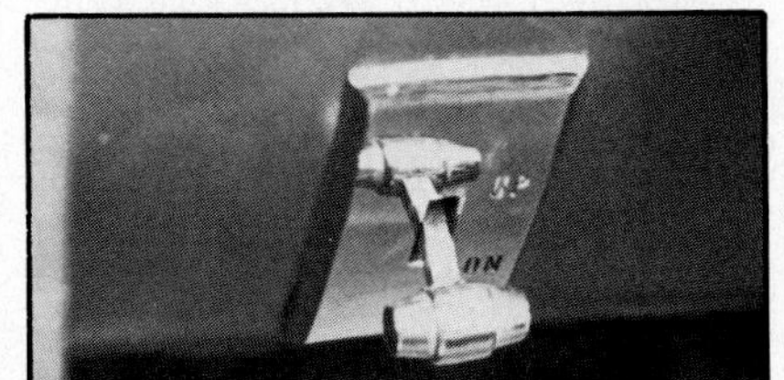

Convertible power-top switch, located on lower left instrument panel.

Pop out cigarette lighter is standard. Early production '65 Mustangs have two, fan blower speeds, with "OFF" in the center position.

Later production models have three, fan blower speeds, with "OFF" in the left position.

The horn ring twists onto the steering column. A large spring holds horn ring off contacts, until depressed. Alternator equipped models have differently configurated horn ring contacts.

Immediately to the right of the cigar lighter is the heater/defroster panel. Three vertical slide controls operate the Heat, Temperature, and Defroster. They are configured respectively, astride each other. The "Heat" lever controls the path of the air in the right heat-ventilating duct. The "Temp" lever controls the amount of warm fresh air discharged from the heater. The "Def" lever controls the path of the air coming out of the heater. A three-position switch is at the top of the controls to operate the fan blower. Initially the switch was wired so that "off" was in the center with "high" to the left, and "low" to the right. Later in production, this was changed to "Off" at the left and increased to three speeds — low, medium, and fast — progressively to the right.

An ash tray is standard on all 1965 Mustangs, and is located directly beneath the radio in the lower center of the instrument panel. On convertible models, two additional ash trays are included, one on either interior rear quarter trim panel. If the car is equipped with an optional console, a fourth ash tray is positioned at the rear of the console.

STEERING WHEEL: The Mustang's steering wheel is deeply dished and has three center spokes. A bright matching horn-ring sets in the wheel's center, having the traditional Mustang insignia thermally engraved beneath the clear ceramic encasement. A sports car effect is accomplished on the Mustang's steering wheel by three, graduated-in-size indentions in each of the bright spokes. The indentions are painted black to create the illusion of pierced holes. "Ford Mustang" is inscribed at the upper and lower circular outline of the horn-ring's center. The turn signal selector lever is mounted on the Mustang's steering column just forward of the steering wheel.

Rally-Pacs, (combination clock/tachometers) were optional on all '65 Mustangs. The Rally-Pac is saddle-mounted onto the steering column. A 24-hour clock is on the right, with an ignition triggered, electrical tachometer on the left. The internal meter movement in the tachometer therefore, varies between six and eight cylinder models. All models except the high performance V-8, use a 6000 RPM tachometer. The "hipo" gets an 8000 RPM tachometer, if the Rally-Pac option is ordered. The calibration is RPMs x 100 in all models. The model at left was installed as a factory, or dealer installed option.

When the GT Equipment Group and Interior Decor were introduced in '65 mid-year production, a low-profile version (at right) was offered as an extra cost option, to accommodate the 5-dial instrumentation in the new option groups. The Rally-Pac at left is painted a black wrinkle finish, while the low-profile version is either black, or color-keyed to the steering column in Interior Decor equipped models. The low-profile tachometer may be graduated in multiples of either 5 or 10, while the other Rally-Pac is graduated only in multiples of 10.

TRANSMISSION SHIFTERS:
1965 Mustangs are outfitted with floor-mount transmission shifters. The standard selector (3-spd manual transmission) is bright metal, extending through a cutout in the tunnel area of the Mustang's floor. A baffled, rubber boot surrounds the base of the shifter. A ceramic ball-type shift knob is screwed onto the end of the shifter, and is inscribed with the shift pattern. On optional four-speed equipped Mustangs a reverse lock-out is configured of two horizontal ears spring/loaded directly beneath the shifter knob. The four speeds are in an "H" pattern. Pulling upward on the spring loaded ears allows the shifter to be moved into the reverse position. In this position the shifter depresses the shifter-mounted back-up light switch on cars equipped with that option. On models equipped with the optional Cruise-O-Matic transmission, the gear selections are labeled on a ceramic strip inside the shifter's domed selector base. The selector base is bright cast metal with "Cruise-O-Matic" inscribed on it. A raised casting mark also appears at the "R", "N" and the normal "DRIVE" position.

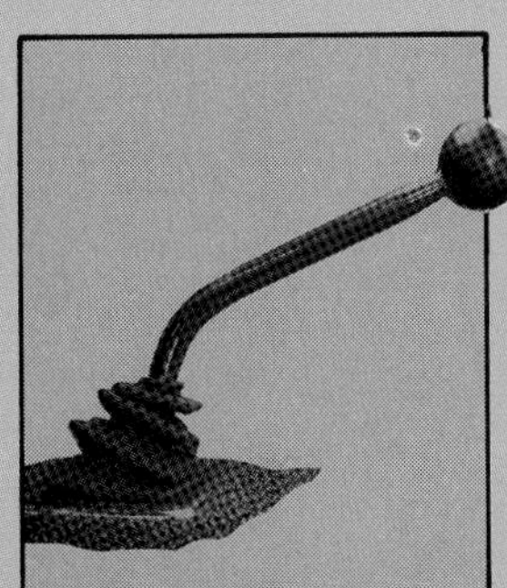

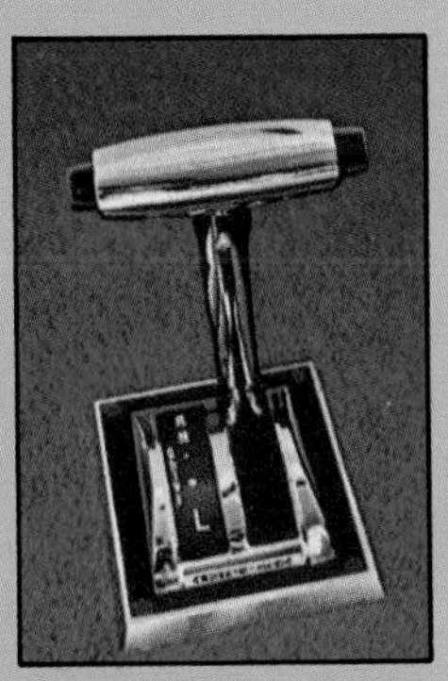

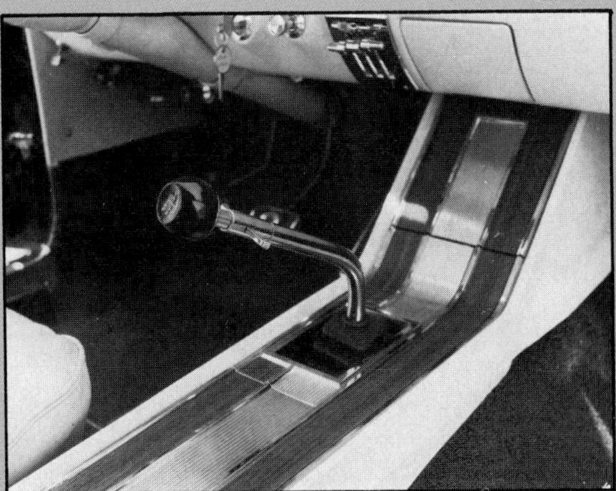

Manual transmission equipped Mustangs, optioned with consoles have a rectangular opening for the shifter to pass through.

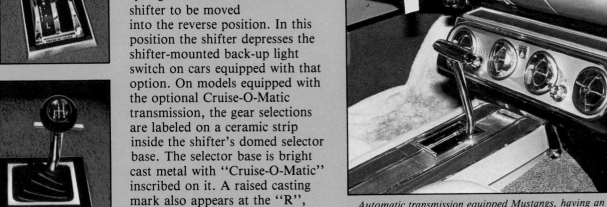

Automatic transmission equipped Mustangs, having an optional console received a unique, shift slide integrally mounted into the console.

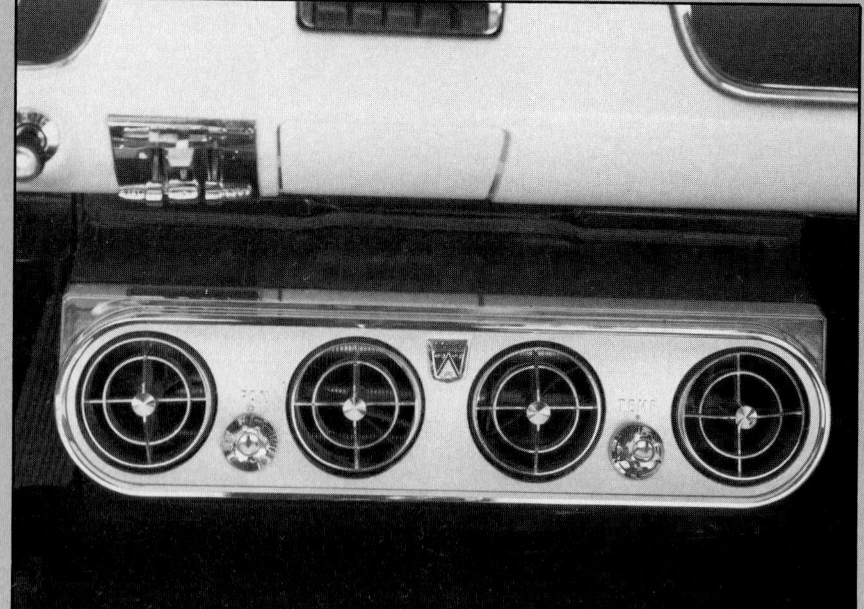

1965 Mustang air conditioning was optional. The air conditioner mounts underneath the center of the instrument panel. In '65, the air conditioner face is painted argent (dull silver), and has four air registers to direct the air. The '65-type air registers also have 2 concentric bright trim rings. '66 air conditioner faces are painted black, and have the inner trim ring deleted in the air registers.

Typical belt-driven air conditioner compressor on '65, V-8 Mustang. Eaton-type power steering pump & reservoir are mounted beneath the compressor. Several versions of Ford & Eaton power steering systems can be found on '65 Mustangs.

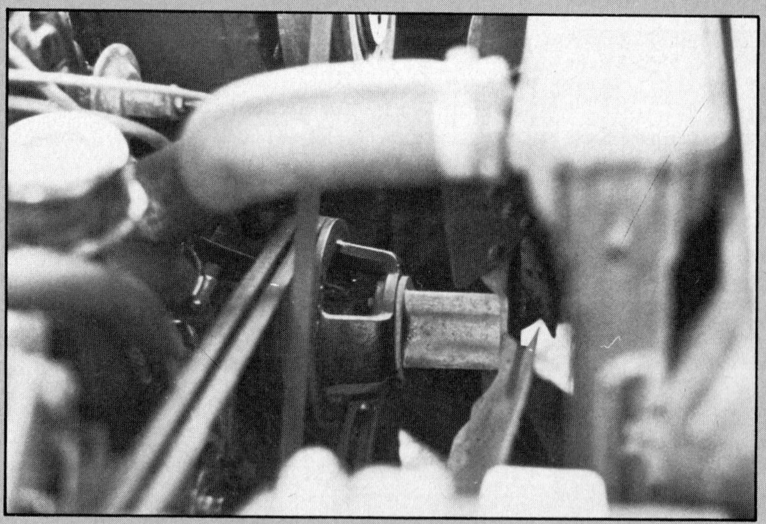

Early production '65 Mustangs have slotted cast iron engine pulleys, while later '65 model pulleys are stamped-steel. Note dual generator belt, found on air conditioned Mustangs with generator charging systems.

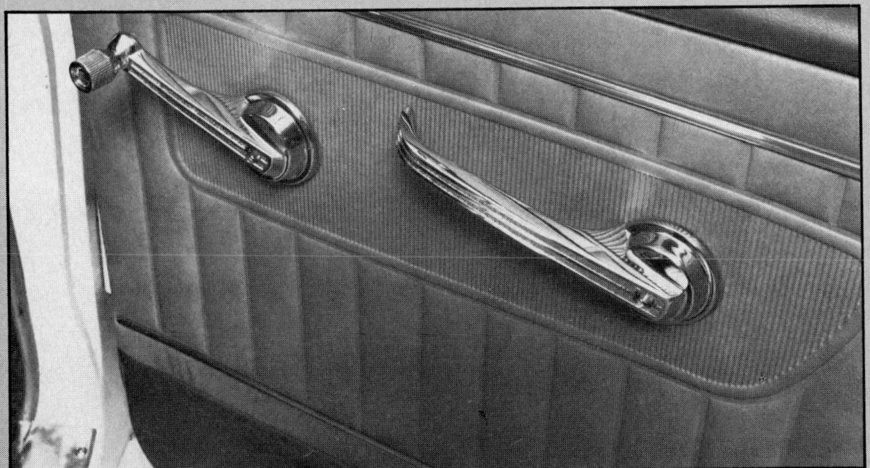

INTERIOR DOORS & DOOR PANELS: The 1965 Mustang's interior door has a leather-like texture cast into the door's metal surface, and is painted to match the interior. At the upper front is the swivel latch that locks or unlocks the vent window. At the upper rear is a plastic door lock plunger. The large cutout area for servicing the door & window crank mechanisms is covered over by a vinyl covered fiber board with cutouts for the door and window cranks. Somewhat inset, and following the panel outline, is a bright mylar trim line. A ribbed pattern, similar to the seat pleats, is heat set, and runs vertically, between the mylar trim.

Early production '65 Mustang interior door handles & window cranks (center photo), are held on with a spring-clip, while later production '65 thru '67 Mustangs have a revised handle (bottom photo), and are held on with allen-head screws.

At introduction, Mustang door-lock plungers were color-keyed to the interior, subsequently, bright mylar (plastic chrome), lock plungers replaced the colored ones.

KICK PANELS: Forward of the door, beneath the instrument panel, the Mustang is fitted with thick vinyl kick-panels on either side. Attached vertically, their outline includes the lower front door jamb, floor, and firewall area.

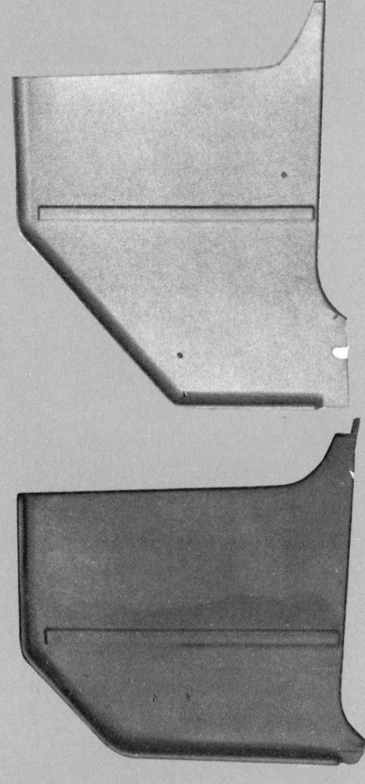

Convertible kick panels are shorter than hardtop or fastback models due to the convertible's re-enforced body platform.

CLUTCH, BRAKE & ACCELERATOR PEDALS: All foot pedals in the 1965 Mustang are suspended beneath the instrument panel. The pedals are covered with thick ribbed pads of black rubber configured to the pedal's outline.

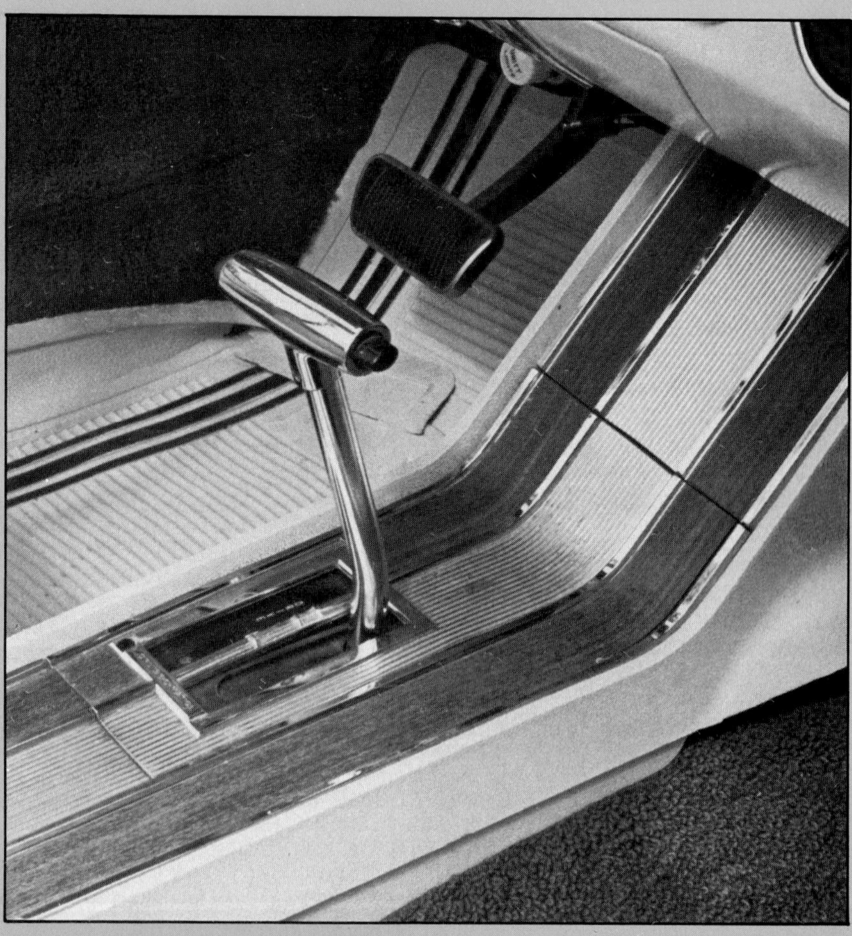

FASTBACK (2+2) INTERIORS

The standard front bucket seats are interchangable between all three '65 Mustang bodystyles. The rear seats however, are different in each. The most apparent difference is the fastback rear seat.

In the up position, the seat is held with a latch, and provides seating for two passengers, therefore the "2+2" identity was assigned to the fastback bodystyle. Releasing the latch permits the seat to be folded forward, to provide an expansive luggage or package compartment. The load floor is carpeted and brightly trimmed with stainless steel molding.

The fastback's interior rear quarter panels are fitted with color-keyed fiberglass panels extending along the sides and into the corners of the load area.

The panel at the rear is textured metal, and can be raised, creating a pass-through from the fastback's trunk compartment, thereby allowing transporting extra-long items, as well as enlarging the fastback's small trunk capacity.

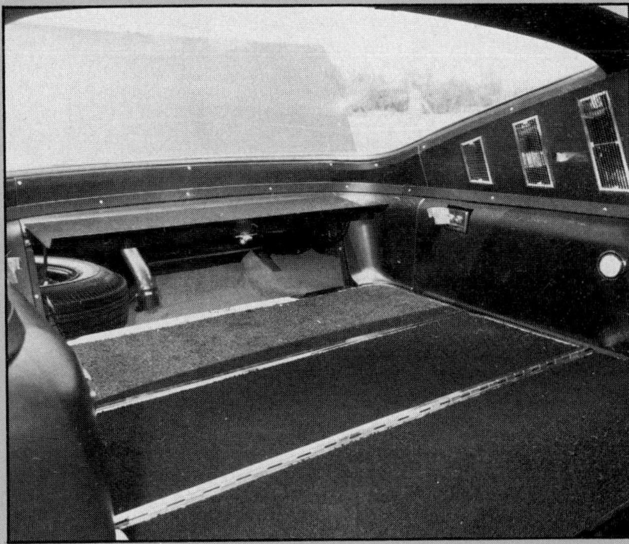

CARPETING: 1965 Mustangs are fitted with a combination Rayon/Nylon carpet, pre-molded to the contour of the car's floor. In two sections, the carpet meets beneath the bucket seats, concealing the surged seams running the breadth of the floor's center. The carpet is milled and sewn in a short-nap, loop-twist design, common to the mid-sixties production era. The fold-down area in the Mustang fastback is also carpeted.

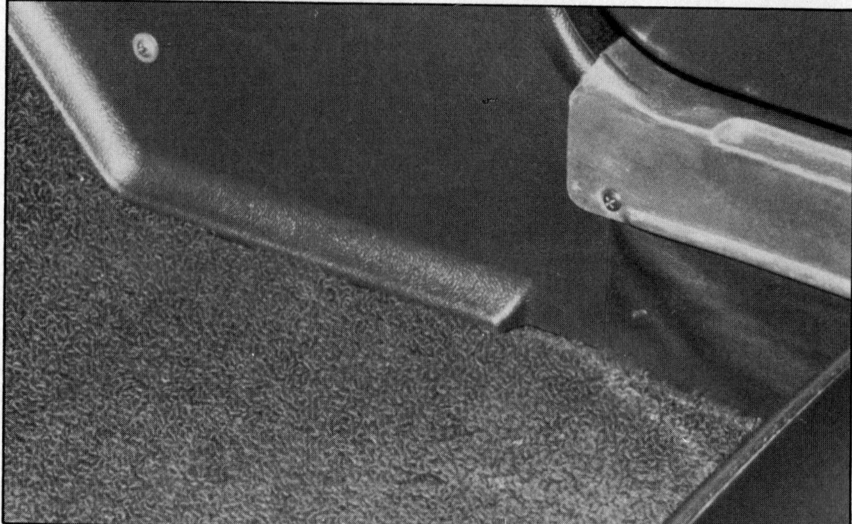

Early production '65 Mustang carpet (upper left), had a color-keyed rubber heel pad, but no toe pad. Later production '65 models have both heel and toe pads (upper right). At right is another variance between early and late '65 Mustang carpet. Notice the carpeting stops at the inner rocker panel. Carpet in later '65 production travels up the rocker panel, and beneath the door sill-plate.

Front seat belts in '65, are of a metal-to-metal configuration. Also available, were deluxe seat belts which are vinyl covered and color keyed to the interior. Rear seat belts were not available, unless an optional dealer installed adapter was put in.

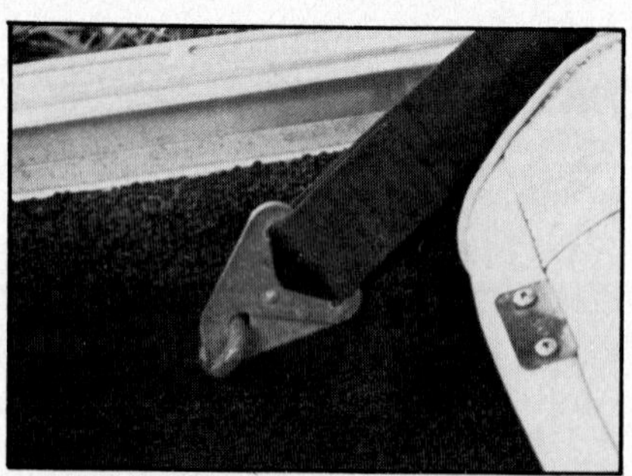

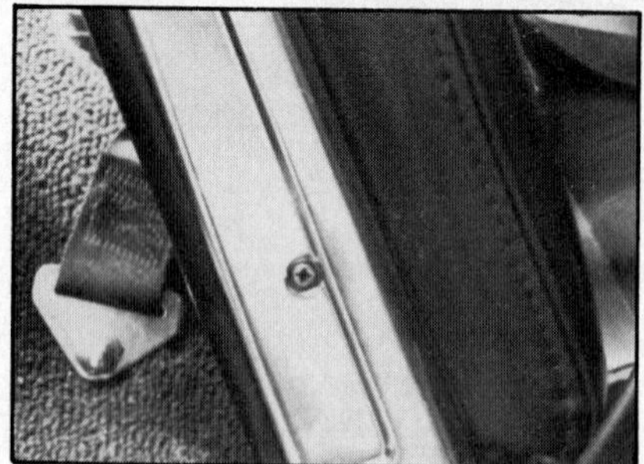

Early '65 production seat belts (at left), are secured to the Mustang's floor with an eye bolt. Later model '65s (center), are secured with a standard hex-head machine bolt.

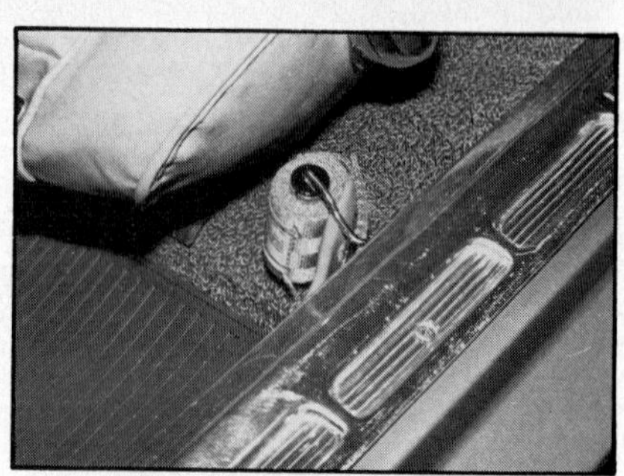

Seat belt retractors above, as well as rubber mounting-boots were optional in '65.

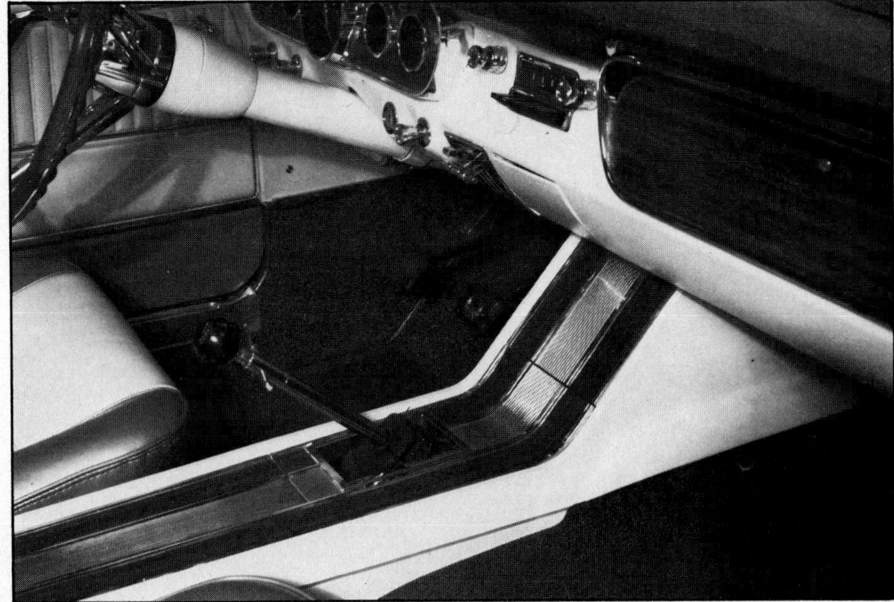

Consoles were a popular option in 1965 Mustangs. The full, or long console, at right is constructed of a leather-grained, molded plastic with a metal top trim that has the side strips painted camera case black. Some models optioned with Interior Decor have the console's black strips covered with simulated walnut appliques.

An ash tray and courtesy light are located at the rear of the consoles. Full consoles have a lighted storage compartment at the front.

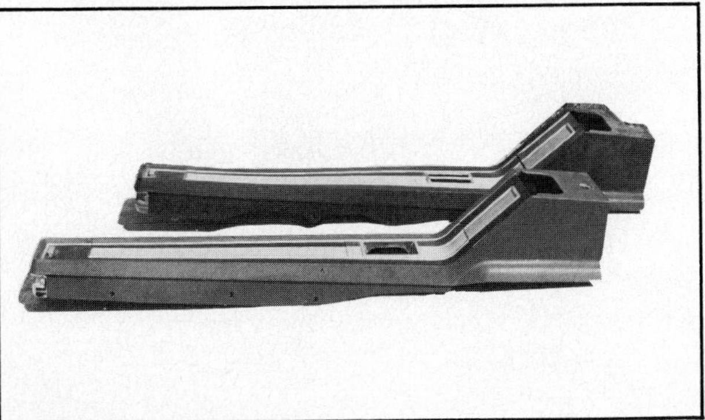

Consoles used in Mustangs with optional air conditioning are cut off, and trimmed with a bright end-cap molding. The '65 console end trim (photo at center left), is about 1" wide at the base and tapers slightly at the top. The console to it's right has a '66-type end trim, which is nearly 3" wide at the base and tapers sharply toward the top. All '65 & '66 consoles are identically constructed. Shortened versions are simplv cut off and then trimmed, as described above. Convertible Mustangs have a reinforced floor, requiring the console's base to be scallop-cut in the areas where it mounts onto Mustang convertible's floor, as depicted by upper console in photo at left.

Introduced as a mid-year option, in March of 1965, the Interior Decor Group includes unique luxury bolstered seats and door panels, padded sun visors, woodgrain appliques on 5-dial instrument panel and glove box door, deluxe simulated walnut grain steering wheel, walnut-look, pistol grip door handles, brightly trimmed foot pedals, partial carpeted kick panels with a bright center-strip molding and red & white courtesy lights located in door.

Most noticeable in the Interior Decor, is the galloping pony inserts on the seats. For this reason, the Interior Decor is often referred to as "Pony" interior.

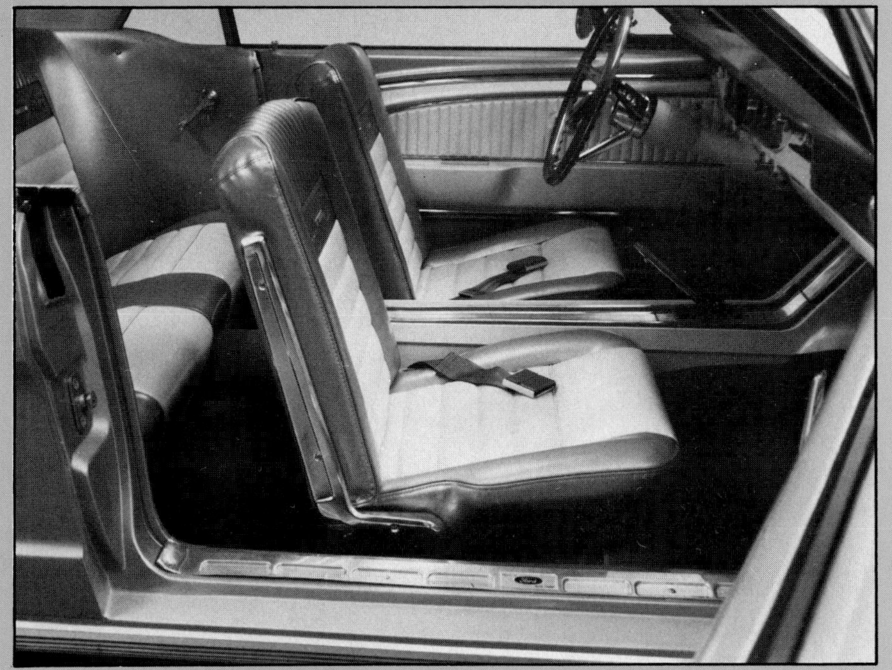

All three '65 Mustang bodystyles (code -65 hardtop, code - 63 fastback, code-76 convertible), were available with optional Interior Decor. The bodysyle code stamped onto the Mustang's warranty plate should include the letter 'B' for factory Interior Decor equipped models. (65B, 63B or 76B). The letter 'A' after the bodystyle code denotes standard interior.

Interior Decor, door courtesy light.

Walnut-look steering wheel option is included in Interior Decor Group.

The "Pony" inserts are sewn into both front bucket seats, as well as either side of the upper rear seat cushion, on hardtops and convertibles. However, Fastbacks equipped with the Interior Decor option, have the rear seat "pony" inserts deleted.

Hardtop models with the Interior Decor option, began receiving a bright trim cap at the upper leading edge of the rear inner panel shortly after the option group was introduced. A few early spring (1965) models were produced without the trim cap.

Mustang Interior Decor door panels are trimmed with two stainless-steel moldings, one around the pleated inner section, and one around the panel's outline. The kick panel in Mustangs with the Interior Decor option, have carpet half-way up the kick panel, and are then trimmed with a bright center molding, lining up with the door panel's lower trim molding.

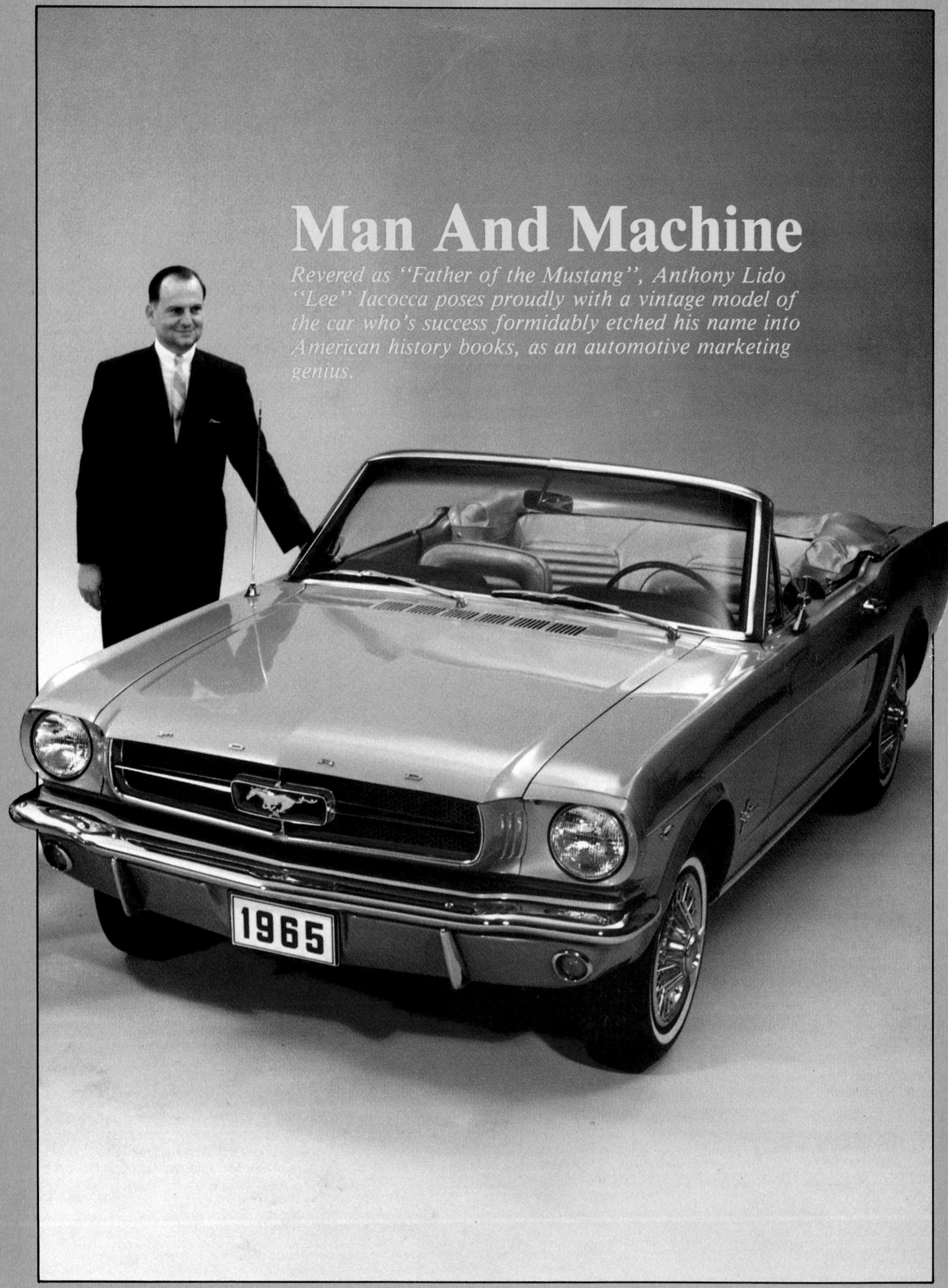

Man And Machine

Revered as "Father of the Mustang", Anthony Lido "Lee" Iacocca poses proudly with a vintage model of the car who's success formidably etched his name into American history books, as an automotive marketing genius.

SCUFF PLATES: The rocker panel on the 1965 Mustang that is exposed when the door is opened, is trimmed with a 2½'' wide stainless steel molding running the length of the door opening. This molding serves to conceal the seam created where the rocker panel meets the body platform, as well as being a scuff plate to protect against scratching the painted surface along the opening. Affixed to the center of the scuff plate is a 1''x3'' manufacturer's identification tag.

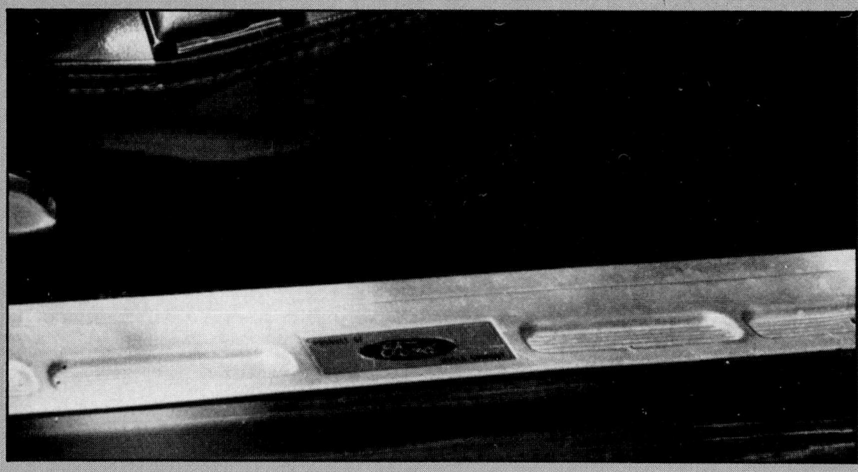

A manufacturer's tag, with an embossed black & silver logo is affixed to the '65 & '66 Mustang's door sill plates.

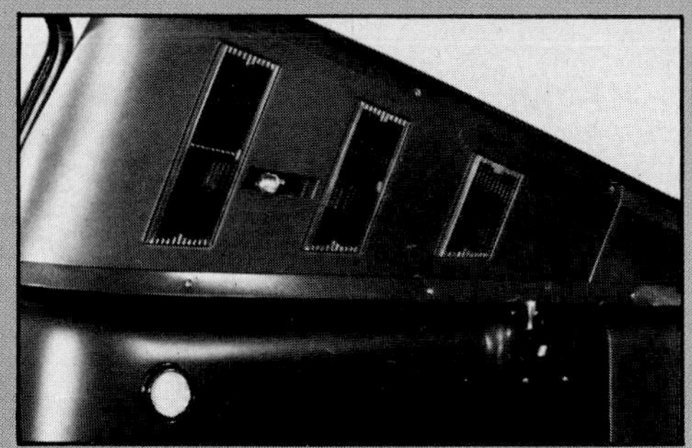

VENTILATION: A swivel-to-open vent window is located forward of the door windows on either side. Further fresh-air ventilation is ducted in from the louvered intakes in front of the windshield. A pull-knob is bracketed beneath the left side of the dash that allows fresh air to come in beneath the driver's side of the instrument panel. A small door is located beneath the passenger side of the instrument panel that brings in fresh air to the passenger compartment, when opened.

Fastback models have three functional air extractor vents on either side in the area where the rear quarter window would appear. An Open/Close slide control is configured into each side to operate the air extractors.

WHEELS: Standard wheels on the 1965 Mustang were 13" in diameter, and had a bead width of 4½". 6-cylinder models had a 4-lug pattern and 8-cylinder models had a 5-lug pattern. 14" wheels were optional, with the engine size again determining lug-pattern. Optional on all V-8 Mustangs, and standard with the 271 horsepower models, was a special handling package. This optional suspension package included 14" tires & wheels. However, at an extra cost, 15"x5" wheels could be ordered with the package. The 15" wheels were discontinued in the fall of 1964 when low-profile 14" tires were introduced.

Styled steel wheel, available in 14", 5-lug pattern only.

TIRES: 1965 Mustangs were outfitted with 6.50x13" 4-ply rayon, black side-wall tires as standard equipment. Premium nylon, as well as white side walls were optional in both the 13" and 14" sizes. 5.70, 5.90x15" tires were available at extra cost on Mustangs equipped with V-8 engines, and then, only if the optional suspension package was ordered. In the Fall of 1964, when low-profile tires were introduced, the Mustang's standard tires & wheels remained 6.50x13", but optional sizes became 6.95x14" instead of the former 6.50x14". 15" tires were dropped, and a premium quality, dual red line, 6.95x14" nylon tire became standard equipment on the high-performance V-8s, and optional on all other models. Buyers of the high performance model could select premium nylon, white side walls instead of the dual red line tires at no extra cost if they preferred.

1965 MUSTANG TIRES

	6.50x13 4 Ply Rating	7.00x13 4 Ply Rating	6.50x14 4 Ply Rating	5.90x15 4 Ply Rating ***	6.95x14 4 Ply Rating	6.95x14 Dual Red Band Premium Nylon
6-Cylinder Models	Std.	Opt.*	Opt.	——	Opt.**	——
8-Cylinder Models	Std.	Opt.*	Opt.	——	Std.**	Opt.**
8-Cylinder Models With Handling Pkg.	——	——	Standard w/handling package	Optional w/handling package	**Std. w/handling package	**Std. w/High Perf. V-8

* Standard with air conditioning
** After September, 1964
*** Dropped in August, 1964

1965 MUSTANG WHEEL COVERS

Top Left - Standard, 13" or 14"
Top Center - Optional, 13" or 14"
Top Right - Optional, 13" or 14"
Bottom Left - Optional, 13" or 14" (early 64½)
Bottom Center - Optional, 14" only (mid 64½)
Bottom Right - Optional, 14" only (fall 1964 intro)

1965 MUSTANG WHEELS

	6-Cyl. Models	V-8 Models	V-8 Models
Type	Stamped steel ventilated disc with integral safety-type rims.		Styled steel ventilated disc fully chromed with safety-type rims.
Number Of Studs	4	5	5
Diameter & Rim Size In Inches	Standard: 13x4.5 Optional: 14x4.5	[1] Standard: 13x4.5 [2] Optional: 14x5.0 [3] Optional: 15x5.0	[4] Optional 14x5.0

[1] Not used on V-8s after September of 1964
[2] Became standard in September of 1964
[3] Discontinued in August of 1964
[4] Introduced in May of 1964

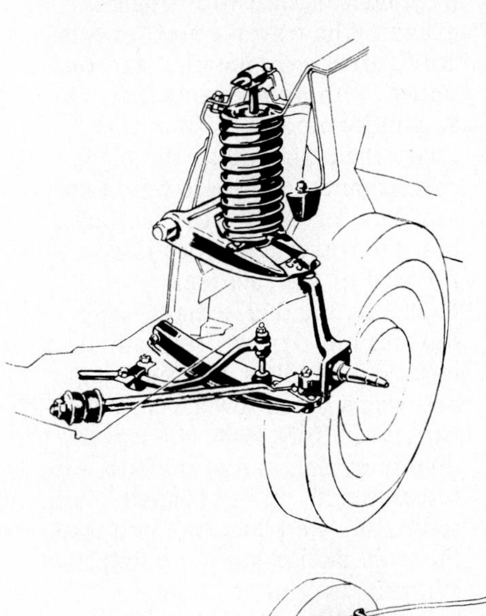

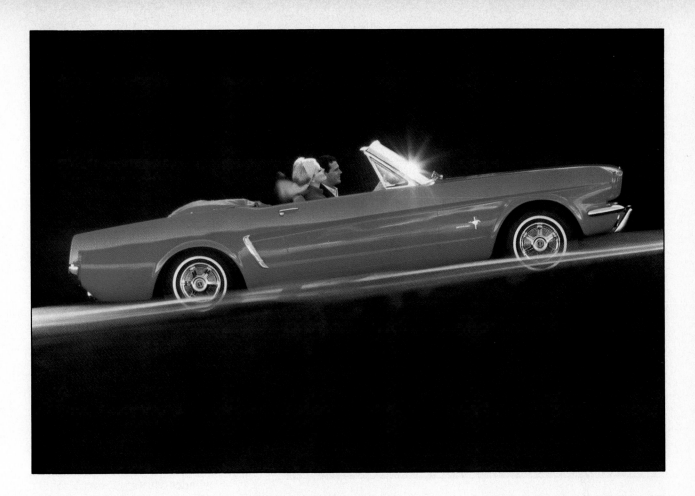

SUSPENSION: The 1965 Mustang's front suspension is independent ball-joint, with single lower arms and A-frame upper arms. 6-cylinder models are fitted with Falcon-type front suspension, while although similar in appearance, heavier duty, Fairlane-type suspension, is on V-8 Mustangs. The Mustangs front suspension is equipped with independent coil springs, an anti-roll bar, and constant rate shock absorbers. The rear suspension is comprised of a combination of two rigid axles attached to semi-elliptic leaf springs on either side, containing four leafs each. The calibrated rear springs vary according to the body type and optional equipment. The springs are offset-shackled at the rear, and along with two angle-mounted shock absorbers provide the aftward portion of the Mustang's ride and stability.

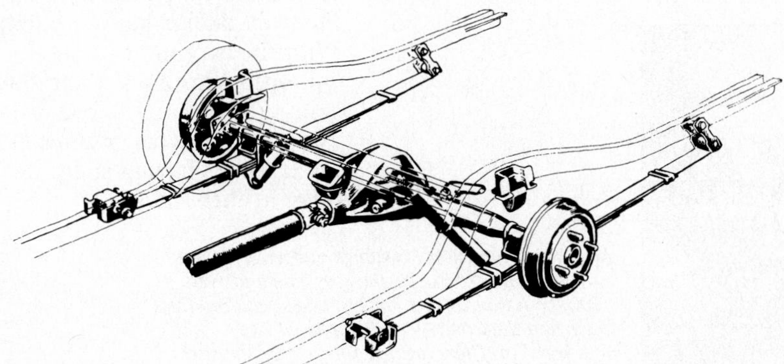

REAR AXLE: The 1965 Mustang is equipped standard with a semi-floating, hypoid-type rear axle. The differential carrier is integral with the axle housing on 6-cylinder models. On 8-cylinder Mustangs, the rear axles have a removable differential carrier, equipped with a straddle-mounted pinion, thereby allowing a variety of interchangeable gear combinations.

Early production '65 Mustang with air conditioning were fitted with 6-blade fans on clutchless pulleys.

COOLING SYSTEM AND HEATER: Two radiator capacities are found on 1965 Mustangs. 8½ U.S. quarts for 6-cylinder models and 14 quarts for 8-cylinder models. Both are pressurized and thermostatically assisted.

An upper and lower radiator hose allows the water to circulate through the engine water jacket and radiator core with a thermostat control located at the upper engine outlet to regulate the engine temperature.

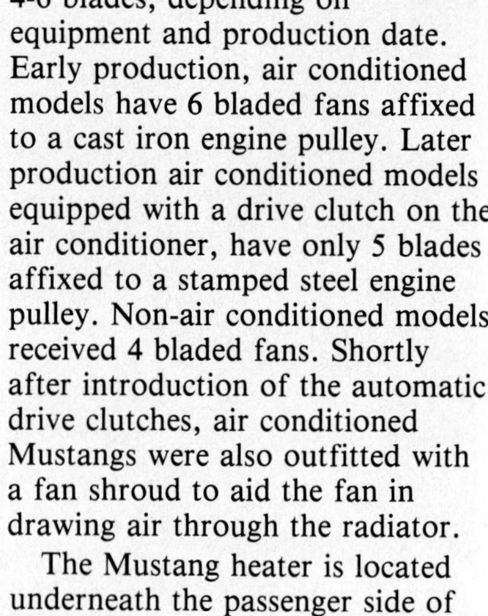

Fans vary in blade count from 4-6 blades, depending on equipment and production date. Early production, air conditioned models have 6 bladed fans affixed to a cast iron engine pulley. Later production air conditioned models equipped with a drive clutch on the air conditioner, have only 5 blades affixed to a stamped steel engine pulley. Non-air conditioned models received 4 bladed fans. Shortly after introduction of the automatic drive clutches, air conditioned Mustangs were also outfitted with a fan shroud to aid the fan in drawing air through the radiator.

The Mustang heater is located underneath the passenger side of the instrument panel and relies on heated water circulated from the engine block to operate.

EXHAUST SYSTEMS: Exhaust systems on all 1965 Mustangs, both single and dual, initially utilized a single traverse mounted muffler just forward of the fuel tank, and behind the rear axle. On 6-cylinder Mustangs, and also 8-cylinder models with single exhaust, the traverse muffler was configured with one inlet and one outlet, both on the same side. On 8-cylinder models, with optional dual exhaust including the high performance 289, there were two mufflers forward of the rear axle, plus the traverse muffler just forward of the fuel tank. However, the dual exhaust type traverse muffler was configured to include dual inlets and dual outlets and was a much lower restriction variety. In July 1964, the traverse dual inlet/dual outlet muffler was discontinued, and two small resonators were incorporated into the truly dual exhaust's tailpipes. With the exception of GT equipped Mustangs, the exhaust exits, just before the rear valance, away from the car, by means of the tailpipes having sharp down-turns at their ends.

All early production Mustangs utilized a traverse muffler located between the rear axle and fuel tank. Those on dual exhaust models featured dual inlets and dual outlets and employed two additional mufflers located forward of the rear axle.

BRAKES: The 1965 Mustang is equipped standard with drum-type brakes, front and rear, with a drum size of 9'' on 6-cylinder cars and 10'' on 8-cylinder models. They have a dual-servo internal design and are self-adjusting in reverse only.

STEERING: The steering gear is of the worm and recirculating ball type. An I.D. tag is attached under one of the attaching bolts on the steering gear housing, just forward of the engine firewall. 27:1 is the standard ratio, with a 22:1 ratio for power steering and models with the optional Special Handling Package.

Master cylinder for optional '65 Mustang power brake system.

Mustang steering-gear box.

POWER BRAKE, is spelled out on the brake pedal of '65 Mustangs with the optional power brake system. Disc brakes were also optional in '65, but the Power/Disc combination was not available until 1967.

Several versions of power steering was optioned on '65 Mustangs. At left is an Eaton-type with pump mounted reservoir. Below left is an Eaton-type pump with hose removed to allow a better view. It was used on early production air conditioned models and had it's reservoir mounted on the Mustang's inner fender panel (lower center). A Ford-type pump is pictured at the lower right, which has the filler neck canted to the rear, to allow clearance for the air conditioning hose. Another Ford-type pump has the filler neck canted to the side (not pictured).

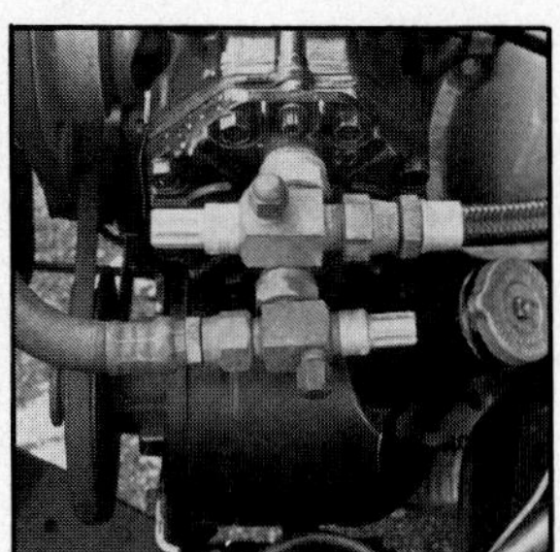

MUSTANG POWER TEAMS

ENGINES; On the day Mustangs debuted at Ford dealerships, they were equipped with one of 3 engines: 170 cubic inch - 101 horsepower, 6-cylinder; 260 cubic inch - 164 horsepower, 8-cylinder; or 289 cubic inch - 210 horsepower, 8-cylinder. Initial brochures stated the 289 cubic inch - 271 horsepower, high-performance 8-cylinder wouldn't be available until June. By the time fall arrived, the 170 cubic inch, 6-cylinder engine had been replaced with a 200 cubic inch version. The 260 cubic inch, 8-cylinder was dropped from the line-up, as was the former low-compression, 289 cubic inch, 8-cylinder. Boasting a 10:1 compression ratio (10.5:1 for the high performance), the updated 289s were available in either 2-barrel or 4-barrel versions. The updated 2-barrel, 289 is rated at 200 horsepower. The 4-barrel engine is rated at 225 horsepower. An additional 10 horsepower is available from the optional dual exhaust. The 271 horsepower V-8 remained basically unchanged throughout the production year, featuring special heads, free-flow cast iron headers, and solid valve lifters and camshaft.

The Mustang Warranty, or Data Plate is located on the rear of the driver's door.

The 260 was fitted with a 2V carburetor and was available only with automatic transmission power teams.

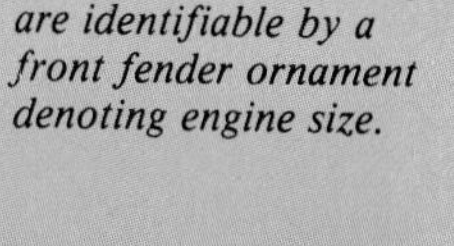
V-8 equipped Mustangs are identifiable by a front fender ornament denoting engine size.

At introduction, the Mustang's standard engine was a 170 cubic inch 6-cylinder.

The 289 was initially offered with 4V carburetors only, but a 2V version was introduced to replace the 260 engine.

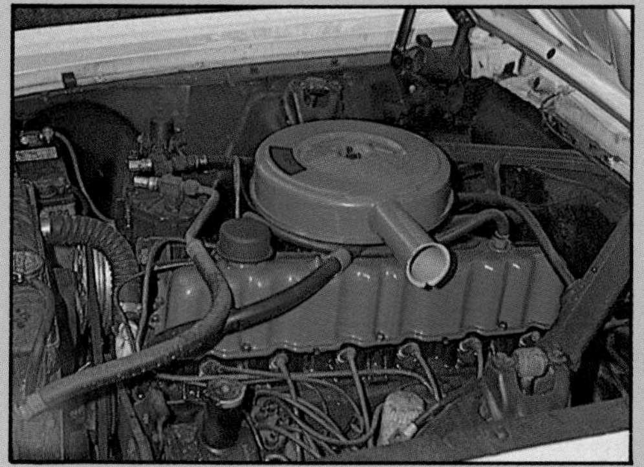
The 200 cubic inch 6-cylinder, replaced the 170 version in the fall of 1964. This engine was much sturdier than the 170, having 7-main bearings, it puts out an additional 19 horsepower, (120).

The lethal high performance 289 began appearing in Mustangs in June of 1964. Horsepower is rated at 271.

POWER TEAM SELECTION CHART

ENGINES	TRANSMISSIONS			REAR AXLE RATIOS					
	3-Speed Manual	4-Speed Manual	Cruise-O-Matic	3-Speed Manual Std.	3-Speed Manual Opt.	4-Speed Manual Std.	4-Speed Manual Opt.	Cruise-O-Matic Std.	Cruise-O-Matic Opt.
170 Six—Std.	Std.	Opt.	Opt.	3.50	—	3.50	—	3.50	—
200 Six—Std.	Std.	Opt.	Opt.	3.20*	—	3.20*	—	2.83*	—
260 2v V-8—Opt.	Std.	N/A	Opt./(Required)	N/A		N/A		3.00	—
289 2v - V-8—Opt.	Std.	Opt.	Opt.	2.80*	—	2.80*	—	3.00	—
289 4v - V-8—Opt.	Std.	Opt.	Opt.	3.00*	—	3.00*	—	3.00*	—
**289 Hi-Perf. V-8—Opt.	N/A	Opt.	N/A	—	—	3.50	3.89 4.11	—	—

*Also available with optional limited-slip differential
**Available after June 1, 1964.

GENERATOR CHARGING SYSTEM (64½ only)

Mustangs produced in the spring and early summer of 1964 were equipped with belt-driven D.C. (direct current) generators. Of the many engineering improvements that transpired during the Mustang's early life, the transition from a generator to alternator charging system is most significant. Pictured below are items to look for on generator equipped Mustangs.

The generator assembly is located on the front of the engine and was originally fitted with a black rubber shroud as shown. A much longer oil dip-stick and tube are required to clear the generator assembly.

The warning light on the Mustang's instrument panel reads GEN, denoting generator.

Generator equipped Mustangs have much larger horns, almost twice the size of horns on alternator equipped models. These early horns are mounted down on the frame behind the radiator.

The coil, on V-8 models must be mounted on the intake, since the generator assembly prevents mounting it on the front of the engine block.

Generator equipped cars have a 3-wire pigtail running to the tail/stop lights assembly.

The radiator core-support panel is configured with air louvers directly in front of the battery box to aid in cooling the battery in the generator charging system.

Introduction of alternators required revamped wiring harnesses, switches and grounding procedures. Although not related to the type charging system employed, the changeover to alternators also moved the Mustang's brake light switch. Generator equipped models have the brake light switch mounted on the master cylinder beneath the hood.

Additional Features Found On Early Production '65 Mustangs

Several variances exists between early to late production '65 Mustangs, based on their assembly time and plant location. Some have been pointed out in this chapter, but there are many more. Here's a listing of a few.

- Stationary (non-adjustable) passenger seat.
- Smaller version of "T"— handle on automatic transmission.
- Owner's manual appearance (cover art is transposed and 170 and 260 engines are included in it's contents).
- Small, flip-open oil cap on distributor base, that requires manual oiling.

Oil filler tube was configured into engine's front cover on early production V-8 Mustangs.

Early production windshield wiper post have threaded base. This was deleted before '65 production ended.

ALTERNATOR CHARGING SYSTEM

Mustangs began receiving alternator charging systems in the summer of 1964 and is likely, the biggest change that took place during the eighteen-month production year of '65 Mustangs. While the detail photos below aren't electrically required with an alternator charging system, they do exist on '65 Mustangs which have the alternator system.

Alternator mounts slightly lower on the engine, with the coil now located on the engine's front cover.

Instrument panel warning light now denotes ALT.

The wiring harness employed with the alternator charging system finds the brake light switch relocated beneath the Mustang's instrument panel.

Four, small rectangular cutouts are in radiator core support, but large air-louvers found on generator models are deleted.

Another revision brought about with the alternator wiring harness, is clip-on, 2-wire connectors on the Mustang's tail/stop light assembly. Removal of the exterior bezel and cover are still required for bulb replacement.

Horns are much smaller and have a higher pitched tone on alternator equipped models. The smaller horns are relocated to the front of the radiator core support.

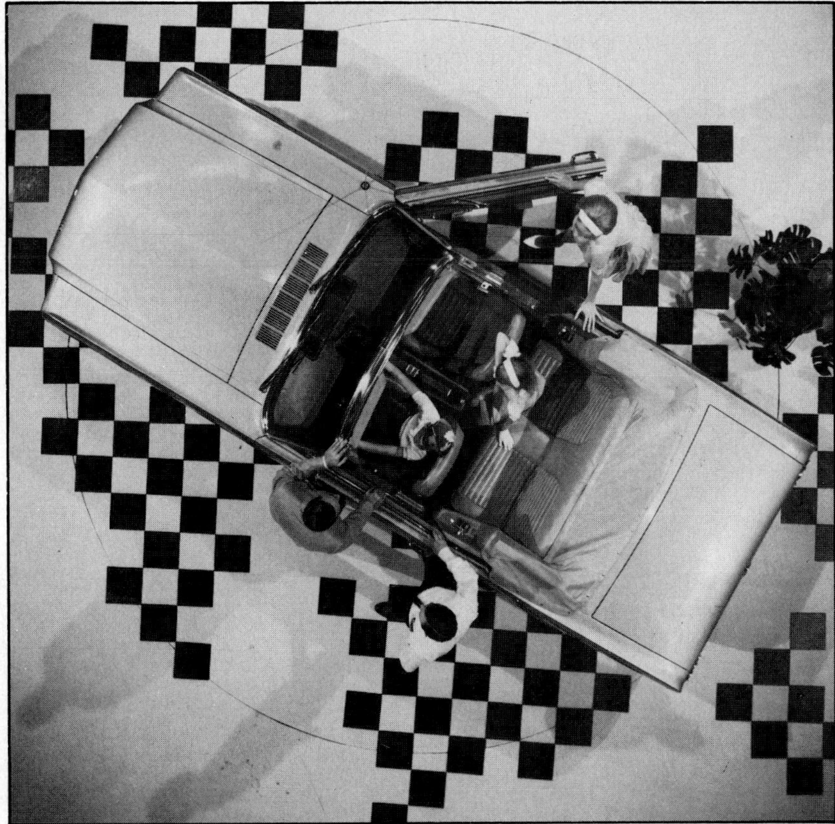

From any view point the '65 Mustang reflects its' sporty, unclutted styling.

1965
RK 7304
MUSTANG

GT MUSTANG

The First Anniversary of the Mustang was April 17th, 1965. Ford celebrated it by introducing two option packages. The "Interior Decor Group", illustrated in preceding pages, was one. The other, and likely most distinctive of all early Mustang options, is the "GT EQUIPMENT GROUP". 1965 Mustang GT equipment is a combination Performance/Appearance package. Ford originally used the European abbreviation of "Gran Turismo" on its famed GT40 racers in the early '60s. Carroll Shelby adopted the designation for his G.T. 350 Mustangs, only a few months prior to introduction of Ford's GT Mustangs.

The mechanical, or performance features included in the 1965 Mustang GT package were taken from an already existing list of RPO (Factory Installed Regular Production Options), which could be ordered separately on any 8-cylinder Mustang. The GT's appearance embellishments were all-new, and unique. Their RPO availability, required the entire GT Equipment group be ordered. At a later date, Ford made the GT appearance items available as Dealer Installed Accessories. The GT appearance items were promoted in major automotive magazines with full-page ads, suggesting: "Make Your Mustang Into A GT! Your Ford Dealer has the goods." Purists differentiate between GT Mustangs of factory origin, and those which are dealer or owner prepared, by looking for identifying features found on factory GT Mustangs. These are:

- Large disc-brake type master cylinder with clip-on cover.
- "DISC BRAKES" denoted on brake pedal.
- Coded I.D. tag on steering gear box contains the letters "HCC-AW" or "HCC-AX" for Mustangs with the quicker, 22:1 steering. Standard steering is 27:1 and is coded HCC-AT.
- Assembly of GT Mustangs did not begin until late February of 1965, therefore the letter in the date code on the warranty plate, must be, "P" through "V".

'65 GT EQUIPMENT GROUP

Available with 225 & 271 HP, V-8 engines only. Includes dual exhaust system with bright extensions through valance panel, special handling package components, front disc brakes, fog lamps and grille bar, GT stripe, 5-dial instrument cluster and GT ornamentation.

The GT's dual exhaust exits through bright trumpet-look extensions, immediately preceded by two throaty resonators, as well as dual mufflers, forward of the rear axle.

Front disc brakes are included in the GT equipment, while power brakes are not available with the GT option

The DISC BRAKE identity is affixed to the GT's brake pedal.

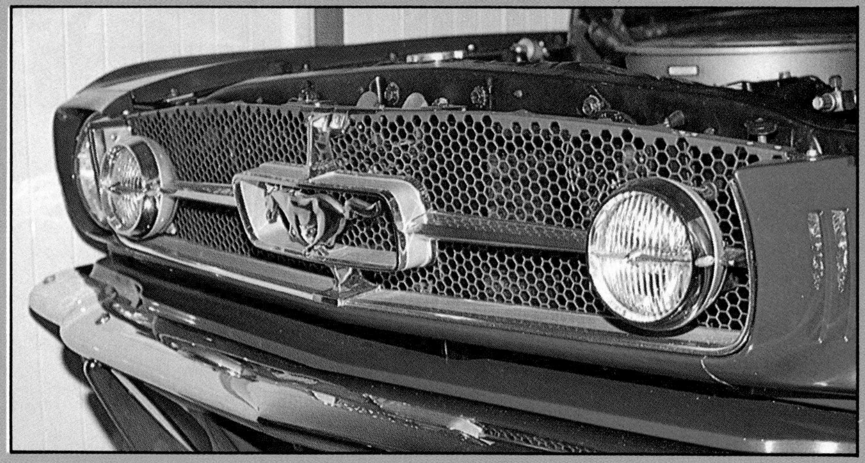

'65 Mustang grilles are painted gun-metal gray. Grilles on GT models are unique in that they have two circular holes configured into the honeycombed grille, one behind each fog lamp. The center portion of the grille's ornament is used on both standard and GT models, however the two horizontal bars on GT models have unique grille arms, onto which the fog lights attach.

- All factory GT Mustangs were equipped with 8-cylinder engines w/4-barrel carburetors, therefore the 5th character in the Vehicle Identificaton Number, which is the engine code, must be an "A" or "K", denoting a 225 hp, 289 cubic inch engine, or 271 hp, 289 cubic inch engine respectively. The low-compression, 210 hp, 289 cubic inch engine was discontinued several months prior to introduction of the GT.
- The two, grille mounted fog light's wiring is routed through two factory-punched holes. One is located on either side of the radiator core support, behind the grille.
- The mesh-type grille in the '65 GT has a pair of circular holes directly behind each bulb assembly through which the fog light wiring is also routed.
- Rear bumper guards are deleted
- A toggle switch, with "FOG" inscribed, is mounted just left of the windshield wiper switch on the instrument panel.
- The GT instrumentation is of the 5-dial, gauge variety. The instrument bezel is black and chrome mylar on standard interior models, or walnut and chrome mylar on models equipped with the "Interior Decor Group". The walnut-style bezel carried over into 1966, while the '65 GT standard bezel was unique only to the '65 model year.

Ford-type lighted grille ornament with horse integrally molded onto light.

Antenna was included with all radio options.

Bright metal horse is an aftermarket accessory which mounts onto the center of the hood's leading edge.

Black & white, rear bumper mounted rubber horse shoes were popular aftermarket items, but more rare, are these front bumper bolt-ons.

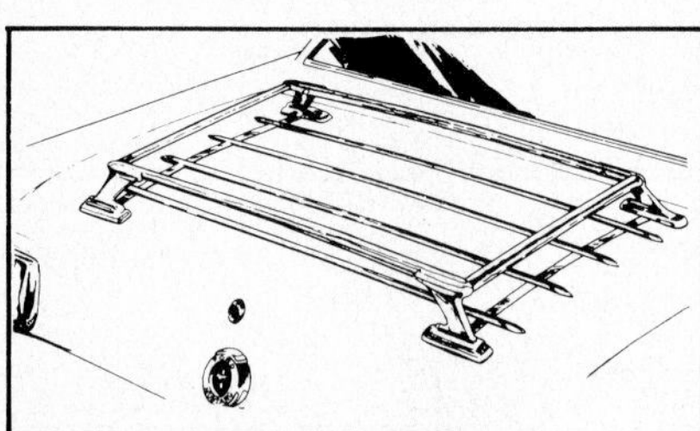

Luggage racks were dealer installed accessories on '65 Mustangs. This type required four strips be mounted onto the rear deck lid.

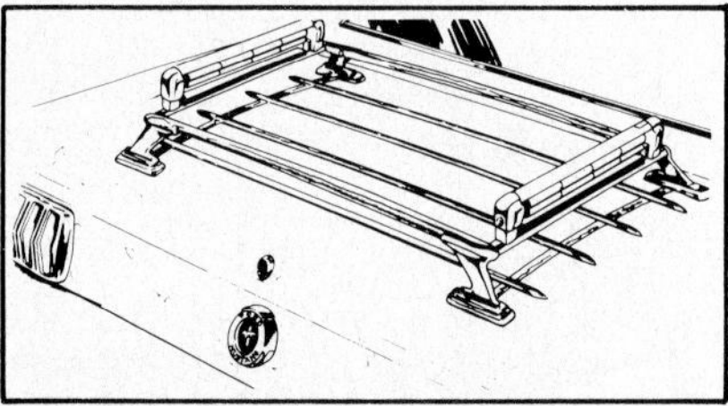

Ski rack attachments were available for both types of luggage racks, at an extra cost.

The "Stand-Off" type luggage rack was most widely used due to the requirement of drilling only four holes for installation.

Extra cost ski rack attachments were also available for the "Stand-Off" type luggage rack.

Options & Accessories

REGULAR PRODUCTION OPTIONS

ENGINES
- 260-2V, V-8
- 289-2V, V-8
- 289-4V, V-8
- 289-4V, V-8 High Performance (6/64) includes Special Handling Package and also 6.95x14 Dual Red Band Nylon Tires after 9/64.

TRANSMISSION
- Cruise-O-Matic — 6-Cylinder
- Cruise-O-Matic — 200 HP and 225 HP V8s (N/A with 271 HP V-8)
- Four-Speed Manual — 6-Cylinder
- Four-Speed Manual — V-8 Engines

PERFORMANCE EQUIPMENT
- Disc Brakes — Front (8-Cyl. — N.A. with Power Brakes)
- Limited Slip Differential
- Rally-Pac — Clock/Tachometer
- Special Handling Package — 200 and 225 HP V-8 Engines — includes increased Rate Front and Rear Springs, Larger Front and Rear Shock Absorbers, 22 to 1 Steering Ratio, and Larger Diameter Front Stabilizer Bar
- GT Equipment Group — Available with 225 & 271 HPV-8 Engines only. Includes Dual Exhaust System with Bright Extensions Through Valance Panel, Special Handling Package Components, Front Disc Brakes, Fog Lamps & Grille Bar, GT Stripe, 5 Dial In--strument Cluster & GT Ornamentation
- Wheels — Styled Steel — 14" (8 cyl. only) 4 or 5

POWER ASSISTS
- Power Brakes
- Power Steering
- Power Top — Convertible

SAFETY EQUIPMENT
- Emergency Flashers
- Padded Visors — 65A and 76A
- Seat Belts, Deluxe, Front — Retractable
- Seat Belts, Deluxe — Rear
- Visibility Group — includes Remote Control Mirror, Day/Nite Mirror, 2-Speed Electric Wipers and Washers
- Accent Group — includes body side paint stripe, rocker panel molding — less rear quarter ornament, 65A or B, 76A or B
- Air Conditioner — Ford (underdash mount)
- Back-Up Lamps
- Battery, Heavy Duty
- Closed Emission System (Calif. type)
- Console, full length
- Console (For use with Air Conditioner)
- Full Width Seat With Center Armrest — 65A & 76A
- Glass — Tinted w/Banded Windshield
- Windshield Only, Tinted & Banded
- Interior Decor Group — Includes Unique Luxury Trim, Padded Visors, Woodgrain Applique Ornamentation & Deluxe Woodgrain Steering Wheel, 5 Dial Instrument Cluster & R/W Door Courtesy Lights
- Radio — Push Button and Antenna
- Radio - AM/Stereosonic Tape Player
- Rocker Panel Moldings — 65A & 76A
- Vinyl Roof — 65A
- Wheel Covers — Knock-Off Hubs
- Wire Wheel Covers, 14"

OPTIONAL TIRES
- Extra Charge For:
  - (5) 6.50x13 4-p.r. WSW
  - (5) 6.95x14 4-p.r. BSW Nylon
  - (5) 6.95x14 4-p.r. WSW
  - (5) 6.95x14 4-p.r. WSW, Nylon
  - (5) 6.95x14 4-p.r. Dual RedBand, Nylon

DEALER INSTALLED ACCESSORIES

ITEM	PART NUMBER
AIR CONDITIONER, FORD	
—6-Cylinder	C5ZZ 19700-F
—8-Cylinder	C5ZZ 19700-G
ARM REST—REAR (PAIR)	C5ZZ 6531600-A-F
AIR HORNS	C5AZ 13800-A
BACK-UP LIGHTS	C5ZZ 15499-A
CIGAR LITE-LIGHTER	C2RZ 15072-A
COBRA HIGH PERFORMANCE KITS (289 C.I.D.)	
—Cobra Engine Performance Kit	C40Z 6A044-C
—Cobra Cylinder Head and Valve Kit	C40Z 6C056-A
—Cobra High Performance Cam Kit	C40Z 6A257-A
—Cobra Distributor Kit	C4DZ 12050-A
—Cobra Heavy-Duty Clutch Kit	C30Z 7A537-A
—Cobra Single 4-V Induction Kit	C5ZZ 6B068-A
—Cobra Two 4-V Induction Kit	C40Z 6B068-E
—Linkage Kit (Std. Trans.)	C5ZZ 9B843-D
—Cobra Three 2-V Induction Kit	C4DZ 6B068-B
—Linkage Kit (Std. Trans.)	C5ZZ 9B843-A
—Cobra Four 2-V Induction Kit	C50Z 6B068-A
—Linkage Kit	C5ZZ 9B843-C

—Cobra Engine Dress-Up Kit C40Z 6980-A
—Cobra Valve Cover Kit C40Z 6A547-A
—Cobra Competition Oil Pan Kit C40Z 6675-A
—Cobra Scatter Shield Kit C40Z 6394-A
COMPASS C4RZ 19A548-A
DOOR EDGE GUARDS C4ZZ 6520910-A
DOOR STOWAGE COMPARTMENT C3RZ 6220130-A
ENGINE COOLANT HEATER
—150 Watt C3RZ 8B152-A
—1000 Watt C3RZ 8B152-B
ENGINE/TRUNK LIGHT C2RZ 15A700-A
FIRE EXTINGUISHER
—2¾ Lb. Unit C3RZ 19B540-A
—5 Lb. Unit C5AZ 19B540-A
FLOOR MATS
—2-Piece Front .... C5ZZ 6513086-A thru E
—Twin Rear .... C5ZZ 6513106-A thru E
GLOVE COMPARTMENT AND CONSOLE DOOR LOCK C4DZ 6206081-A
LAKE PIPES C4AZ 5C246-A
LICENSE PLATE FRAME (Pkg. of 2) C4AZ 17A387-A
LIMITED-SLIP DIFFERENTIAL C40Z 4880-A
LUGGAGE RACK — DECK-MOUNT C5ZZ 6555100-F
—Ski Carrier C3AZ 2555100-C
—Ski Rack — mounts on Luggage Rack C5ZZ 6555100-F C5ZZ 6555100-G
—Luggage Rack Clamp Kit — for making a temporary installation of Luggage Rack C5ZZ 6555100-F C5ZZ 6555196-A
LUGGAGE RACK — ROOF MOUNT
—Basic Kit C5ZZ 6555100-E
—Luggage Carrier C5ZZ 6555100-D
MIRROR, INSIDE NON-GLARE REAR VIEW ... C5ZZ 17700-B
MIRROR, VANITY B9AB 17A679-A
MIRRORS, OUTSIDE REAR VIEW
—Round Head B5AZ 17696-A
—Universal Round Head C3RZ 17696-A
—Remote Control C5ZZ 17696-A
—Matching Right Hand Non-Remote C5ZZ 17696-B
—Racing Type (June Availability) C5RZ 17696-A
PARKING BRAKE WARNING LIGHT C4DZ 15A852-A
POWER BRAKES C5ZZ 2A091-B
POWER STEERING .... Several kits available for specific model application
RACING STRIPE (RED, WHITE, BLUE) .... C5ZZ 1077-A, B, C
RADIO, AM/FM (INCLUDES ANTENNA) C5ZZ 18805-BA
RADIO, TWO-WAY CITIZEN'S BAND C5AZ 18805-E
REAR SEAT SPEAKER C3AZ 18875-A
ROCKER PANEL MOLDING C5ZZ 6510176, 77-A
SEAT BELTS (METAL-TO-METAL)
—Deluxe .... C5AZ 6261200-A thru K
—Standard .... C5AZ 6261200-L thru W
—Rear Seat Adapter Kit C3RZ 6261156-A
SEAT BELT BOOT AND RETAINER KIT (FRONT SEAT) C4AZ 25611A32-A
SEAT BELT RETRACTORS C4AZ 62611A06-A
SPOTLIGHT C5ZZ 15313-A
STUDIOSONIC SOUND SYSTEM C5AZ 18875-E
—Foot Control Switch C5AZ 18876-A
TACHOMETERS
—8-cylinder, 8000 RPM, 4" Rotunda C2RZ 17A326-B
—Mounting Bracket C2RZ 17368-B
—6-cylinder, 6000 RPM, 3" Rotunda C3RZ 17A326-A
—8-cylinder, 6000 RPM, 3" Rotunda C3RZ 17A326-B
—8-cylinder, 9000 RPM, 4" Sun C4AZ 17A326-A
—Mounting Bracket C2RZ 17368-A
—Rally-Pac (Clock-Tachometer Combination)
—6-Cylinder C5ZZ 10B960-B
—8-Cylinder C5ZZ 10B960-C
TISSUE DISPENSER C3RZ 19A549-A
TONNEAU COVER
—White C5ZZ 76501A42-A
—Black C5ZZ 76501A42-B
TOOL KIT B7A 17003-A
TRUNK RELEASE, REMOTE CONTROL C4AZ 62432A00-A
TURN SIGNAL—FENDER MOUNTED C5AZ 13A310-A
WHEEL COVERS (SET OF FOUR)
—Deluxe With Spinner 13" (ea.) C5ZZ 1130-B
—Deluxe With Spinner 14" (ea.) C5ZZ 1130-D
—Simulated Wire 13" (set of 4) C30Z 1130-J
—Simulated Wire 14" (set of 4) C50Z 1130-C
—Style-Steel Wheels (ea.) C5ZZ 1007-B
—Nut (ea.) C5ZZ 1012-A
—Cap, 2¼" (ea.) C5ZZ 1130-G
WHEEL TRIM RINGS
—13" C5AZ 1211-A
—14" C5AZ 1211-B
WINDSHIELD WASHERS
—Single Speed Wiper C5ZZ 17A603-A
—Universal C1RZ 17A603-A

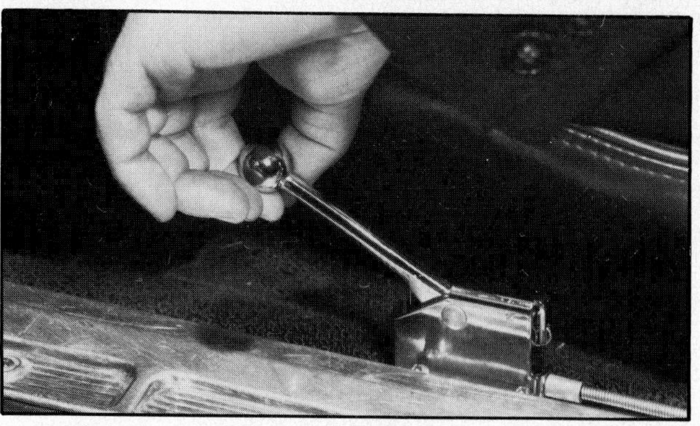

Remote trunk release employs a cable operated latch, actuated by a bright metal lever mounted between the driver's seat and door sill.

Several dealer installed tachometers, ranging from 6000-9000 RPMS, were offered.

Dealer installed lock could be used on optional console, as well as glove box door.

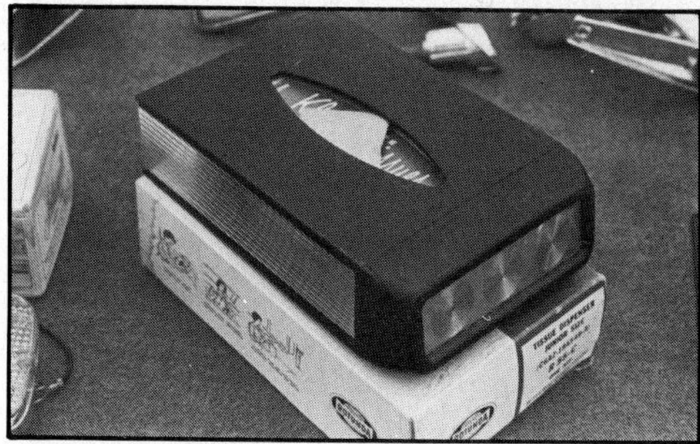

Tissue dispensors were offered in the above normal capacity size, as well as a junior version. Both mount beneath the Mustang's dash.

Dealer installed clocks were offered for '65 Mustangs, and mount in the top-center of the dash.

Parking Brake warning light is a dealer installed accessory

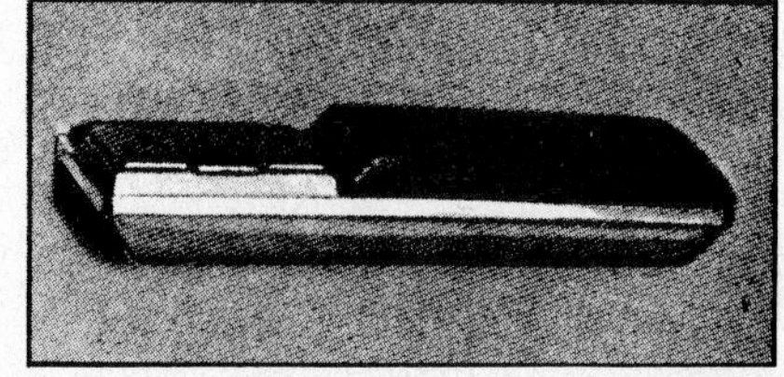

Rear seat, ash tray/arm rest is a rare dealer installed accessory mounted beneath the rear window crank

1965 SHELBY

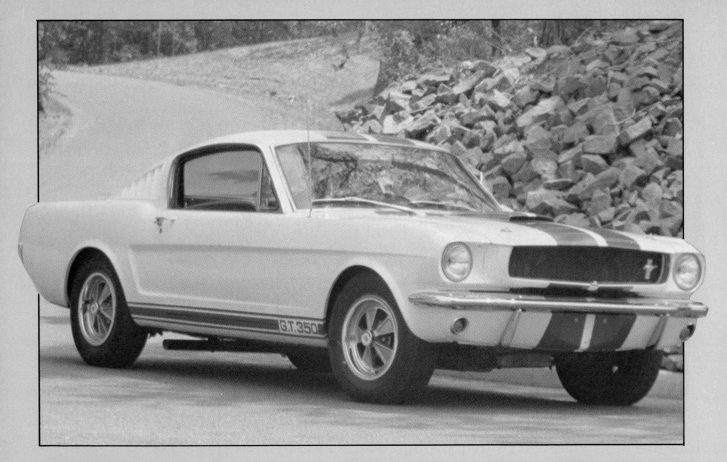

In late 1964, Ford asked Carroll Shelby to create a sports car based on the then-new Mustang fastback. The goal was to have a Ford alternative to GM's Corvette: road racing victories and showroom excitement. Shelby's edition of the Mustang, unveiled on January 27, 1965, fit the bill in all respects. It looked like a Mustang fastback at first glance, but upon closer inspection, the difference took precedence over the similarities.

SHELBY EXTERIOR:

Outwardly, the 1965 Shelby is a Mustang. A lightweight fiberglass hood carries a functional hood scoop and the grille is cleaned up by deleting the large Mustang running horse and corral. Racing-type hood pins are standard. The Mustang running horse/tri-color bar is relocated in the driver's side of the grille. All other Mustang emblems are removed (except for the stock Mustang gas cap). The cars all carry bold blue side stripes along the rocker panels and a "GT350" designation just behind the front wheel well. All 1965 GT350s are white. Some, but not all, include a small rectangular GT350 emblem attached to the passenger side of the rear panel.

INTERIOR:

Shelby interiors in '65 are black only. The steering wheel is flat, 3-spoke aluminum with a wood rim. A special instrument pod carrying a tachometer and oil pressure gauge mounts in the top center of the dash, at eye level, canted toward the driver. Large 3 inch competition seat belts are standard. In place of the production Mustang's deleted fold down rear seat, the '65 Shelbys feature a one-piece fiberglass shelf that mounts the spare tire.

ENGINE:

The Shelby GT350s are equipped with a Shelby-modified 289 High-Performance engine rated at 306 horsepower. Shelby unique parts include an aluminum "COBRA" high-rise intake manifold and 715 cfm Holley center-pivot float carburetor, finned aluminum "COBRA" valve covers, an extra capacity aluminum oil pan, and Tri-Y exhaust headers. Glasspacked bullet mufflers are employed with exhaust pipes exiting just forward of the rear wheels.

Transmissions are all Borg Warner T-10 aluminum case units with close ratio gears. Rear ends are large 9 inch units, shortened and carrying a Detroit Automotive "No Spin" ratcheting differential.

SHELBY SUSPENSION:

The 1965 Shelby suspensions are modified with a larger 1 inch front stabilizer bar, special pitman and idler arms, lowered upper "A" arms, Koni adjustable shock absorbers, and rear torque control arms (traction bars). Travel-limiting cables are attached to the rear axle housing. Under the hood, the Shelby front end is stiffened with a one-piece export-type brace, replacing the standard Mustang two-piece unit. This brace attaches to both shock towers and the firewall. Also, a "Monte Carlo" bar is utilized between the fender wells.

Early '65 Shelbys had their batteries mounted in the trunk for better weight distribution. Later cars retained the stock Mustang under-hood battery placement.

Front brakes are large Ford disc; Galaxie station wagon drums fit on the rear — sintered metallic linings are used on both the front and rear.

WHEEL:

The standard Shelby wheel is a 15x5½ station wagon rim, painted silver with chrome lug nuts, mounting special Goodyear Blu Dot 7.75x15 tires.

SHELBY VIN PLATE

All 1965 Shelby GT350s have a special Shelby VIN plate pop-riveted over the Ford VIN number on the driver's side inner front fender. The Mustang fastbacks delivered to Shelby were all built at the San Jose, California, assembly plant and all were equipped with the 289 High-Performance engine, so the Ford serial number (found under the Shelby VIN plate or stamped on the passenger side inner fender) will always begin with 5R09K.

LEMANS STRIPES

The wide, twin Guardsman Blue racing stripes were a dealer-installed option on the Shelby models. Some cars received them at the factory.

OPTIONAL WHEEL

A special 5-spoke Shelby wheel, manufactured to Shelby's specification by Cragar, was available optionally. The 15x6 wheel is aluminum, and features a chrome die-cast center cap with "CS" in the center.

1966

Supply the demand! That was Ford's major goal with the 1966 Mustang. Close to 700,000 Mustangs were built in that first extended model year — a record for first season sales of a totally new car. Mustang remained the most talked about car in America, and it was still alone in Ford's newly outlined "ponycar" market.

Obviously, then, the Mustang was far short of requiring a major styling revision, and no sheetmetal changes were made. Still, Ford added many styling "refinements" — several which are easy to recognize. Most Mustang owners will quickly point out the new 1966 grille — no bars flanking the galloping horse emblem (unless the GT Equipment Group was ordered). Also, the simulated air scoop forward of the rear wheels now contained three bars, to give the look of channeling air to the rear brakes. On the inside, every 1966 Mustang has a five dial instrument cluster, whether or not it's a GT. The option/accessory list was also evolving and expanding. Options in '66 totaled over 70, up from 50 in 1964.

Then too, some mechanical changes were made. For example, in '66 you could get an automatic

'66 Mustang with optional Interior Decor and styled steel wheels. Shortly after model-year change over, the all-chrome wheels were redesigned, with only the honeycomb center remaining chrome, with the rest of the wheel being painted black. A bright trim ring is used to give the newly designed wheel an all-chrome appearance.

BODYSTYLES

The 1966 Mustang's exterior body sheetmetal is identical to its' 1965 predecessor. The visual differences are achieved by subtle revisions in trim appointments. All exterior body panels will interchange between the two model years.

transmission with the 289 high performance "K" engine (although not air conditioning).

What about the GT350? Refinements here too. Overall, the "bean-counters" back in Detroit (GT350's were assembled in California) wanted to see more sales, and less red ink. The "Detroit-Locker" 4.30 rear axle was made an option. Plexiglass rear quarter windows replaced the side vents found in the '65 — giving the car a more fashionable look. Sales increased about 500%, aided dramatically by an order of close to 1,000 GT350's from Hertz Rent A Car.

FORD

'66 Mustang with optional Interior Decor, accent stripe and styled-steel wheels. Note: hood lip and rocker panel molding are standard on '66 Mustangs.

EXTERIOR

GRILLE: The 1965 honeycomb, stamped grille was changed on 1966 Mustangs to extruded aluminum, configured in an egg crate design, with hundreds of rectangular openings. The thin, horizontal strips of the grille structure are chromed. On GT equipped Mustangs, the chrome strips are blacked out. Other grille features, recognizable as '66 Mustang are the absence of horizontal chrome spikes fitted astride the grille ornament, as well as deletion of the stubby chrome, vertical attachments. The grille ornament's suspended appearance gives the Mustang emblem an even greater running-free look in 1966. The only other change to the '66 Mustang's front, is the bright metal hood lip, becoming standard on all models. Whereas in '65, only GT equipped Mustangs received the hood lip molding. FORD is spelled out, widely spaced, across the hood's leading edge, in bright letters, as in the previous model year.

ROOF: The 1966 Mustang roof line remained unchanged, on hardtop and 2+2 fastback, body styles. On convertible Mustangs, the power top remained optional, but color choices were reduced, from 3 to 2, black or white only. Top material was 5-ply vinyl laminated canvas, structurally reinforced. The top boot is constructed of vinyl coated canvas, color keyed to the car's trim scheme on convertible models.

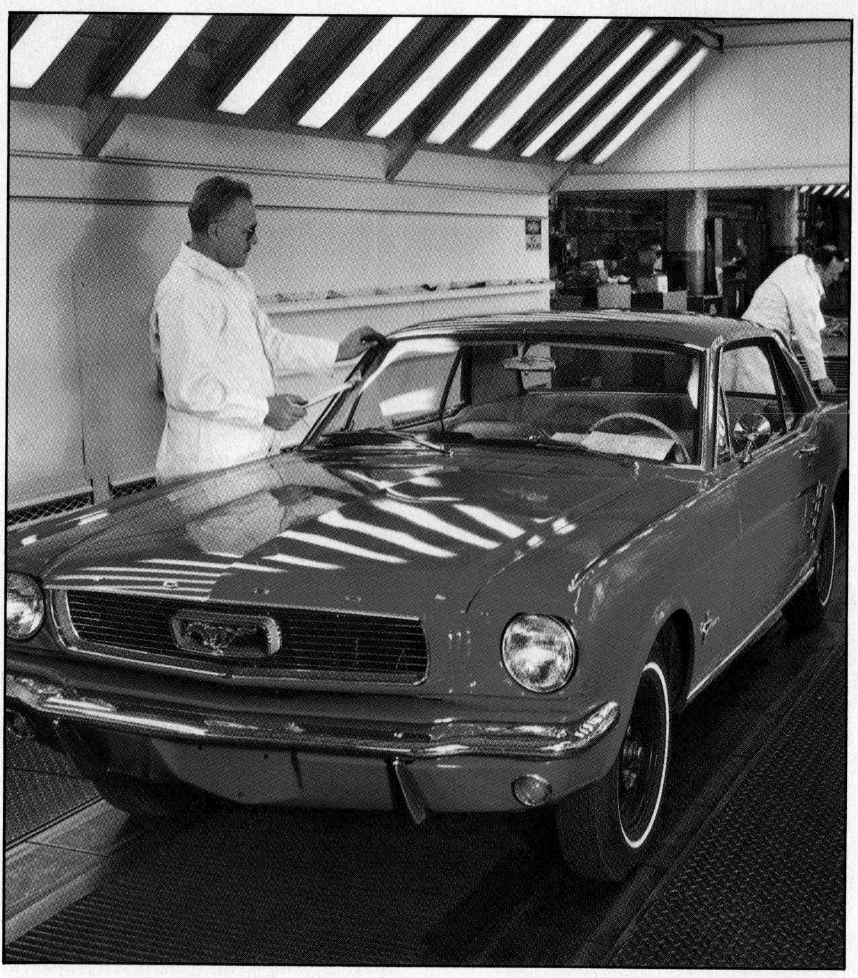

SIDE EXTERIOR: The sculptured side view of the '66 Mustang, received a visual revision to its' simulated rear quarter air scoops. The appearance of a functional opening in the scoop, is more closely simulated, by the 1966 chrome ornament's center, being blacked out. Three chrome spires, six inches in length, extend forward from the ornament, giving the appearance of scooping air into the rear brakes. The simulated air scoop ornament is deleted on 2+2 Mustangs, those with the GT equipment group option, or Accent Group pin stripe option.

ROCKER PANEL MOLDINGS: The rocker panel moldings, that were previously standard only on 1965, 2+2 Mustangs, became standard trim on all 1966 bodystyles. Only, the accent pin stripe, outlining the Mustang's sculptured side remained optional throughout 1966. GT equipped Mustangs have the rocker panel molding deleted. The pin stripe, was likewise, unavailable with the GT equipment group.

EMBLEMS: The V-8 engine equipped Mustangs are again identified in '66 with the cubic inch displacement cast atop a bright-metal, shallow "V" emblem affixed to the upper center of car's front fender. On high performance models, a backing plate is affixed behind the emblem with "HIGH PERFORMANCE" stamped onto a checkered background.

The running horse and tri-colored vertical bar emblem appears behind the front wheel opening, affixed onto the fender panel. Also, MUSTANG is spelled out, on a one-piece bright-metal casting. Both emblems are eliminated on GT models.

Tri-colored front fender emblem carries over from '65.

Fastback models receive a unique "2+2" identity.

289 is the only V-8 offered, however three horsepower versions were available.

HIGH PERFORMANCE identifies the 271 hp 289 V-8s. Note: Cobra medallion was a dealer added item, included with Cobra performance kits, available through participating Ford dealers.

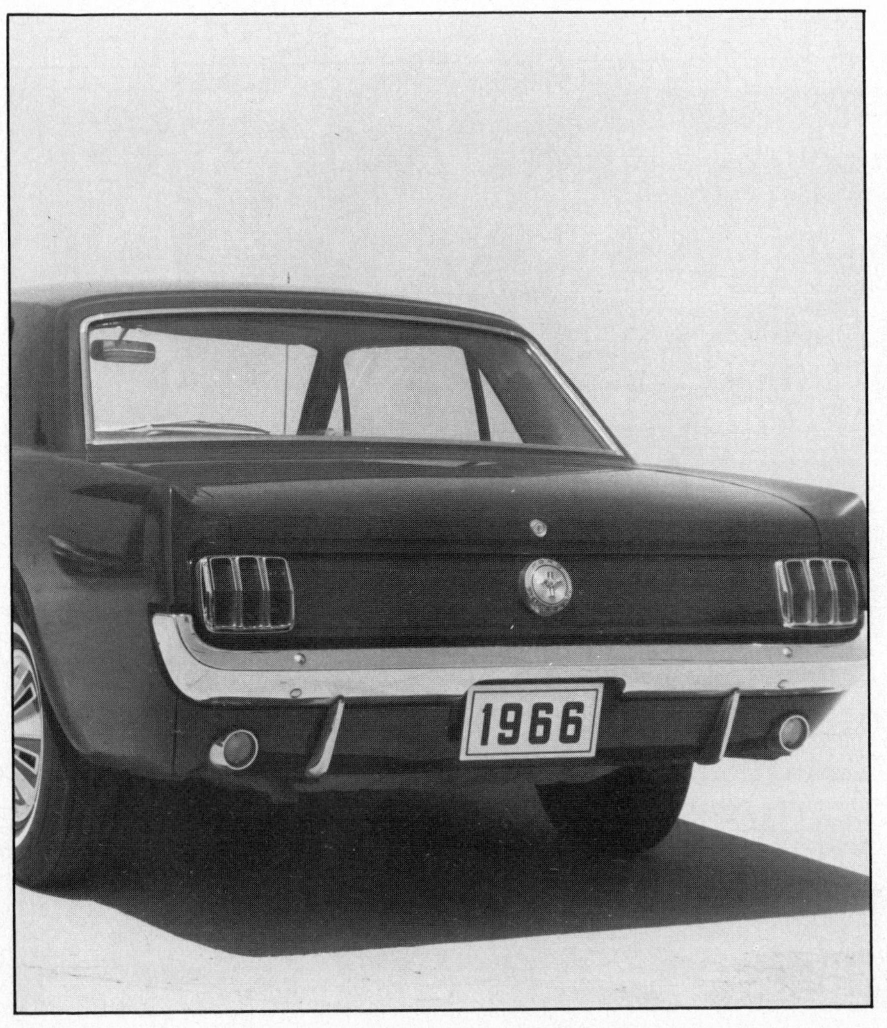

BUMPERS: Identical to 1965, the '66 Mustang bumpers contour to the sheet metal of the Mustang's front and rear, highlighting the car's sculptured appearance.

GAS CAP: The 1966 fuel filler neck and fuel tank are unchanged from 1965, however the gas cap underwent a major revision. The ceramic center is eliminated from the '66 gas cap. The cap's edges are grooved, and the words, "FORD MUSTANG" are stamped concentrically, into the brushed bright-metal surface. A cast-metal version of the running horse and tri-colored bars are affixed to the gas cap's center.

BACKUP LIGHTS: Here-to-fore optional, backup lights became standard equipment on '66 Mustangs.

EXTERIOR AIR VENTS: Just forward of the windshield, in the Mustang's cowl area, there is a series of slender openings to gather air into the passenger compartment fresh air ducts, as well as into the heater/defroster assembly.

On the fastback bodystyle there is a series of five louvers, configured into the upper exterior quarter area. Each louver becomes progressively smaller, front to rear. The louver openings are latticed with chrome trim. Ford, referred to the louvers as ''Silent-Flo ventilation''. The primary function, when open, is to extract stale air from the passenger compartment.

GLASS: Tempered safety-glass continued, all-around on '66 Mustangs with tinting optional, on the windshield only, or to the entire glass area. The convertible retained it's zip-out clear vinyl rear window. Folding-glass rear windows, were not a factory (RPO) production option until the 1967 model year.

'66 Mustang, optional vinyl roof included a bright molding at the roof base.

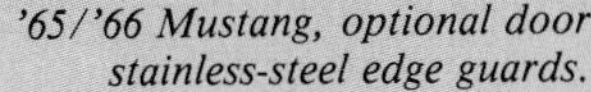

'65/'66 Mustang, optional door stainless-steel edge guards.

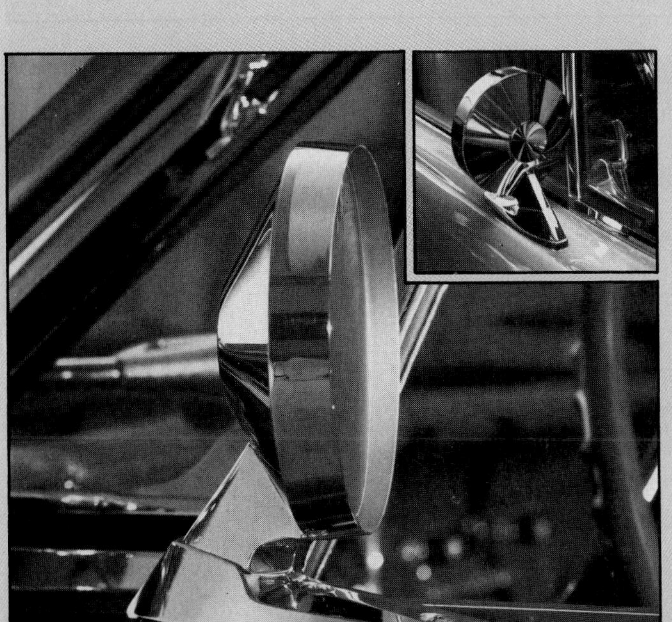

Optional remote controlled mirror was included in the visibility group. A matching, right hand mirror was also offered, although it's fixed-head position rendered it non-functional to the driver.

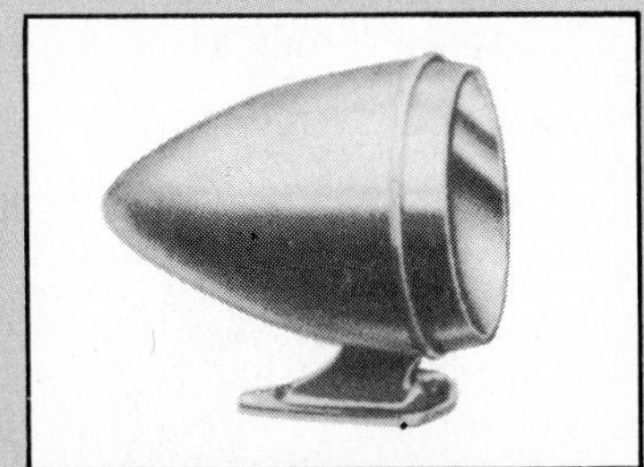

Mustang & Shelby racing mirror was a dealer installed option.

Bright-metal hood ornament is an aftermarket accessory, but was offered over the counter by many Ford dealers. Ornament requires holes to be drilled into the center leading edge of the Mustang's hood.

TRUNK

LUGGAGE COMPARTMENT:

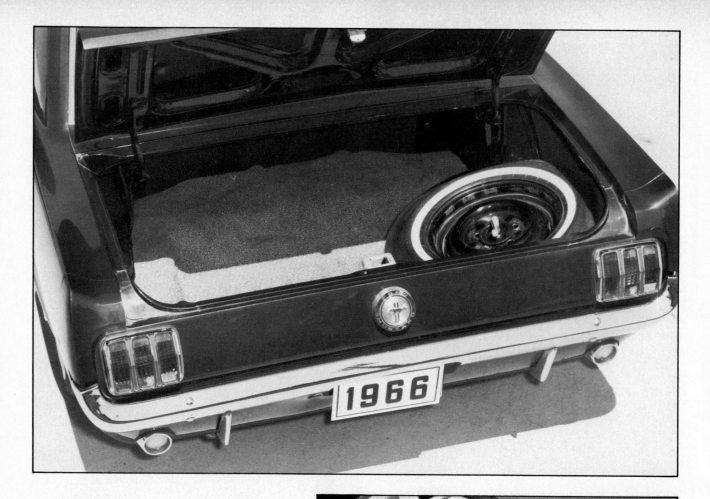

The 1966 Mustang luggage compartment was again 9.0 cubic feet in hardtop models and 7.7 cubic feet in convertibles. Ford publicized that usable luggage space in the 2 + 2 is tripled when the rear seat is folded down, and the pass-through to the trunk is open. Otherwise, usable trunk space is only about 5.0 cubic feet in the 2 + 2.

In the up position, rear seat in fastback model seats two adults.

Luggage compartment provides storage for spare tire on the right. Mats were plaid or speckled, depending on assembly plant.

Folded down, the 2 + 2's rear seat becomes a carpeted cargo area.

Standard '66 Mustang interior.

INTERIOR

Interior differences between '65 and '66 Mustangs are far more apparent than the minor exterior variances.

INSTRUMENT PANEL: The '66 Mustang's standard instrument panel received an all-new instrument bezel, glove box door, and reshaped crash pad.

Five-dial instrumentation using gauges, instead of warning lights, is standard equipment on '66 Mustangs. The 140 mph speedometer, formerly used on GT models, or those with Interior Decor, is standard in all '66 Mustangs, including 6-cylinder models. The instrument bezel, or housing varies with some option packages, as well as model years, as illustrated on the accompanying artist renderings.

'65/'66 INSTRUMENT BEZEL COMPARISON

'65 standard interior.

'65 standard interior with GT Equipment Group.

'65/'66 with Interior Decor. (Includes walnut applique.)

'66 standard interior. (Note concentric outline trim rings.)

1966 INSTRUMENT BEZELS

Standard Instrument Bezel

Interior Decor Instrument Bezel

INSTRUMENT LAYOUT

The '66 Mustang's circular speedometer is inset directly in the center of the instruments.
To the left are the fuel and oil pressure gauges. To the right are the amp and temperature gauges. '65 Mustang standard instrument panels had only one turn signal indicator, while '66 models are equipped with two. The instrument bezel is molded plastic with a black camera-case finish, trimmed in bright mylar, (plastic chrome). The glove box door matches the instrument bezel outline, but is made of metal instead of plastic.

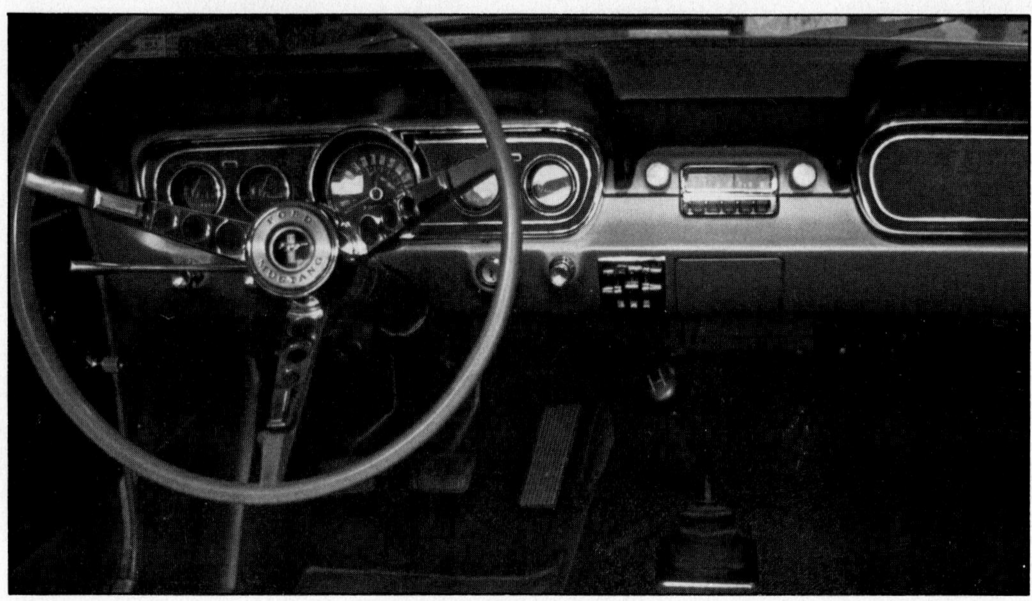

CRASH PAD

The '66 style crash pad retains the dual-hooded appearance, contouring to the instrument panel on one side, and the glove box door on the other, but is shaped slightly different from the '65.

STEERING WHEEL

The standard steering wheel and steering column are color keyed to the Mustang's painted metal instrument panel, and have a 3-spoke design. The steering wheel center is trimmed with a bright metal matching 3-spoke horn ring, containing nine, black circular depressions, to simulate holes. The words FORD MUSTANG are stamped around the center of the horn ring. The traditional 3-color Mustang insignia is molded into the horn ring's ceramic center.

CONTROLS & SWITCHES

The windshield wiper switch is at the extreme left, beneath the instrument bezel. The light switch is located directly to the left of the steering column. The four-position ignition switch is located to the right of the steering column. A "pop-out" cigarette lighter is located to the right of the ignition switch. The fresh air heater-defroster controls and fan blower switch are located to the right of the cigarette lighter. A large pull-out ash tray is located beneath the radio. Emergency flashers are standard equipment on '66 Mustangs. The switch is located inside the glove box.

Fresh air is available to the driver side by pulling out the air vent knob, located beneath the instrument panel directly to the left of the steering column.

To the left of the vent knob is the parking brake lever labeled, BRAKE.

AM/FM radio, offered as service part, beginning in July of 1965 - RPO, (regular production option), for '66 model year only.

RADIOS:

- AM — The optional AM radio in '66 is located between the instruments and glove box. It is of the push-button variety and utilizes a single speaker, mounted flush into the top of the crash pad, covered with a louvered metal grille. If the radio is not optioned, a color-keyed blanking plate covers the area cut out for the radio.
- AM RADIO/STEREOSONIC TAPE SYSTEM — Offered as a factory option in '66, this radio was AM only, but received an integral stereo, 8-track tape player. The stereo speakers are mounted into the lower inside of the Mustang's doors. Each speaker is covered over with a color keyed grille. The normal speaker in the top of the instrument panel is not used with this option. Push-buttons are deleted. A black camera-case chrome trimmed face plate is used to mount the AM/Tape player in the Mustang's instrument panel.
- AM/FM — Most rare of Mustang radios is the AM/FM. Similar in appearance to the AM model, the AM/FM fits into the same opening and also has five push buttons. A horizontal, AM to FM slide-bar selector, determines the radio mode. F-O-R-D, is stamped into the slide-bar.

DELUXE STEERING WHEEL

An optional simulated walnut steering wheel was available on '66 Mustangs with all bodystyles and interiors. Studded with eighteen, bright recessed dots, the deluxe steering wheel features brushed metal spokes, pierced with 12 circular holes. In addition, each spoke has a cutout to accommodate the back-mounted horn ring ends. The deluxe steering wheel's center appears quite similar to the standard type, but is configured differently. The deluxe steering wheel is included in the Interior Decor option.

Low-profile Rally-Pac has the RALLY-PAC wording deleted. Often referred to as the '66 style Rally-Pac, the low-profile version was actually introduced along with 5-dial instrumentation in the spring of 1965. It retains the wrinkle finish of its' predecessor, however it was often painted to match the steering column.

RALLY-PAC

The low-profile Rally-Pac introduced along with 5-dial instrumentation in the 1965 mid-production year, carried over to '66, remaining an individual option, available with any bodystyle or powerteam. A clock is located on the right side, and a tachometer is located on the left. The Rally-Pac straddles the steering column and is painted with a wrinkle-finish. All, early style Rally-Pacs were painted camera case black, while the low-profile version used in all '66 Mustangs may be either black, or color-keyed to the steering column. The Rally-Pac's exterior housing, as well as the 24-hour clocks are all alike. There are many variations however, of the Mustang Rally-Pac's tachometers. The tachometer is driven by electrical impulses from the car's ignition system. Therefore 6-cylinder cars require a different internal meter movement than those for cars equipped with 8-cylinder engines. The tachometer is calibrated from 0-6,000 RPMs on all models, except those equipped with the high-performance, 271 horsepower V-8. These models have a 0-8,000 RPM tachometer. All Rally-Pac tachometers are read in RPMs x 100. Some are graduated in multiples of 5, while others are graduated in multiples of 10. "FORD" is imprinted in the lower center of the Rally-Pac's tachometer face.

CONSOLE

Mustang consoles for '66 are unchanged from the previous year. The console is constructed of molded plastic, with a bright metal top panel. An ash tray is located at the rear of the console. The rear portion also houses two integral mounted lights, wired to the interior lighting system. The transmission shifter passes through the console, which contains a plate with a large opening for manual transmissions, or a unique console transmission indicator plate for automatic equipped cars. A storage compartment is located at the front of the console. The storage compartment illuminates when its' door is opened. The storage compartment area is cut away on Mustangs with air conditioning. The cut end is capped with a bright metal end trim, about twice the size of the console end trim used in '65.

Air Conditioning option was under dash type in 1965 and 1966 Mustangs. If optional console is also installed, the storage area is cut off and capped with a bright end trim.

AIR CONDITIONING

The '66 Mustang air conditioning remained an underdash version in 1966, but there are subtle differences from '65. The face is painted a camera-case black, and the four air registers no longer have two concentric trim rings. A small red, white and blue Ford crest emblem is affixed to the upper center.

SHIFTERS

Both automatic and manual '66 transmissions received identical shifters to their '65 predecessors. The manual transmission shift pattern is stamped into the knob, while automatics have a base mounted transmission shift indicator.

Cruise-O-Matic shifter.

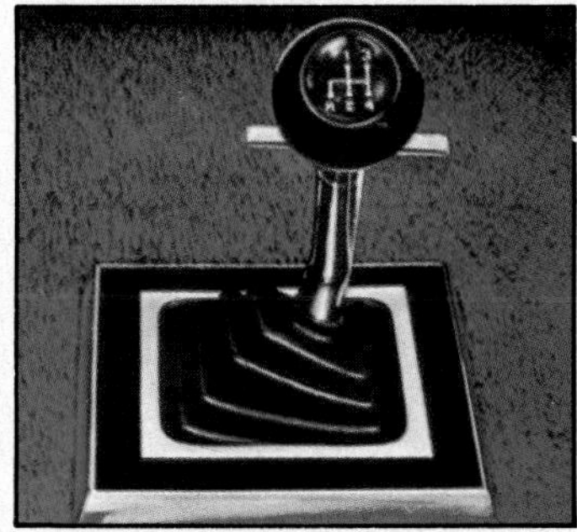

4-speed shifter.

The accelerator pedal, brake pedal and clutch (if so equipped) are suspended on linkage rods beneath the Mustang's instrument panel. The headlight dimmer switch is located at the upper left on the driver's side floor. A small red indicator light illuminates inside the circular speedometer when the high beam lights are operative.

SEATS

The standard '66 Mustang seats received knit-weave vinyl inserts in their center sections, while '65 were constructed entirely of smooth grained vinyl. The '66 blue interiors are lighter than '65, while the '66 red interiors are much darker.

DOOR PANELS

The '66 Mustang standard door panels feature horizontal, embossed pleats, running the length of the panel's lower half. (The '65 door panel's pleats were vertical.) The standard door and window cranks, as well as the arm rest pad and base are direct carry-overs from '65. The door panel has a bright mylar (plastic chrome), concentric trim inset around its' outline.

REAR SEATS

The rear seating area varies between the three bodystyles and therefore each bodystyle has a different size rear seat. The hardtop is widest of the three, the convertible cushions are shortened to accommodate the inner convertible quarter trim panels. Least wide of the three, is the fastback's narrow two-passenger rear seat.

The convertible rear, upper seat cushion is affixed with a grooved molding for the top boot to attach.

The convertible rear, inner trim panels have an ash tray configured in either side, but the quasi arm rest area is too far forward to be usable. Fold-down rear seats are standard on fastback models. A latch mechanism is located on the right inner trim panel to release the seat. A flip-up pass-through allows extra long articles to be transported. Fastback models have two circular interior lights recessed into the rear inner trim panels.

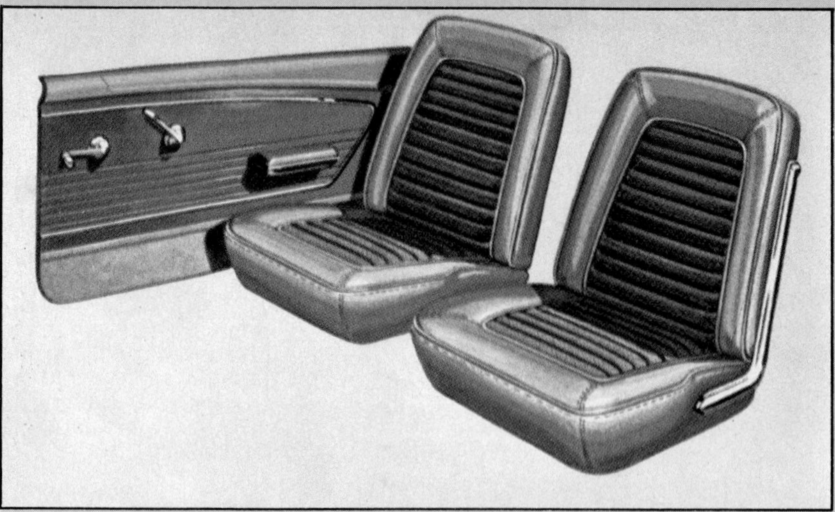

'66 standard bucket seats and door panels.

'66 optional bench seats. Not available with Interior Decor or fastback models. Ford referred to the fastback as 2+2, and the bench seat would have conflicted with the 2-passenger front, 2-passenger rear, theme suggested by the 2+2 nameplate.

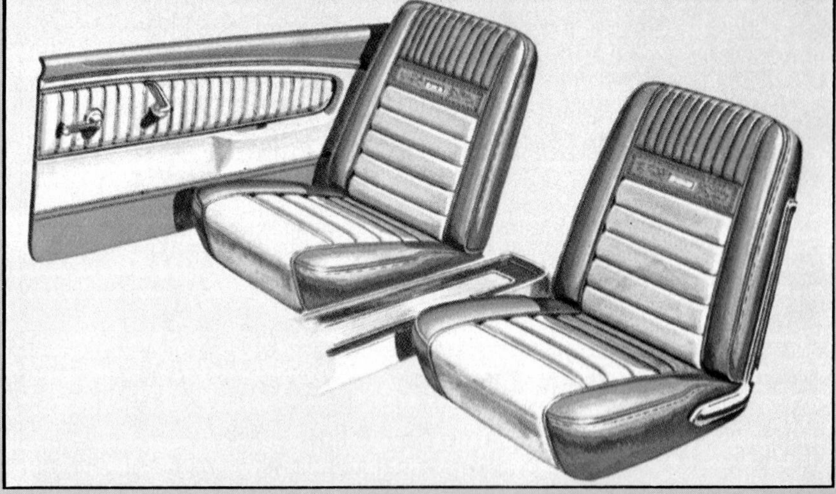

'66 Interior Decor option. Door panels and front seat buckets are uniquely bolstered and the seat's knit-weave centers are replaced with a contrasting color, grained vinyl. Running Pony inserts perpetrated the now popular "Pony" interior reference.

OPTIONAL INTERIORS

- Interior Decor: Often called Pony, Deluxe or Luxury interior, was virtually unchanged from '65 to '66.
  Pistol grip door pull-handles.
  Simulated walnut trim on the instrument panel and glove box door.
  Deluxe steering wheel.
  Luxury padded door panels, with integral arm rest.
  Courtesy/Warning lights in doors.
  Unique foam bolstered seats with embossed running pony inserts front and rear, (pony inserts deleted on rear seat of fastback models).
  Brightly trimmed foot pedals.
  Partial-carpeted kick panels, with unique trim.
- Bench Seat: Optional on hardtops and convertibles, while not available on fastback models, or those with the Interior Decor Option.

Seat belts, front and rear, are standard on '66 Mustangs. Deluxe, push-button release, seat belts were optional, and included retractors for front belts and a reminder light centered on the instrument panel beneath the ignition switch and cigarette lighter. Seat belt retractors were also optional.

Interior Decor option included a plush door trim panel with integral molded arm-rest. Red & white courtesy lights are also part of the luxury interior. Speaker grille is included with radio/tape player option.

Padded visors are standard in '66. Convertible top latches into clamp affixed to inner windshield frame.

Mirror attaching arm includes a trough recepticle for visor tips. Convertible visors are shortened to allow clearance of top latches.

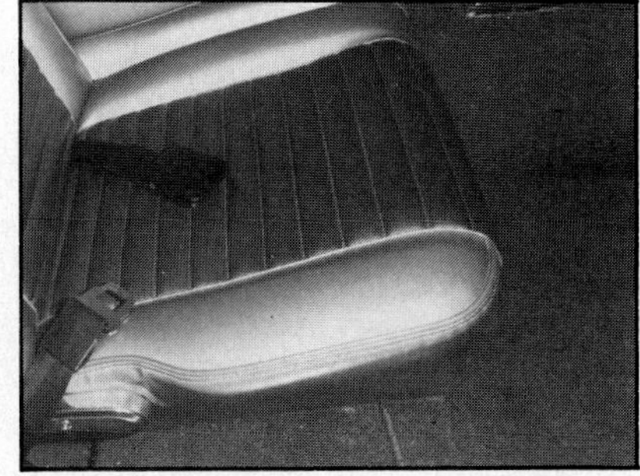

Standard seat belts are color-keyed in '66. Optional deluxe belts have a push button release.

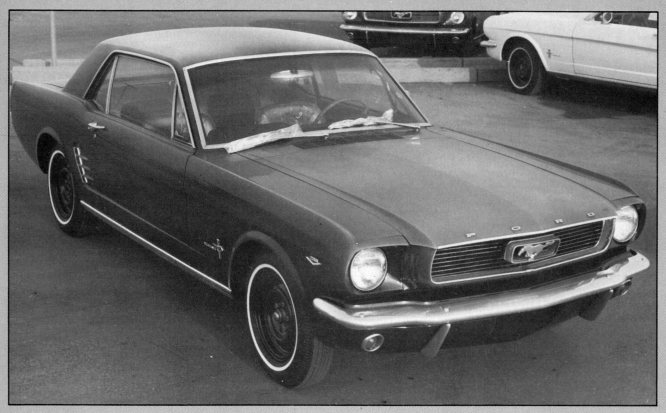

'66 Mustang awaiting shipment from assembly plant storage yard.

WHEEL SPECIFICATIONS		
	6-Cyl. Models	V-8 Models
Type	Stamped Steel Ventilated Disc with Safety-Type Rims	
Number of Studs	4	5
Diameter and Rim Size (in.)	14x4.5	14x5

WHEELS

Standard wheels for '66 Mustangs are 14" on all models. 6-cylinder models are equipped with wheels having a 4-lug pattern, while 8-cylinder models are fitted with 5-lug, wheels.

WHEEL COVERS

Slotted, full disc wheel covers are standard on '66 Mustangs. The tri-colored Mustang insignia is thermal embossed in the wheel cover's plastic center.

TIRE SPECIFICATIONS			
	6.95x14 4 PR Rayon	6.95x14 4 PR Nylon	6.95x14 4 PR Premium Nylon
Six-Cylinder Models	Std.	Opt.	—
"289" 2v and "289" 4v V-8 Model	Std.	Opt.	Opt.
"289" High-Perf.**	—	—	Opt.*

* No-Cost Option — black or white sidewalls
**Includes dual red band premium nylon tires.

TIRES

6.95x14, 4-ply rayon black sidewall tires were standard on '66 Mustangs.

OPTIONAL WHEELS

The Mustang's all-chrome styled steel wheels were redesigned early in the '66 model year. Only the honeycombed center remained chrome, while the rest of the wheel was changed to black. A beauty ring is used to trim the black, outer portion of the wheel, so there is little visual difference. The hub is capped with a small red center-cap with a thermal embossed Mustang insignia. The styled steel wheels were an individual option, not included with any other option package. These wheels were made in 14", 5-lug patterns only.

OPTIONAL WHEEL COVERS

OPTIONAL TIRES

Whitewall tires were available in rayon or premium nylon. Optional High Performance V-8 models received dual red band, premium nylon as standard equipment, or buyers of the high performance could instead, opt for premium nylon whitewalls at no extra cost.

EXHAUST SYSTEM

Mustang exhaust was unchanged for '66. Single exhaust was standard on all but the 225 or 271 hp V-8's.

COOLING SYSTEM

1966, 6-cylinder Mustangs have a 9.5 quart cooling system capacity. 8-cylinder models have a 14.5 quart cooling system capacity. Both these figures are U.S. measure and includes one quart for the heater system.

FUEL TANK

'66 Mustangs have a 16-gallon (U.S. measure) fuel tank mounted beneath the luggage compartment.

SUSPENSION

'66 Mustang suspension is the identical to the '65 models. The front suspension is comprised of independent ball joints, with single lower arms and A-frame upper arms. Both are attached to the body with threaded bushings. A coil spring is fitted atop the A-frame, and is cushioned with rubber mounts, which along with fluid filled shock absorbers dampen the suspension system.

At the rear, the suspension utilizes two long leaf spring units comprised of 4 leafs each. The Mustang's powerteam determines the type and rigidity of the leafs employed. The springs are bushion mounted to the frame on the leading end, and shackled to the frame rails at the rear.

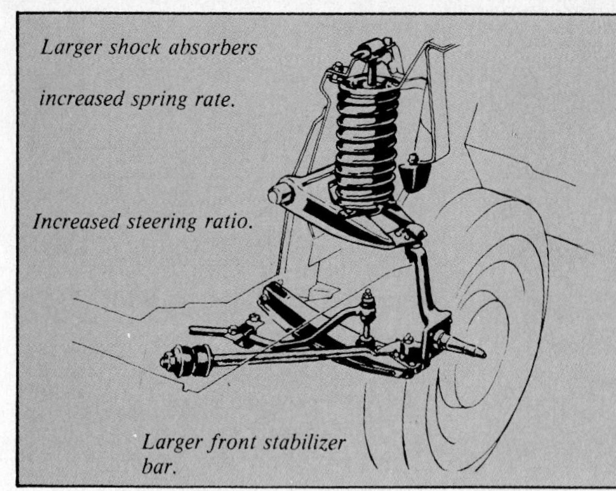

SPECIAL HANDLING PACKAGE

This suspension is included in the High Performance V-8 package and optional on all other V-8 equipped Mustangs. It consists of increased front and rear springs rates, (101# vs. 89# front, 130# vs. 101# at rear). Larger front and rear shock absorbers, increased (22:1) overall steering ratio, and a larger diameter front stabilizer bar (0.84 vs. 0.69 inches).

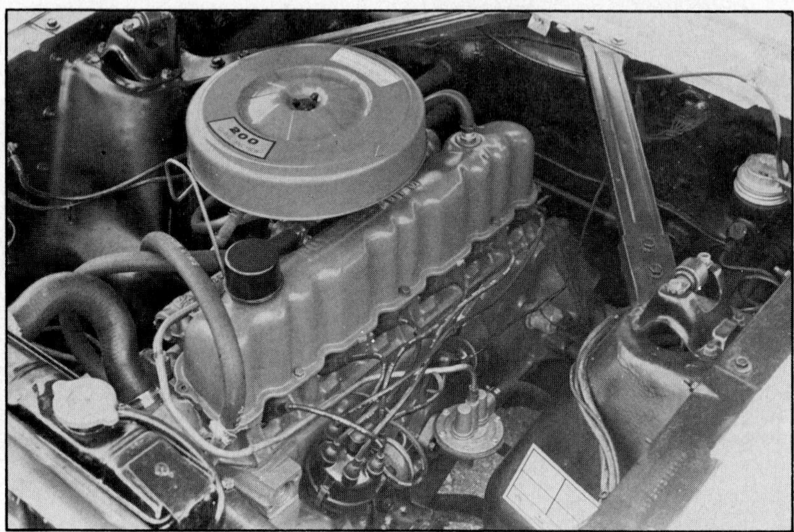

POWERTEAMS

The engine color mystery was eliminated in '66 as Ford painted all '66 Mustang engines blue. Buyers received a 200 cubic inch, 120 horsepower 6-cylinder as standard equipment. With a 9.2:1 compression ratio, the '66 Mustang 6-cylinder engine has 7 main bearings, a single barrel carburetor, self-adjusting hydraulic lifters and uses regular fuel.

TRANSMISSIONS

Five transmissions were offered on '66 Mustangs. The non-synchronized, 3-speed manual-type was standard equipment.

REAR AXLE

The standard rear axle for '66 is an integral (fixed) axle housing with a 3.20:1 ratio on 6-cylinder Mustangs equipped with manual transmissions, and 2.83:1 on 6-cylinder Mustangs with automatic transmissions. V-8 models received a removable differential carrier, with a straddle mounted pinion, thereby allowing a variety of gear ratios.

POWER TEAM SELECTION

ENGINES		TRANSMISSIONS			REAR AXLE RATIOS					
	Engine Code	3-Speed Manual	4-Speed Manual	Cruise-O-Matic	3-Speed Manual Std.	Opt.	4-Speed Manual Std.	Opt.	Cruise-O-Matic Std.	Opt.
200 Six - Std.	T	Std.	Opt.**	Opt.	3.20*	—	3.20*	—	2.83*	3.20
289 2v-V-8—Opt.	C	Std.	Opt.	Opt.	2.80*	—	2.80*	—	2.80*	—
289 4v-V-8—Opt.	A	Std.	Opt.	Opt.	3.00*	—	3.00*	—	3.00*	—
289 Hi-Perf. V-8-Opt.	K	N.A.	Opt.	Opt.	—	—	3.50*	3.89	3.50*	3.89

*Also available with optional limited-slip differential.
**Dagenham type, available with 6-cylinder only.

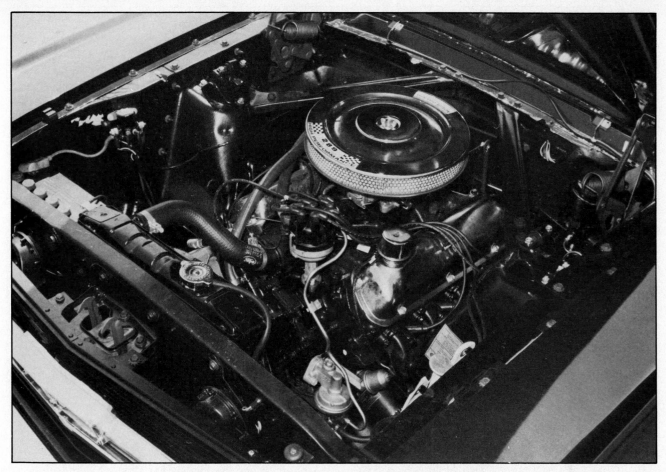

Racing-type air cleaner and valve covers are bright metal on the high performance engine option.

OPTIONAL POWERTEAMS

Three versions of the 289 cubic inch V-8 were offered in '66. The "Challenger V-8" option is a 200 horsepower, 2-barrel carburetor, hydraulic valve equipped model, with a 9.3:1 compression ratio, and uses regular fuel. The "Challenger Special V-8", while still equipped with hydraulic lifters, boasts a 10:1 compression ratio, is equipped with a 4-barrel carburetor, requires premium fuel, and is rated at 225 hp.

The most potent engine offered in '66 Mustangs is the "COBRA V-8". This is also the rarest of '66 Mustang engines, often referred to as the "High Performance", or "K" engine. 271 horsepower is obtained from the small block 289 engine with an increased 10.5:1 compression ratio, solid valve lifters, performance camshaft, manual choke type, 4-barrel carburetor, dual point distributor, and dual exhaust with free-flow cast iron headers.

Optional transmissions include a fully-synchronized 3-speed manual, available with any engine, except the 271 hp V-8, a unique, English design (Dagenham), 4-speed manual, optional with the 200 cubic inch, 6-cylinder model. Ford, 4-speed manual transmissions in close, or wide gear ratio choices were optional on V-8 Mustangs. High Performance V-8s were equipped with Ford type, as well as the Borg Warner type 4-speeds. The Cruise-O-Matic transmission was optional with any engine choice, including the 271 hp, V-8 in '66.

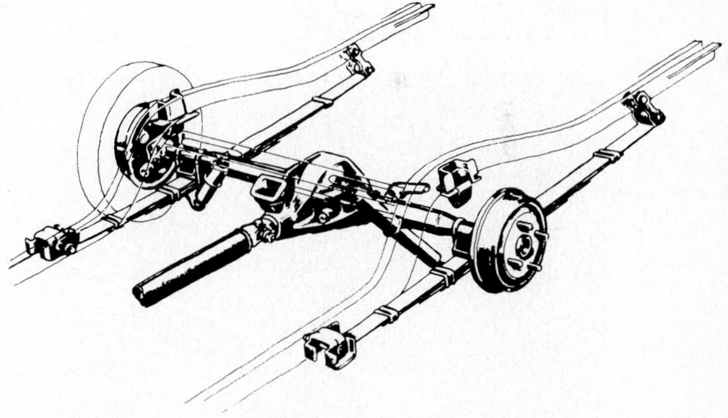

High performance (271 horsepower), Mustangs received a Galaxy-type 9" rear axle ring gear, and larger housing, while other V-8 models were equipped with an 8" rear axle ring gear. Limited-slip was optional on V-8 models.

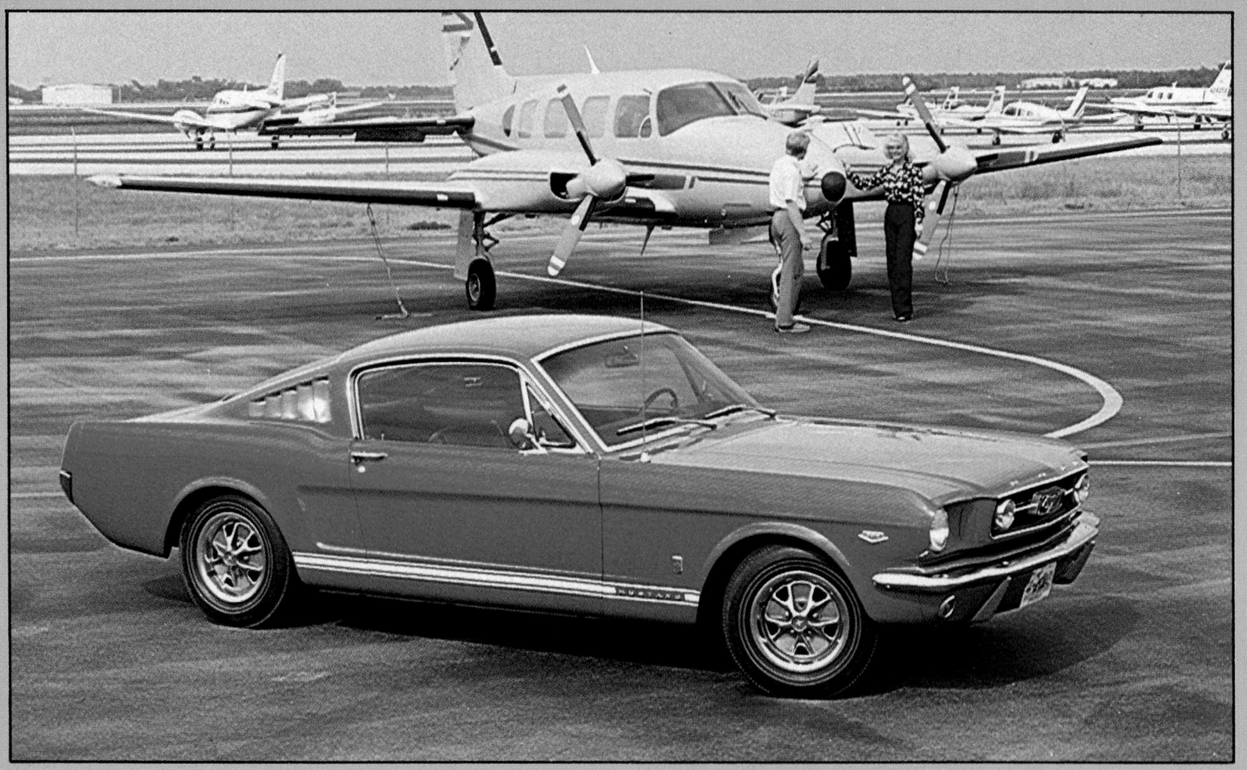

'66 GT MUSTANG

Gran Turismo adaptations were quite prevalent in the '60s. The Mustang climbed on the bandwagon in the spring of 1965, introducing the GT as a mid-year option. When the model year changed over to '66, few changes were made to Ford's desirable Mustang GT.

The "GT Equipment Group" consists of a combination of performance and appearance options, available with all Mustang bodystyles.

'66 Mustangs equipped with the factory GT Equipment Group must have either the 225 horsepower, or 271 horsepower, 289 cubic inch V-8 engine. Although required, the optional engine is not a part of the GT group. The GT option did include the fully synchronized 3-speed manual transmission. The 4-speed, or automatic was an optional extra.

'66 GT EQUIPMENT GROUP*

- GT badges on front fenders.
- M-U-S-T-A-N-G spelled out on fender behind front tire.
- GT stripe running front to rear along the lower body.
- A pair of 4-inch fog lamps (clear lens) mounted in the grille.
- Low-restriction dual exhaust system.
- Chrome flared tail pipe extensions through the rear valance.
- Special Handling Package.
- Front disc brakes.
- Unique GT gas cap.

*The normal Mustang insignia is deleted from the front fender. The quarter panel ornament and rocker panel molding are deleted. The grille is blacked out. The rear bumper guards are deleted. Either the "Challenger Special" or "Cobra" engine is required, but not included in the GT Equipment Group price.

JOIN OUR
MILLIONTH MUSTANG SUCCESS SALE
Featuring This Specially Equipped, Specially Priced, Limited Edition Mustang Hardtop

HERE'S YOUR CHANCE TO SAVE BIG DURING OUR

MILLIONTH MUSTANG SUCCESS SALE

LOOK AT ALL THE EXTRA VALUE YOU GET IN THIS LIMITED EDITION MUSTANG HARDTOP:

SPRINT 200 OPTION GROUP
- Body Side Accent Stripe
- Chrome Air Cleaner
- Engine Decal
- Wire-Style Wheel Covers
- Center Console

SAFETY EQUIPMENT GROUP
- Padded Instrument Panel and Sun Visors
- Outside Rearview Mirror
- Seat Belts Front and Rear
- Backup Lights
- Emergency Flasher*
- Windshield Washer and Electric Wipers

*Where Permitted by Law

PLUS THESE STANDARD FEATURES
- Sporty Bucket Seats
- All-Vinyl Interior
- Full Carpeting
- 200-cu. in. Six Engine
- 3-Speed Manual Floor Shift
- Suspended Accelerator Pedal
- 5-Dial Instrument Panel and many more
- Plus a personalized nameplate

Your choice of colors, trims, and options too!

All this at a low, low price during our big Millionth Mustang Success Sale!

HURRY IN! QUANTITIES ARE LIMITED!

Remember... you're ahead in a Ford all the way!

VOL. 66CM45L5

Ford celebrated selling one million Mustangs by offering a specially equipped 200 cubic inch, 6-cylinder hardtop. This postcard was used by dealers to promote the sale

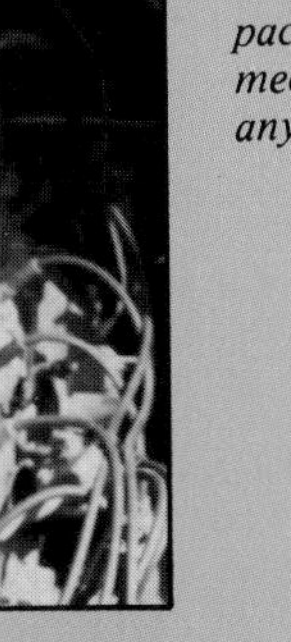

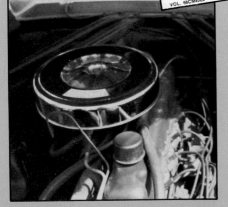

Chrome air cleaner with unique MUSTANG POWERED SPRINT 200, decal was included with package. The car was however, mechanically like any other 6-cylinder Mustang.

Although not a special model, all Mustangs going to Germany, (from Ford), had the Mustang name deleted from fenders, wheelcovers, horn ring etc. A German manufacturer already had rights to the Mustang name and Ford chose to alter a few emblems, rather than pay an exorbitant royalty fee.

SHELBY VIN PLATE

Like the 1965 Shelby, the 1966 model used a Shelby American VIN plate, riveted over the Ford VIN number, on the driver's side inner fender panel.

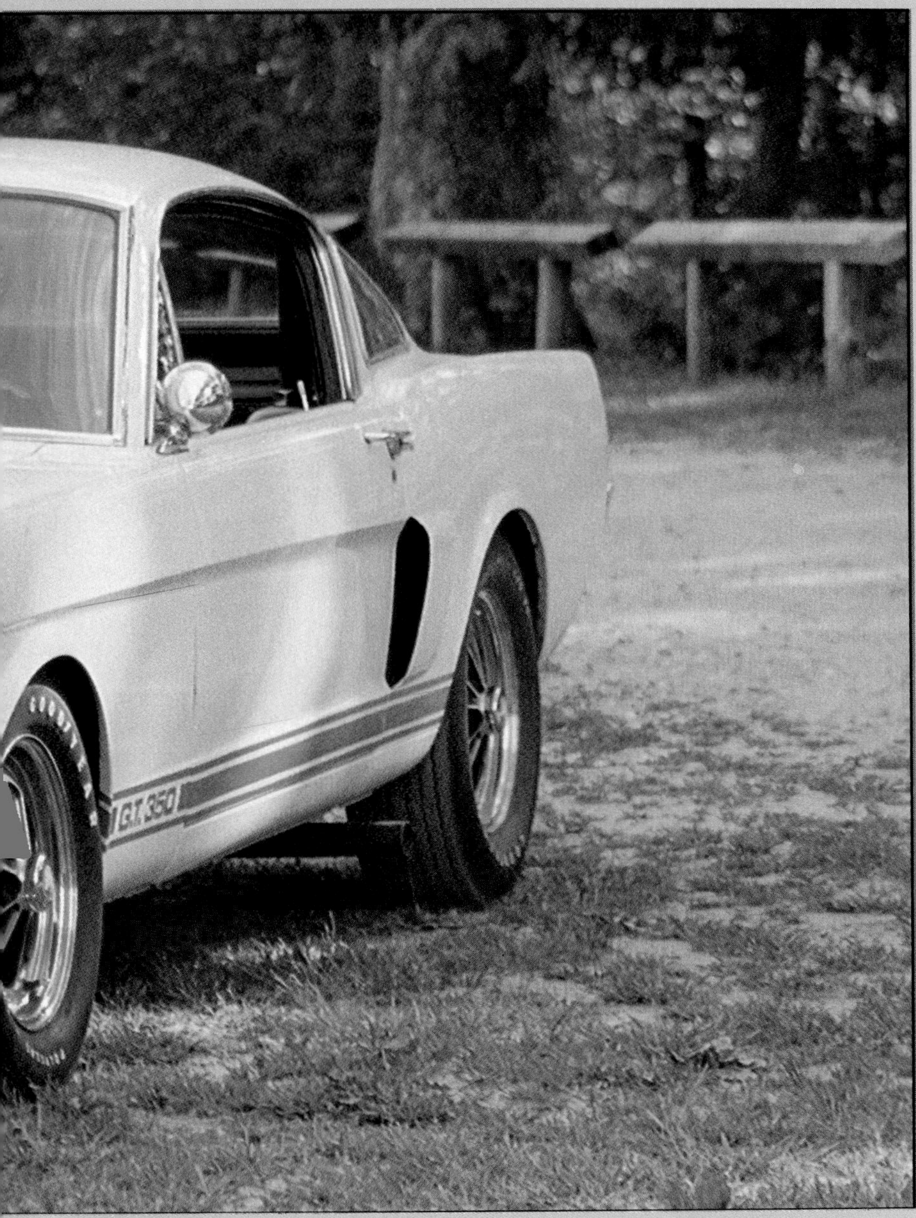

1966 SHELBY

When the 1966 Shelby was being planned, the basic concept of the car was untouched; however, two new things were thrown into the equation. Cost effectiveness (Ford wanted Shelby to break even at the very least on the cars he sold) and increased sales (which meant eliminating the items that turned prospective buyers off. As a result of these two factors, the 1966 Shelby Mustangs required less fabrication — which took time and money (upper "A" arm lowering and rear over-ride torque control arms) — but buyers were offered more choices (five colors as opposed to take-it-or-leave-it white, plus, automatic transmissions). The most objectionable features were either eliminated entirely, (noisy side-exiting exhausts were replaced by rear exiting pipes; rear seat made available), or put on the option list (Koni shocks, Detroit Locker).

EXTERIOR:

To differentiate the 1966 Shelby from stock Mustangs (and also to differentiate the cars from the 1965 GT350s), functional rear quarter panel side scoops and clear plexiglass rear quarter windows were installed. The rear quarter windows replaced the stock Mustang's air extractor louvers.

The '66 Shelby's side stripes are tape, slightly narrower than the '65's and positioned higher on the car. White cars received blue stripes, while all other colors got white stripes.

The special Shelby fiberglass hood with integral scoop continues for 1966. Most are secured by racing-type hood pins, but a few '66 cars are equipped with regular steel hoods (with scoop) and utilize the stock Mustang hood latch. The production Mustang grille is used, but without the chrome Mustang running horse and corral. Instead, the Shelby has a small Mustang running horse/tri-color bar attached to the driver's side of the grille.

A new "GT350" gas cap is used in 1966.

INTERIOR:

The 1966 Shelby uses the standard Mustang's 5 dial instrument panel, which includes an oil pressure gauge, so the tachometer/oil pressure bezel from the '65 Shelby is eliminated. In its place, bolted to the top of the crash pad in the center, is a Cobra 9000 rpm tachometer mounted in a bracket facing the driver. The steering wheel is the Mustang optional deluxe walnut wheel, with simulated wood rim. A chrome

GT350 center cap contains the same "GT350" logo that appears on the gas cap.

The spare tire is moved out of the rear interior in 1966 and placed in the conventional luggage compartment position. A small number of early '66 Shelbys (probably less than 100) have a rear "package tray" similar to the one used in '65, but the large majority of '66 Shelbys are equipped with the Mustang fold-down rear seat. Front seat belts continue as 3" competition units.

ENGINE:

The "Cobra-ized" 289 High-Performance engine continues as the only GT350 powerplant. Like 1965, it is modified with "COBRA" finned aluminum valve covers, "COBRA" aluminum intake manifold with a 715 cfm Holley carburetor, "COBRA" high-capacity aluminum oil pan, and Tri-Y headers. The 1966 exhaust systems continues to use glass-packed mufflers, but the exhaust pipes exit at the rear of the car.

The standard Shelby transmission is the Borg Warner T-10 close ratio.

A 9 inch rear end is standard, but the differential is an open type. The Detroit Locker differential, a standard 1965 item, is relegated to the option list in 1966.

SHELBY SUSPENSION:

Several of the 1965 handling modifications were deleted in 1966 (however, the first 252 '66 Shelbys were actually left-over '65s — these cars include the '65 suspension modifications). The 1966 "A" arm retain their stock Mustang position, and the rear over-ride torque control bars (traction bars) are replaced by simpler-to-install under-ride units. The '65 Koni shocks move to the option list, replaced by Ford "heavy-duty" shocks.

WHEEL:

Until the supply was depleted, the early 1966 Shelbys received 15" 1965-type Shelby 5-spoke Cragar mags. Later cars got 14" Magnum 500 wheels painted gray with black centers and "GT350" hub caps.

AUTOMATIC TRANSMISSION

The Ford C-4 automatic transmission became a Shelby option in 1966. Cars so equipped also received an Autolite 595 cfm carburetor in place of the standard Holley.

OPTIONAL WHEELS

Two optional wheels were available for the 1966 Shelby: a chrome 14" Magnum 500 and a new-for-'66, 14" aluminum 10-spoke. Both wheels carry the "GT350" center cap.

SUPERCHARGER

In mid-April, 1966, the Paxton Supercharger became a GT350 option for 1966 Shelbys. Included in the package was the belt-driven supercharger, an Autolite 460 cfm carburetor, and a special "COBRA" carburetor enclosure. A gain of 46% additional horsepower was advertised.

1966 SHELBY CONVERTIBLES

A total of 6 Shelby convertibles were built in 1966. These cars were the final 6 to be built, and all were equipped with automatic transmission. Otherwise, they were identical to the standard GT350 fastback (the side scoops, due to the convertible top mechanism, were not functional). All 6 were given away by Shelby to friends and employees.

HERTZ

In a special deal with Hertz Rent-A-Car, 936, 1966 Shelby GT350s were built as rental cars. Most were black, but other colors were produced — all had the gold GT350 side stripes and most got gold LeMans racing stripes. They were basically standard GT350s with the optional chrome Magnum 500 wheels. The earliest Hertz Shelbys were equipped with 4-speed transmission, but all later cars got the C-4 automatic. Mustang-type front disc brakes with a modified master cylinder, lowered the required brake pedal pressure somewhat. A special instrument panel reading "This vehicle is equipped with competition brakes. Heavier than normal pedal pressure is required" was applied to the instrument panel.

1967

In 1967, Ford restyled the Mustang for the first time. Why? Primarily to give the Mustang a fresh look, to remain a jump ahead of upcoming competition from Camaro, Firebird, Barracuda — and even Cougar (from sister division Mercury).

Increased performance and extra safety features highlight this major restyling — but done so as to keep intact the character and "look" of the original. For example, the '67's have the familiar side sculpturing, but now with "twin" simulated air scoops. The unique wide mouth grille cavity is noticeably wider and taller. Even the rear taillight board is similar to past years, but now recessed, reminiscent of the "Kamm-back" on the fabulous GT-40. Underneath, performance was also increased. The 390-4V "Thunderbird Special" was added in 1967, giving the Mustang its first big block. Overall, the Mustang in 1967 is wider and longer, but still resting on the same 108 inch wheelbase.

Added safety features, also a key to changes in 1967, included such items as energy absorbing arm rests, impact absorbing steering wheels (with a deep padded hub), safety designed instrument panel and controls — plus a host of other features.

Big news for the Shelby Mustang was the new GT500 fastback, with a 428 big block. Since the Mustang got a 390, Shelby had to go with even more cubic inches. The GT350 and GT500 fastbacks were still two-seaters, with a fold-down rear seatbut this year emphasis was switching from SCCA amateur racing to SCCA professional Trans Am sedan racing. Ford and Chevrolet were capitalizing on the new Trans Am races as a way to showcase their popular ponycars.

BODYSTYLES

The 1967 Mustang was changed, yet unchanged. Although restyled from the rocker panel up, the '67 models closely resemble their 1965-66 counterparts, retaining the classic lines that had earned the original Mustang the coveted Tiffany Award, for Excellence in American Design.

The long hood/rear "hop-up" appearance that made the first 1964½ Mustang so popular was preserved in all 3 1967 models — hardtop, convertible, and fastback. The big news was the addition of Ford's big-block 390 Thunderbird Special to the Mustang's engine line-up: to accommodate the broad-shouldered powerplant, Ford designers widened the

Mustang sheetmetal a total of 2.7 inches, from 68.2" to 70.9". Convertible buyers were given the option of ordering a new-for-'67 folding-glass rear window, in place of the standard plastic window. And the 2+2 became a true fastback with a sloping roof that extended all the way to the rear panel.

EXTERIOR

GRILLE: The '67s grille opening is considerably larger than the '65-66 version, stretching from the hood to the top of the bumper. The rectangular-mesh grille itself is deeper-set, surrounded on the sides and bottom by a wide trim strip, argent in the center and chrome on the outer edge. The ever-present running horse is attached to grille center, encircled by a new type corral that is wider at the bottom than at the top (just the opposite from the '66 corral). A long horizontal bar extends from each side of the corral, nearly reaching the grille's corners. Smaller vertical bars, short stubs in comparison to the horizontal bars, jut out from the top and bottom of the corral.

HEADLIGHTS: The 1967 headlights, in true Mustang fashion, are swept-back towards the outside of the car. Each headlight is surrounded by a color-keyed bezel, fastened by 3 screws. The simulated air intake louvers that were used in previous models are eliminated.

VALANCE PANEL: The front valance panel contains new-style parking lights, deep-set with color-keyed bezels and new-for-'67 clear lens, and a recessed license plate attaching bracket. The valance also serves as a mounting point for the standard chrome bumper guards with rubber inserts.

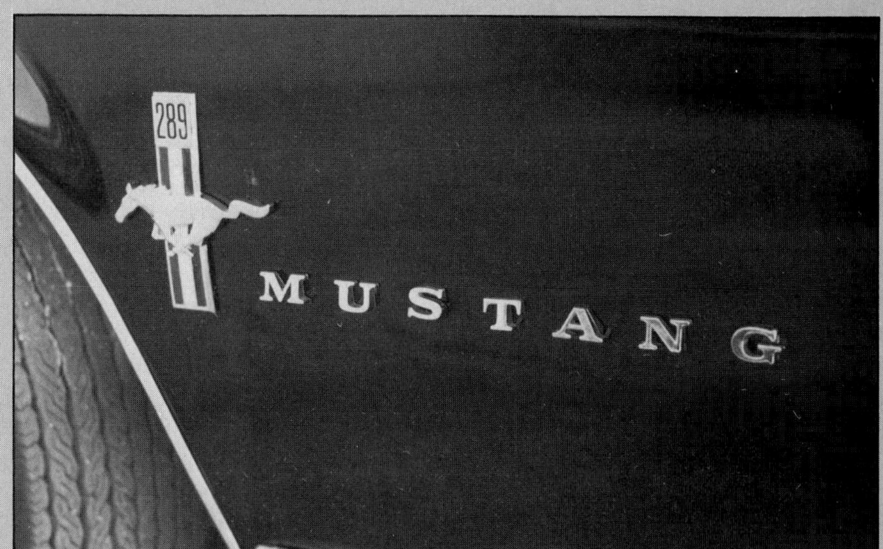

HOOD: The '67 hood slopes downward slightly more at the front than the '66, ending at the top of the grille with chrome trim. The letters F-O-R-D are stretched across the leading edge. A "wind-splitter" ridge runs the entire length of the hood at the center. The hood fastens with a more refined latch mechanism than the one used previously in '66: the latch mounts on the hood and fastens to a bar located between the radiator support and the grille. A safety catch is also part of the mechanism.

SIDE EXTERIOR: The easily recognized Mustang side sculpture in the rear quarter panels is very prominent in the 1967 models. To achieve more of a performance look, Ford designers made the sculpture deeper, and inserted a pair of simulated scoops behind the door, color keyed in place of the '66's chrome ornamentation. A running horse/red, white, and blue vertical bar and chrome M-U-S-T-A-N-G lettering attaches to each fender. The tri-color bar, with V-8 models, has the engine size stamped into a bright section above the colors.

Keyless locking was introduced as a standard Mustang feature in 1967. In addition, the entire Ford fleet began using convenient reversible keys. The remote control rear-view mirror became standard equipment for '67. Chrome rocker panel moldings were standard on the fastback only.

WINDOWS: The 1967 front windshield is identical to the 1965-66, trimmed with bright moldings. The tempered side glass is curved, blending the roofline into the body side panels. A side quarter vent window is standard on all models. Hardtops and convertibles include rear quarter windows that will retract fully into the quarter panels. The rear corner of the fastback's side window is curved to match the shape of the roof. Also, the fastback's large rear window is tinted to maintain a cooler interior temperature. The rear glass on hardtops and fastbacks is trimmed with a bright molding.

ROOF: The basic roof designs of the Mustang hardtop and convertible were little changed for '67, but the 2+2 underwent a dramatic revision. The fastback roofline sweeps from the top of the windshield all the way to the rear of the car, a true fastback. A simplified 12 louver vent on the side replaces the 5-gill assembly from the '66. The little raised "windsplitter" on the hood continued across the roof and rear deck on the fastback only.

The most noticeable change in the hardtop roof is the elimination of the '66's embossed area around the rear window.

The standard 5-ply convertible top employs a conventional zip-out plastic rear window. Tops were available in either black or white, with an all-vinyl top boot, color-keyed to the interior.

REAR EXTERIOR: The rear panel on the '67 Mustang is concave, obviously influenced by the "Kamm-back" styling of Ford's GT-40 and Daytona Coupe race cars. The taillights appear as 3, on either side; however, there is actually only one unit per side. Three individual chrome bezels trim the triple slots in each side of the rear panel.

EXTERIOR DECOR GROUP

- Bright wheel lip moldings.
- Special hood with functional rear-facing louvers and integral turn signal indicators.
- Bright rear deck moldings on hardtops and convertibles (standard on fastbacks).
- Pop-open gas cap with running horse/tri-color bar emblem (GT equipped Mustangs have a GT emblem).

CONVERTIBLE OPTIONS

Sixty-seven was the first year to offer a folding glass rear window for the Mustang convertible. Made from tempered glass and hinged at the center with transparent silicone rubber, the new window added extra convenience by resisting discoloration and scratches.

A power top was available for '67 Mustang convertibles. The switch is located on the instrument panel between the heater controls and the speedometer. The chrome bezel is stamped "TOP".

wire-on gas caps closely resemble the units used in '66, but are distinguished by the 3-blade "knock-off" bars that extend from the ceramic center. The familiar running horse/tri-color bar is centered on the cap with the words "Ford Mustang" positioned above and below respectively. The luggage compartment lock, found on the deck lid during '65-66, moved to the rear panel above the gas cap, in 1967.

DECK LID: The rear of the '67's deck lid differs substantially between the fastback and the hardtop/convertible. On the

VINYL ROOF

A vinyl roof covering was optional for the hardtop only — in 2 colors only: black and parchment. With the vinyl roof, a bright metal trim covers the edge of the vinyl at the base of the roof.

MORE MIRRORS

Three optional exterior mirrors were available from Ford dealers in 1967: a matching right-hand remote, a chrome bullet-shaped racing model, and an extended trailor towing version.

fastback, the embossed line (with its standard chrome molding — fastback only) curves upward in the area between the taillights with the chrome letters M-U-S-T-A-N-G positioned below. But, on hardtops and convertibles, the embossed line curves downward with the M-U-S-T-A-N-G lettering attached above.

REAR VALANCE PANEL: The rear valance panel contains the standard back-up lights and license plate bracket, and provides the attaching point for the standard rear bumper guards (color-keyed to the exterior with rubber inserts).

GT EQUIPMENT GROUP

The GT Equipment Group was available on any 1967 Mustang equipped with one of the 4 V-8 engines. For '67 only, automatic versions received a special GT/A designation — for GT Automatic.

- 4 inch driving lamps at each end of the horizontal grille bar (a small switch marked "fog" is mounted beneath the instrument panel under the ignition switch)
- Power front disc brakes
- Low restriction dual exhaust with chrome quad outlets (1)
- GT stripes along the rocker panel, broken on the fender by a GT or GT/A emblem.
- F70x14 Wide-Oval white side-wall tires
- GT emblem on standard gas cap (2)
- Special Handling Package with higher rate springs and shocks, and larger front stabilizer bar.

(1) Optional 4-barrel engines only
(2) Pop-open gas cap if car is also equipped with th Exterior Decor Group.

LOWER BACK PANEL GRILLE

A special ribbed lower back panel grille was available for all models, but only if equipped with the Exterior Decor Group.

PROTECTION GROUP

- Front and rear color-keyed floor mats
- Door edge guards
- License plate frames

ACCENT STRIPE

Mustang buyers in 1967 could individualize their car with an Accent stripe, a thin pin stripe that ran along the top of the body line, stretching from the edge of the front fender to the rear edge of the quarter panel. The stripes were available in red, white, or black.

OTHER 1967 EXTERIOR OPTIONS

- Tinted glass
- Two-tone paint (lower back panel, dark gray only)
- Rocker panel molding (standard on fastback)
- Rear deck luggage rack.

INTERIOR

Refinement is the best word to use when defining the 1967 Mustang interior. Ford designers took the already sporty 1966 interior and molded it into an even better looking, more functional passenger compartment.

INSTRUMENT PANEL: The 1967 Mustang instrument panel only vaguely resembles the earlier style. The "twin-hood" theme from the '65-66 era is readily apparent, but the "eyebrows" are more rounded, giving the instrument panel more of a cockpit appearance. The instrument layout differs entirely from the '66. For 1967, the instrument cluster consists of a 2 large, 3 small pod arrangement. The 2 larger pods straddle the steering column and house the 120 mph speedometer (on the left, with a red warning sector above 70 mph) and combined oil pressure and alternator gauges (on the right). The 3 smaller pods, positioned above the large pods, contain (from left to right) the fuel level gauge, clock (if equipped — a blank face is supplied without the clock), and temperature gauge. The windshield wiper switch is located directly above the

OPTIONAL TACHOMETER

The tachometer option displaces the oil pressure/ammeter gauge in the large pod on the right side of the steering column. Rectangular openings at the bottom of the tachometer face serve as oil pressure and ammeter warning lights. The tachometer is calibrated from 0 to 6000 on all models, except those equipped with the 289 High Performance engine (0 to 8000 rpm). A trip odometer, located in the speedometer face, is also included with the tach option.

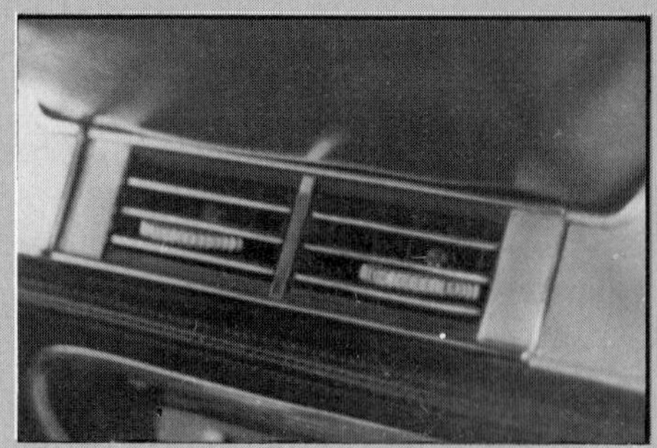

SELECTAIRE AIR CONDITIONING: With air conditioning, a new style heater/air control panel replaces the standard unit. All functions are controlled with 3 handles that slide up and down within vertical slots. A round air vent mounts below the control panel and at the same location on the opposite end of the instrument panel. Two additional rectangular vents mount side by side in the center of the instrument panel above the radio.

speedometer, and a matching (in size) brake warning light is positioned opposite.

Standard instrument panel trim is camera-case black. A safety-inspired padded strip runs the entire length of the panel, from the gauges to the end of the panel on the passenger side.

INSTRUMENT CONTROLS: The heater/defroster control panel is positioned to the very left side of the dash, housing 3 vertical sliding knobs that control the heater, temperature and defroster, and the horizontally-controlled blower switch. The light switch, with its new large-style knob, is mounted on the instrument panel to the left side of the steering column, while the ignition switch mounts on the opposite side of the column. A pull-type emergency brake handle and a small black air vent knob attach below the dash. The windshield washers are controlled by a foot-operated lever just above the headlight dimmer switch. The cigarette lighter is concealed within the ash tray, positioned in the dash next to the ignition switch. As an ever-increasing safety measure, a seat belt warning light - standard -was mounted under the dash beneath the ash tray.

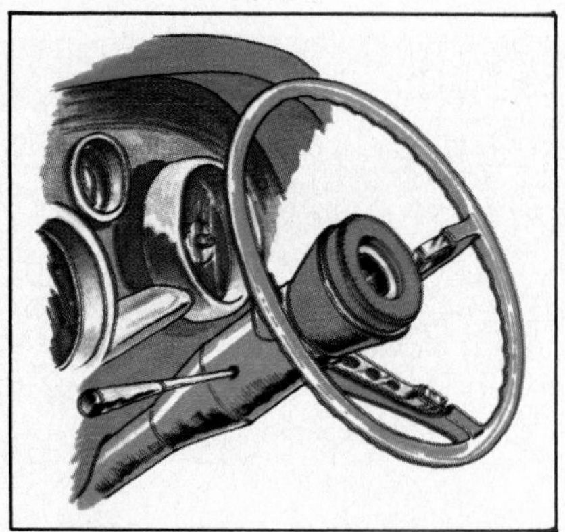

STEERING WHEEL: The 1967 Mustang steering wheel is unique because of its round, heavily padded safety cushion, color-keyed to the interior with the Mustang running horse in the center. The wheel itself is a one-piece 3-spoke unit, also color-keyed, with a chrome 3-spoke horn ring featuring black recesses to simulate holes.

The emergency flasher switch is located on the steering column for the first time in 1967, a much more convenient location compared to the glove box switch used before. Another first time improvement is the "lane-changing" turn signal that allows the driver to briefly operate the turn signals by holding the handle in an intermediate position. When the handle is released, a spring returns it to the straightaway position, cancelling the signal. A second position will lock the handle in the conventional manner.

SHIFTER: The shifter furnished with the standard 3-speed manual transmission (except 289 High Performance and 390 4-barrel models) is a round chrome unit that curves rearward toward the driver. The shifter knob is a round design made of black plastic and engraved with the shift pattern.

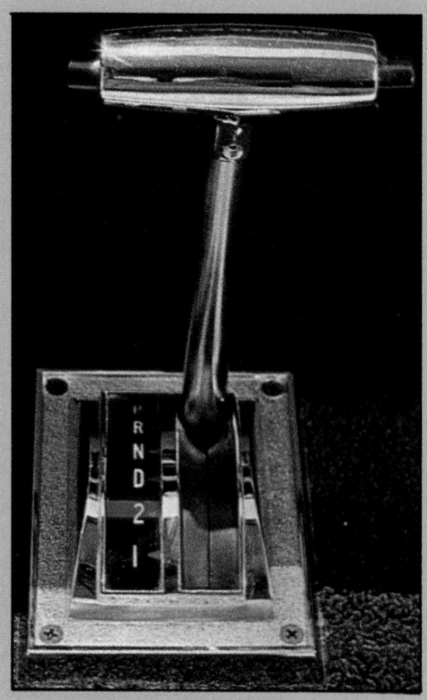

STEERING WHEEL OPTIONS

DELUXE STEERING WHEEL: The optional steering wheel features a wood-like rim. The 3 brushed aluminum spokes are perforated with 4 holes each, small at the outer end and becoming increasingly larger toward the steering wheel center. A horn button is located at the end of each spoke.

TILT-STEERING: 1967 was the first year for the tilt-steering column option in the Mustang. By pushing the turn signal lever forward, the driver can adjust the steering wheel to one of 9 different positions. Also, the steering wheel swings up and over when the driver's door is opened, signaled by a small switch located in the door jamb.

SHIFTERS WITH OPTIONAL TRANSMISSIONS

AUTOMATIC: The automatic shifter is a T-handle design with a push button on the driver's side that, when depressed, releases the handle for gear selection. The mounting plate is square with a semi-circle selector. The T-handle is chrome on standard interiors; vinyl-covered with the Decor Interior.

FOUR-SPEED: The 1967 Mustang 4-speed shifter is a Ford built unit. The chrome handle curves rearward toward the driver and is topped by a round black shifter knob with engraved shift pattern. A reverse lock-out is included, identical to the '66.

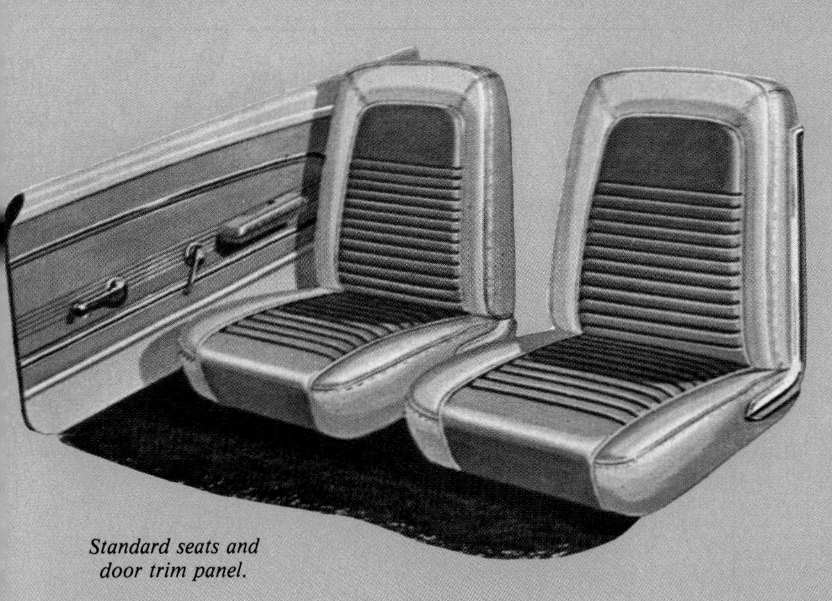

Standard seats and door trim panel.

Bench seat.

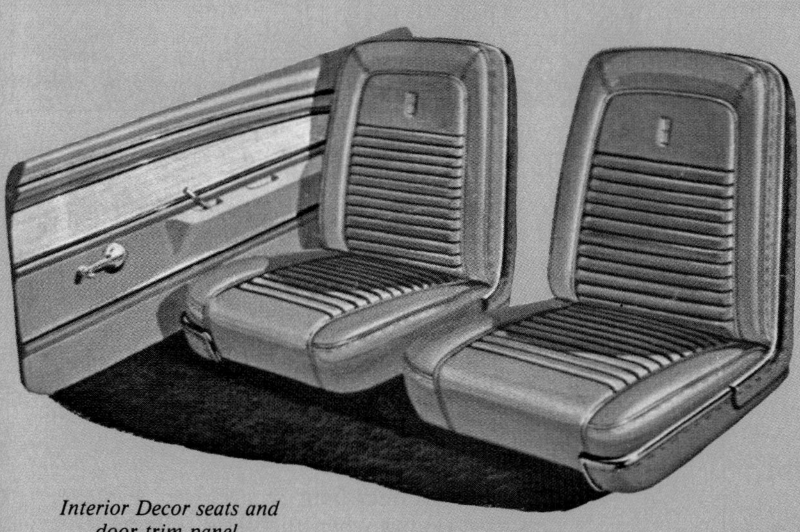

Interior Decor seats and door trim panel.

BUCKET SEATS: The new style Mustang bucket seats appear flatter, similar to the Deluxe seats from '66. The center portions of both the bottom and back cushions contain width-wise pleats enclosed by a wrap-around foam-padded cushion covered with vinyl. Bright metal side shields are used on the outboard sides.

Seat belts are furnished as standard equipment, featuring front retractors and a push-bottom release.

REAR SEAT: The 1967 Mustang's rear seat is a bucket-styled bench type with horizontal pleats to match the front. The standard fastback seat is no longer a fold-down; it is fixed with a rear package shelf similar to the hardtop. Convertibles include a rear seat arm rest with an ash tray on either side. On fastbacks only, a sliding knob above each quarter trim operates the functional side vents that draw air out of the interior.

DOOR PANEL: The standard door interior consists of a textured metal frame with a vinyl-covered door panel, all color-keyed to the interior. The arm rest attaches at the rear of the door panel. A window crank and pull-type door handle mount forward of the arm rest.

Door lock design differs slightly from the '66 style: the center of the '67 button is funnel-shaped; the '66 was dish-shaped. The lock mechanism also changed; to unlock the door from the interior, the lock button must first be raised — the door handle will not override the lock.

The vent window remains standard equipment, but with a new style latch.

The remote control mirror lever mounts in the upper left corner of the driver's side door panel, fastened in place by a round bezel.

REAR VIEW MIRROR: A new-for-'67 plastic-backed rear view mirror is attached at the top of the windshield with a bracket that also serves as a catch for the sunvisors. Also, the rear view mirror is a day/night unit, used as a standard Mustang feature for the first time in 1967.

INTERIOR LIGHTS: The 1967 Mustang interior lights can be operated 2 ways: manually by turning the headlight switch to the left, or automatically through a door switch mounted inside the door jamb — the lights come on when either door is opened.

Hardtops have a large courtesy light attached to the headliner. Convertibles, however, contain concealed lights under each end of the instrument panel. Likewise, fastbacks also utilize the underdash lights, but the 2+2s feature additional lights in the rear quarter trim.

CONVENIENCE CONTROL PANEL

The Convenience Control Panel consists of 4 red warning lights mounted in the center of the dash above the radio (without air conditioning). When air conditioning was ordered, the Convenience Control Panel could be ordered only with the console — the warning lights were integrated within the console, 2 lights on either side of the storage compartment.

- Parking brake warning light
- Door ajar.
- Seat belt reminder light
- Low fuel (glows when fuel level falls to 4 gallons).

OPTIONAL CONSOLE

The center-mounted console for the '67 Mustang is a complete unit that attaches to the dash in place of the radio housing. From the dash, it drops down to the floor, then runs aftward between the required bucket seats. One of the 3 Mustang radios is required with the console. A lighted storage compartment with a unique door that slides upward fits below the radio. Automatic transmission cars have special shifter indicator lights mounted behind the shifter marked P-R-N-D-2-1. The light covers are shaded red, except for the green "D" indicator. Seat belt holsters are inserted near the seats. The rear of the console contains an ash tray and courtesy light. Console finish consists of a wide strip of brushed aluminum in the center paralleled by thin camera case black strips on each sides. The side panels are keyed to the interior color.

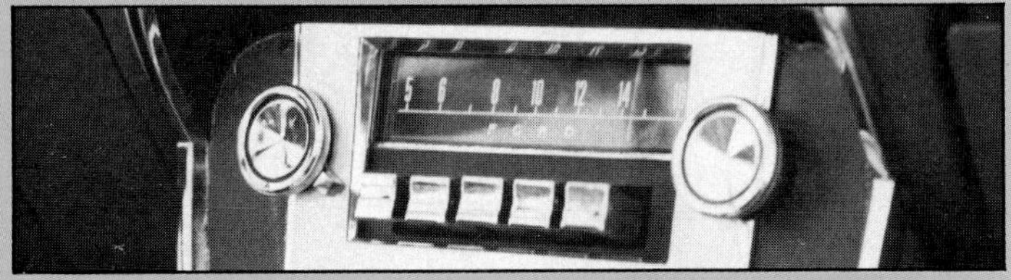

INTERIOR DECOR OPTION

The Interior Decor Group is the luxury version of the 1967 Mustang's interior. Included in the package are:

- Special door panels with brushed aluminum appliques and molded arm rests. The door handle is a pull-back type mounted in the forward section of the arm rest.
- Special grille in the lower door with courtesy lights mounted at the center of the door.
- Brushed aluminum instrument panel appliques.
- Molded seat backs and side shields, plus insert trim buttons on the seat back cushions.
- Roof console with twin map lights and switches (except convertible).
- Bright trim on brake and clutch pedals.
- Vinyl grip insert on automatic shifter (Cruise-O-Matic only).
- Electric clock mounted in instrument panel.
- Padded quarter trim panels (hardtops only)

OPTIONAL RADIOS

All 3 1967 Mustang radios mount in a special housing that fastens below the center of the instrument panel (unless equipped with the optional console — the console bolts in place of the radio housing). The controls are larger than the '66 style, and the tone and speaker balance (with stereo) are controlled by small knobs behind the volume and selection controls.

AM: The Mustang AM radio is a push button type with the word FORD printed on the face. A single speaker is mounted under the center of the crash pad.

AM-FM: The optional AM/FM stereo radio appears similar to the AM unit, but the dial shows 2 sets of numbers and a sliding AM/FM selector. A speaker mounts in the lower front corner of each door. Stations can be pre-selected with the push buttons below the radio dial.

STEREOSONIC TAPE/AM RADIO: The AM radio with the stereo tape system uses the same dial as the standard AM radio, but the push buttons are deleted entirely to make room for the 8-track tape slot.

COURTESY LIGHT GROUP

The Courtesy Light Group includes an under hood and luggage compartment light, and a glove box lock. Also, hardtop models received under dash courtesy lights that operate in conjunction with the single overhead light.

OTHER 1967 INTERIOR OPTIONS

- Fold-down rear seat — Fastback only.
- Bench seat — The full-width bench seat was available for hardtops and convertibles with the standard interior only. It features the same horizontal pleats found in the bucket seats. A fold-down arm rest attaches in the center between the seat backs.
- Speed control — The speed control was a first-time Mustang accessory in 1967. The ON/OFF switch is located on the instrument panel to the lower left of the headlight switch. An engagement switch mounts in the tip of the turn signal lever. The resume switch is a knurled ring around the turn signal stalk.
- Electric clock — mounts in the center of the instrument cluster
- Deluxe seat belt — With push button release and seat belt warning light mounted under the dash.
- Seat belt for third passenger.
- Comfortweave vinyl trim — Knitted vinyl seat inserts.
- Front shoulder harness — Deluxe seat belts required.

TRUNK

LUGGAGE COMPARTMENT

MAT: The luggage compartment floor in all 1967 Mustangs is covered with a patterned rubber mat.

SPARE TIRE: A spare tire was furnished with every 1967 Mustang, mounted on the right side of the luggage compartment with a threaded hook and large wing nut. A scissors jack and handle (which also serves as a lug nut wrench) was also supplied, stored under the spare tire.

WHEELS

STANDARD TIRE AND WHEEL: All 1967 Mustangs were originally equipped with 14 inch wheels and 6.95x14 tires (7.35 with 390 engine — other sizes available optionally).

WHEELCOVER: The base 1967 Mustang is equipped with a 10½" hubcap and color-keyed wheel. Some hubcaps have a Mustang running horse/vertical bar in the center, and others have a Ford crest. However, most '67 Mustangs were delivered to the dealer with a one-piece "radial spoke" wheelcover featuring 21 bright spokes with argent in between. The center is red ceramic with the running horse/tri-color bar in the center. The letters M-U-S-T-A-N-G is placed mirror-imaged on opposite sides of the center.

The 1967 Styled Steel wheel, because of its extra width, uses a wider trim ring, (right) than the '66 version (left). Also, the center of the '67 wheel includes a special slot that aligns the 5-spoke hub cap in the correct position.

OPTIONAL WHEELS AND WHEELCOVERS

STYLED STEEL: Due to the wider tires available for the 1967 Mustang, the '67 styled steel wheel is wider than its '66 counterpart. In addition, the bright trim ring is also deeper to cover the wider wheel. The redesigned center cap, has a blue center, with 5 "fingers" that spread out to meet the spokes on the wheel. The wheel center has a slot cutout that matches the center cap, in order to align the cap with the spokes.

WIRE WHEELCOVER: The optional 14" wire wheelcovers (lower right) are identical to the '66 versions, except for the plain red center that replaces the blue spinners used previously.

WIRE WHEELCOVER WITH SPINNER: A second wire wheelcover, solid and heavier than the first, had spinners that, because of new safety standards, were laid back toward the wheelcover. These wheelcovers (lower left) also used a blue center.

PERFORMANCE OPTIONS

- 55 amp. battery (standard with 390 automatic)
- Extra cooling package (15 quart radiator, 6 blade fan - standard with air conditioned models)
- Limited-Slip differential (all models with V-8 engine)
- Axle Ratios.

POWERTEAMS

The 1967 Mustang was available with 13 engine/transmission combinations — ranging from the standard 200 cubic inch six with a 3-speed manual transmission to the 390 4-barrel V-8 with four-on-the-floor.

SELECT SHIFT AUTOMATIC: The Select Shift Cruise-O-Matic automatic became available for the Mustang in 1967. The Select Shift permits both automatic and manual operation — whichever the driver desires for the immediate road conditions or driving situation.

POWER TEAM SELECTION

ENGINES	TRANSMISSIONS			REAR AXLE RATIOS					
	3-Speed[1] Manual	4-Speed Manual	Cruise-O-Matic	3-Speed[1] Manual		4-Speed Manual		Cruise-O-Matic	
				Std.	Opt.	Std.	Opt.	Std.	Opt.
Std.—200 Six—120 HP	Std.	N/A	Opt.	3.20	—	—	—	2.83	3.20
Opt.—289 2v V-8—200 HP	Std.	Opt.	Opt.	2.80	3.00[5]	2.80	[2]3.00[3]	2.80	[2]3.00[3]
Opt.—289 4v V-8—225 HP	Std.	Opt.	Opt.	3.00	—	3.00[3]	—	3.00[3]	—
Opt.—289 4v Hi-Perf. V-8—271 HP	N/A	Opt.	Opt.	—	—	3.50	3.89	3.50	3.89
Opt.—390 4v GT V-8—320 HP	[4]	Opt.	Opt.	3.00	3.25[5]	3.00	3.25[5]	3.00	3.25[5]

[1] 3-Speed fully synchronized transmission.
[2] Mandatory ratio with F-70-14 Wide-Oval tires.
[3] Also available with optional limited-slip differential.
[5] Available only with optional limited-slip differential.
[4] HD 3-Speed Manual required at extra cost.

SUSPENSION

FRONT: The '67's front suspension received several new design improvements. All chassis attaching points are through rubber bushings to reduce friction. The lower arm is 2½ inches longer and the A-frame is lowered. A separate cam adjustment for both the camber and caster eliminates the need for adjustment shims used previously.

REAR: The '67 Mustang continued using the Hotchkiss-type rear suspension with 4-leaf springs and angle-mounted shock absorbers.

STEERING: The same Parallelogram steering system with cross link and idler arm used on the '66 Mustang was utilized on the '67. However, new components accommodate the '67's new front suspension and increased tread width. Also, polyethylene filled ball joints reduce friction and overall steering effort. The manual steering ratio was changed to 25.3 to 1, standard, instead of the '66's 27 to 1.

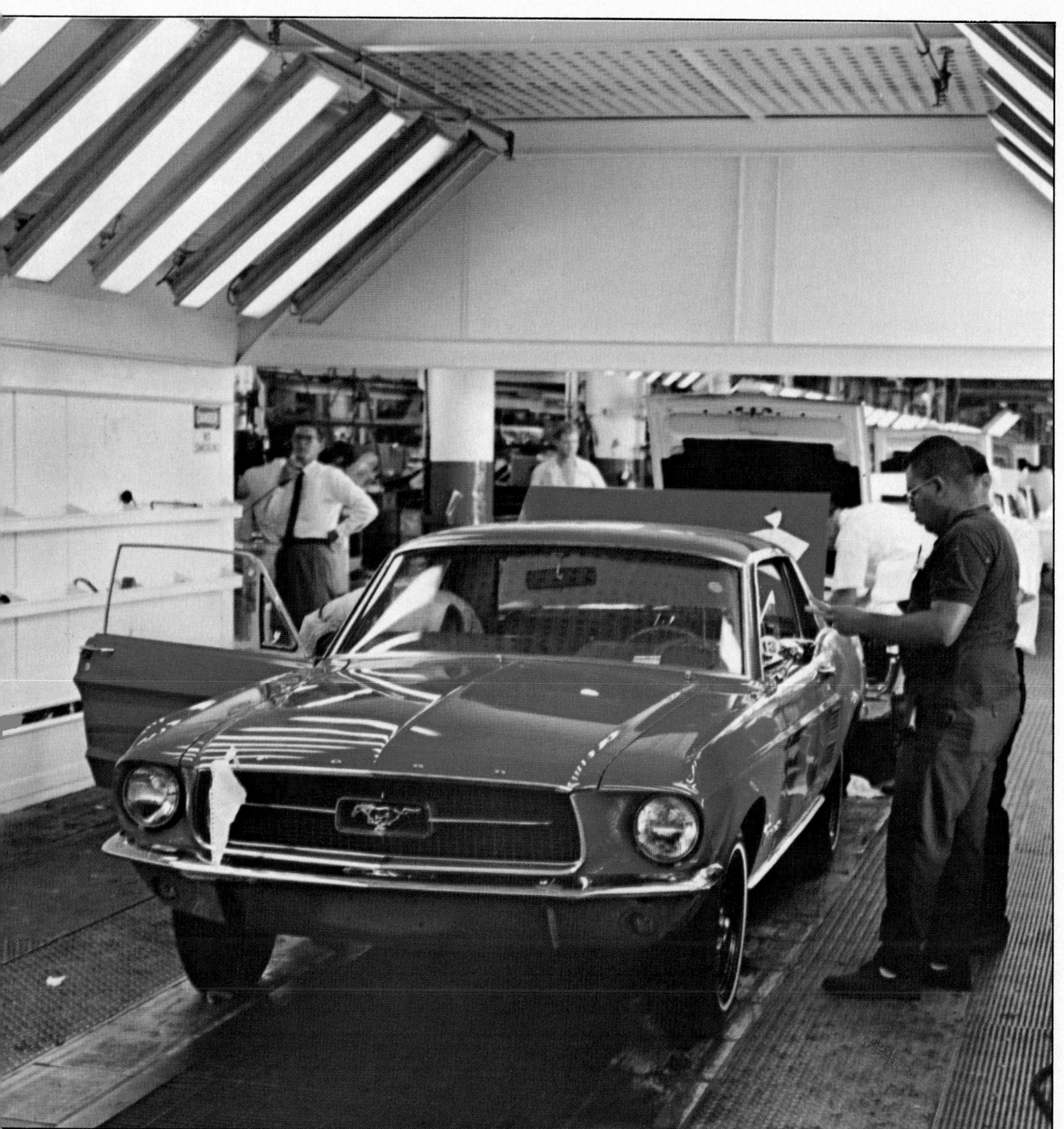

BRAKE SPECIFICATIONS			
	6-Cyl.	289 V-8	390-V8
Brake Drum Diameter	9"	10"	10"
Lining Material	Molded Asbestos		
Lining Attachment	Riveted		
Total Lining Area — Gross (Sq. In.)	131.0	154.7	163.1

OTHER MECHANICAL COMPONENTS

BRAKES: The '67 Mustang was the first to incorporate the dual hydraulic brake system. With this system, dual master cylinders control the front and rear brakes independently.

COOLING SYSTEM: The 1967 engine cooling system requires 9½ quarts for 6 cylinder cars and 15 quarts for V-8 models. Standard fan is a 5 blade unit. A 6 blade fan is furnished with air conditioning.

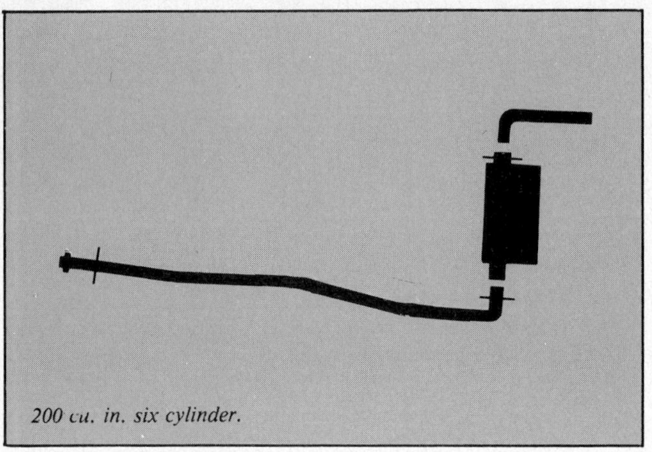

200 cu. in. six cylinder.

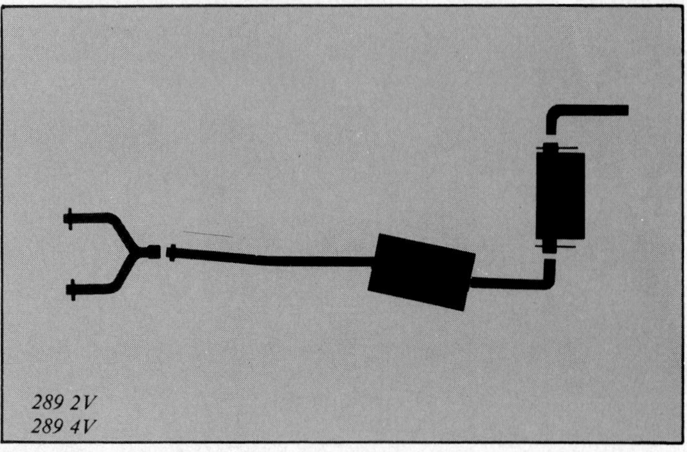

289 2V
289 4V

EXHAUST SYSTEM

The 1967 Mustang exhaust system uses cross-flow mufflers mounted behind the rear axle. V-8 models use a single forward mounted resonater, while 4-barrel versions utilize a pair of bullet-shaped resonators in front of the rear axle. All exhaust tips point downward just forward of the rear valance panel, except for GT models with their unique chrome quad exhaust extensions.

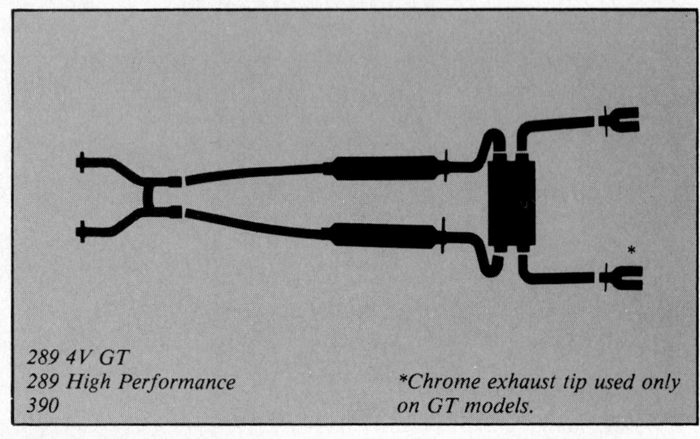

289 4V GT
289 High Performance
390

*Chrome exhaust tip used only on GT models.

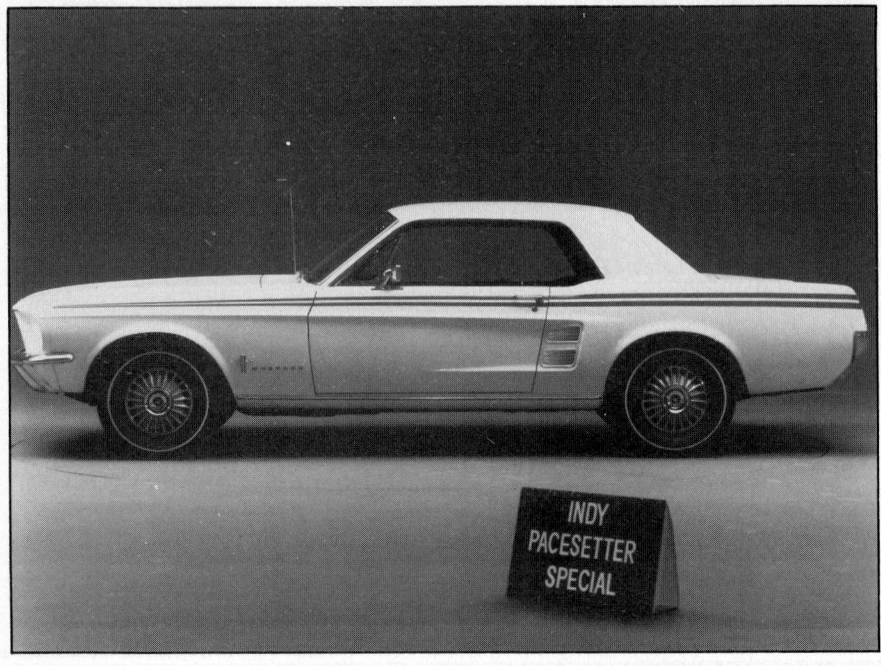

INDY PACESETTER SPECIAL

A limited edition Indy Pacesetter Special was offered in 1967 in conjunction with the Indianapolis 500 race, even though the Mustang was not the official pace car for that year. The Pacesetter was a hardtop only with special dual side stripe that ran the length of the car just below the upper body line.

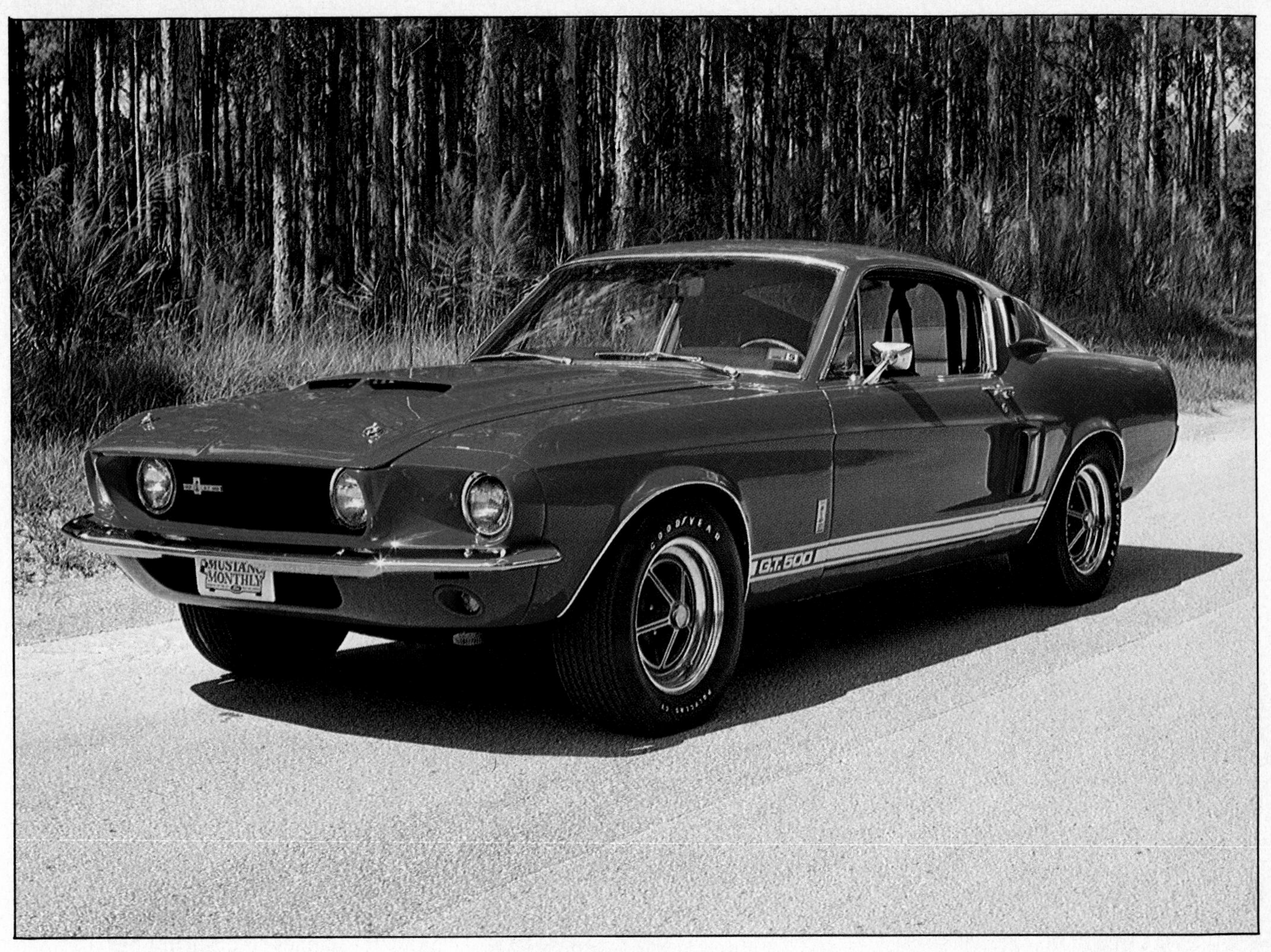

'67 SHELBY

The 1967 Shelby is a radical departure from the 1967 Mustang. Fiberglass parts are extensive, completely changing the character of the car. Shelby's emphasis in 1967 was changing from solely performance and handling, to include styling and appearance, and the new look given the second generation Shelby barely identified the car as a Mustang.

The big news for the '67 Shelby was the addition of another model — the GT500, powered by the big block 428 cubic inch engine with dual quad carburetors. Ford opened the door for the GT500 by adding the 390 to the Mustang engine line-up. The 428, with the same physical dimensions of the 390, was a natural for the Shelby image — it produced nearly 50 more horsepower than the Mustang big block.

The 1967 Shelbys were the last of the Shelby Mustangs to be built at the Shelby-American plant in Los Angeles. Beginning with the first 1968 car, production moved to the A.O. Smith assembly plant in Ionia, Michigan.

EXTERIOR

The '67 Shelby front end is 3 inches longer than its Mustang counterpart. This is accomplished by a fiberglass nosepiece replacing the conventional Mustang sheetmetal. A unique grille sports a pair of 7-inch driving lights (originally, these lights were mounted side by side in the center, but some states enforced a "minimum distance between headlights" law, so cars destined for those states required the driving lights be moved outboard, flush to either edge inside the grille). The stock Mustang front bumper is used, but without the bumper guards. The fiberglass front valance features a large cut-out that allows more cooling air to reach the radiator. A new hood, also molded from fiberglass, contains an integral scoop with dual inlets, separated in the center by a "windsplitter" that continues down the center of the hood. The stock Mustang latching mechanism is retained, and racing style hoodpins fasten the hood securely. Cars with factory-installed air conditioning also include a pair of functional louvers, one on either side of the scoop.

The wide, over-the-top "LeMans" stripes were a dealer-installed option.

The Shelby's rear exterior is dominated by the huge '67 Cougar Shelby-ized taillights (without the chrome trim), and large rear spoiler formed by the fiberglass deck lid and quarter panel extensions. A pop-open gas cap is used, with a "Shelby Cobra" applique. The rear valance contains cut-outs for the 3-inch round chrome exhaust pipe extensions.

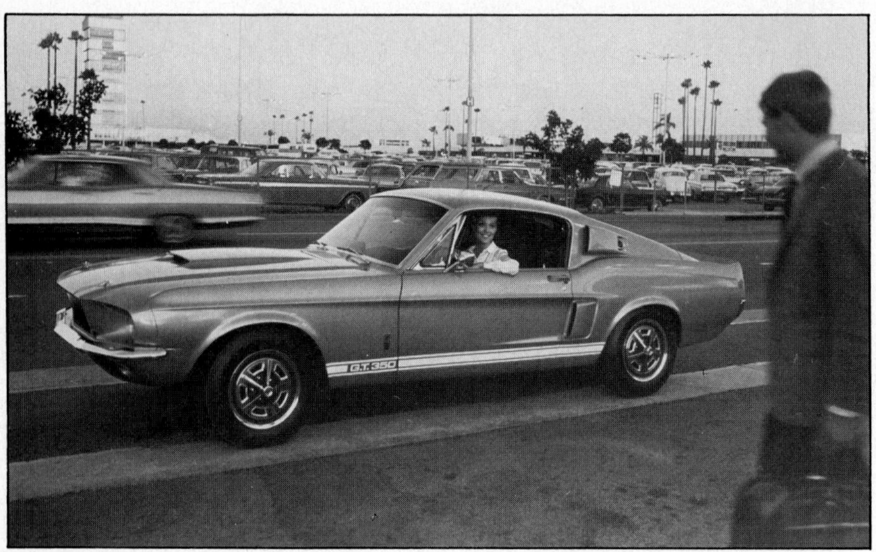

The side exterior of the 1967 Shelby features bolt-on twin scoops, one mounted behind the door in place of the Mustang's simulated scoops, and the other attached in place of the standard fastback roof louvers. The lower scoop is functional in most cars (although possibly due to an interruption of parts flow, some cars never received the actual ducting) directing fresh air to the rear brake area. The upper scoops actually draw air out of the interior. Very early production Shelbys have a small red circular running light attached to the rear of the scoop. A small gold rectangular emblem with a new-style snake is mounted on the front fender. Rocker panel stripes are standard on all 1967 Shelbys, with either GT500 or GT350 lettering inserted on the lower front fender.

1967 SHELBY INTERIOR

The Shelby's interior is basically stock Deluxe Mustang. An 8000 rpm tachometer and 140 mph speedometer are standard. Since the tachometer deletes the all-important oil pressure and ammeter gauges, the Shelby has a special under-dash unit that houses a Stewart Warner oil pressure and amp gauge. The steering wheel features a real wood rim with a perforated 3-spoke stainless center and round horn button with a gold "Shelby Cobra" applique. A unique roll bar includes a pair of inertia-reel shoulder harnesses. The fold-down rear seat, optional in the Mustang, is a standard feature of the Shelby. On Shelby produced Mustangs, the Ford oval and "Product of Ford" wording that designates the manufacturer's identity on the door sill plate is changed to read "Shelby American Inc." along with a '67-style snake insignia.

427 GT500

A limited number of 1967 Shelby GT500s were produced with the 427 medium riser engine. The actual production figure is unknown, but is estimated at less than 50. These cars were specially built for dealers and individuals. However, some high performance dealers offered the 427 engine as a dealer-installed special option.

WHEELS

The standard '67 Shelby wheel is a 15 inch steel rim with a mag-style hub cap. A 15 inch Kelsey Hayes "Mag Star" aluminum center/steel rim wheel and the Shelby 15 inch 10-spoke aluminum wheel were available optionally.

SUPERCHARGER

A very limited number of 1967 GT350s were factory equipped with a Cobra supercharger manufactured by Paxton Products. This option included the blower and a special sealed carburetor enclosure. Advertisements claimed a power increase of up to 46%.

SHELBY ENGINES

GT350: The small-block GT350 is equipped with the 289 High Performance engine, just like the '66 model. However, the '67s do not use the Tri-Y headers (the stock Ford Hi-Po exhaust manifolds are retained) but the 306 horsepower rating remains anyway. The additional power (over the Mustang's 271 horsepower) is gained from the high-rise Cobra aluminum intake manifold and Holley 715 4-barrel carburetor (on 4-speed models; automatic GT350s are equipped with a 595 cfm Autolite.) Most '67 Shelbys used the stock Ford oil pan instead of the aluminum Cobra unit from '66. Valve covers are the "COBRA POWERED by FORD" finned aluminum type.

GT500: The Shelby 428 engine, rated at 355 horsepower, is impressive with its dual quad aluminum intake and 2 Holley 600 4-barrel carbs. An oval finned aluminum air cleaner with the word "COBRA" across the top mounts on the carburetors. "COBRA LEMANS" finned aluminum valve covers have the words cast side by side, while some aftermarket units place the word "LEMANS" under "COBRA".

SHELBY SUSPENSION

The Shelby's performance handling is achieved with the Mustang Heavy Duty suspension, but with a thicker front stabilizer bar, adjustable shock absorbers, and export brace. Power front disc brakes and power steering were standard Shelby items.

TRANSMISSIONS

4-Speed Shelbys are equipped with the Ford top-loader manual transmission. GT350 automatics received the C-4, while the GT500s got the heavier-duty C-6.

1968

The newly restyled 1967 Mustang had beaten the competition, outselling Camaro, Cougar, Firebird, and Barracuda. Looks like Ford had succeeded with their worrisome restyling. Of course, no new sheetmetal was planned for '68 — not after the complete revision of 1967. Therefore, the 1968 cars received minor styling refinements. In fact, at a glance, it's difficult to tell a '67 from a '68. Government safety requirements continued to play games with the interior. Safety even altered the exterior, as side marker reflectors were added to front and rear quarters.

A cubic inch race began when Camaro topped Ford's 390 "Thunderbird Special" with a 396. Ford countered with an optional 427. But production of the 427 was severely limited, expensive, and automatic was the one transmission available with this motor. To realistically top the Camaro 396, in early calendar year 1968, Ford introduced their famous (or infamous) 428 Cobra Jet, deceptively rated at 335 horses. With its new high flow heads, the CJ was able to blow away the SS 396 Camaro.

Some special edition Mustangs also began to appear this year. In addition to the GT, available since year one, Ford sold a special Mustang "E", a Mustang Sprint, and a California Special.

In the Shelby camp, production shifted from California to the A.O. Smith Company in Ionia, Michigan. Of course, with no major styling changes in the regular Mustang lineup, the '68 Shelby also looked very similar to the '67's. A redesigned front end, changed taillights, and a new fiberglass hood with a large scoop are some of the more evident revisions. Also, a convertible was offered for the first time, as well as a new model — the GT500 "KR".

BODYSTYLES

All three Mustang body styles — hardtop, convertible, and fastback — received minor updates in 1968. Some of the changes can be contributed to the U.S. government's ever-increasing safety requirements (side lights and reflectors), and others are obviously an attempt by Ford to differentiate the '68 from the '67 (deletion of the grille bars and new side scoop ornamentation).

EXTERIOR

GRILLE: The 1968 grille opening is identical to the '67 version. However, the '68 front end achieves a unique look by deleting the traditional Mustang bars and replacing them with a smaller and simpler chrome running horse and corral. The rectangular-mesh grille is updated slightly to include a concave shape. Attached to the grille is a thin bright trim that follows a concentric pattern around the grille opening perimeter.

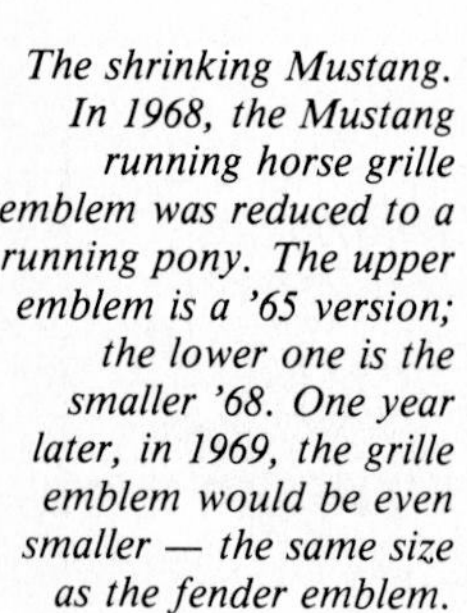

The shrinking Mustang. In 1968, the Mustang running horse grille emblem was reduced to a running pony. The upper emblem is a '65 version; the lower one is the smaller '68. One year later, in 1969, the grille emblem would be even smaller — the same size as the fender emblem.

HEADLIGHTS: Single headlights are set at either side of the grille in a sweptback housing identical to the '67. Again, a color-keyed bezel surrounds each bulb.

VALANCE PANEL: The front valance panel continues to contain the recessed parking/turn signal lights with clear lens and the integral license plate bracket. Front bumpers guards are no longer standard equipment, but relegated to optional status.

HOOD: The 1968 Mustang hood is identical to the standard hood used on the '67. The chrome molding on the leading edge of the hood continues, but the F-O-R-D block letters that extended across the front of the '67's hood are deleted.

SIDE EXTERIOR: The basic sheetmetal design of the '68 Mustang is the same as the '67. A chromed-trimmed side marker light, with clear lens, is inserted into the front fender just below the wrap-around bumper. The familiar Mustang running horse/red, white, and blue vertical bar emblem attaches to the rear portion of the front fender behind the front wheel opening. If the Mustang is equipped with a V-8 engine, the cubic inch size is stamped into a bright section at the top of the bar. The block style M-U-S-T-A-N-G fender emblem used on previous year models is changed to an updated script style, mounted in the same fender position behind the running horse/tri-color bar.

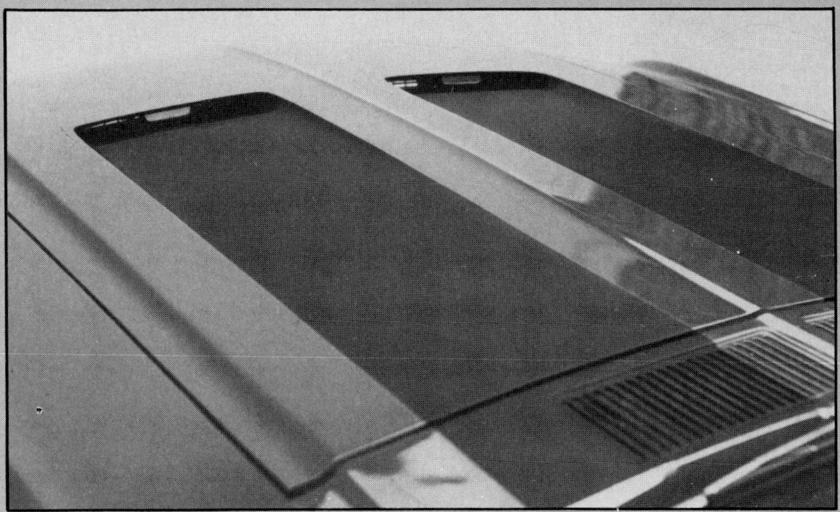

LOUVERED HOOD

When Ford dropped the Exterior Decor Group from the Mustang line-up in 1968, the louvered hood became a separate option. The hood included the same functional louvers and integral turn signal indicators from the 1967 models.

TWO-TONE PAINT

The Two-Tone Paint option was offered only in 1968 for Mustangs with the louvered hood. With the option, special low gloss black paint stripes extended from inside the hood louvers to the base of the windshield.

ACCENT STRIPES

Mustangs in 1968 could be individualized with an Accent stripe, a thin pin stripe that stretches across the top body line from the leading edge of the front fender to the rear of the quarter panel. The stripes were available in 4 colors for 1968: black, white, red and blue.

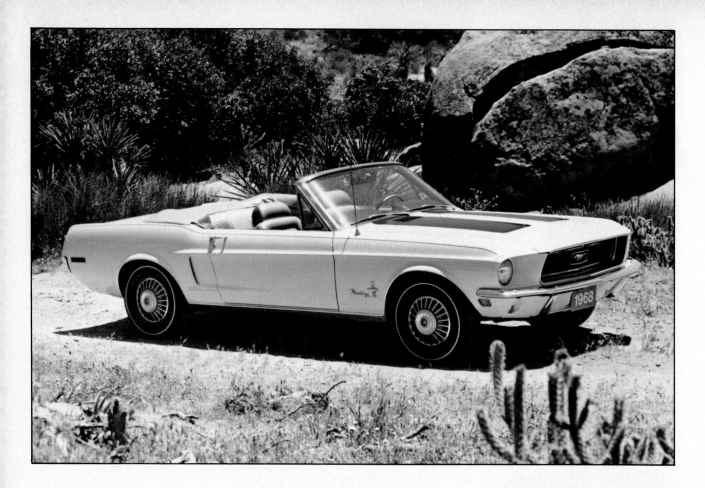

The chrome rocker panel molding is a standard item on all 1968 Mustangs (in 1967, it was standard only on the fastbacks — optional on the hardtops and convertibles).

The chrome rectangular outside rear view mirror is like the '67 unit, however, the remote control feature is no longer standard equipment. The '68 mirror is manually adjustable.

On the rear quarter panel, the twin non-functional scoops of the '67 Mustang are replaced by a simple vertical ornament. This simulated scoop is chrome with black paint inside the front leading edge. 1968 Mustangs built prior to February 15, 1968 are equipped with a rectangular red reflector, with color-keyed bezel, inserted into a cut-out in the rear of the quarter panel. Models assembled after February 15 are equipped with a bolt-on red reflector with oval-shaped chrome trim. Later quarter panels do not contain the cut-out.

WINDOWS: The curvature of the 1968 front windshield is slightly different from the '65-67, creating the need for new windshield glass. The side glass on all models is curved, blending the roofline into the door sheetmetal. Quarter vent windows are standard on all models, and the hardtop and convertible continue with the fully retractable rear quarter windows. The fastback's side window is curved at the rear upper corner to match the roofline. Also, the rear window in the fastback remains tinted, and includes a thin line down the center that continues the "windsplitter" from the roof to the rear deck lid.

Windshield washers for 1968 are a new dual stream type that directs 2 jets of water to each side of the windshield. The nozzels are mounted in the cowl vents.

ROOF: The 1968 roof design on all three models remains identical to the '67s. Both the hardtop and the fastback continue to use the

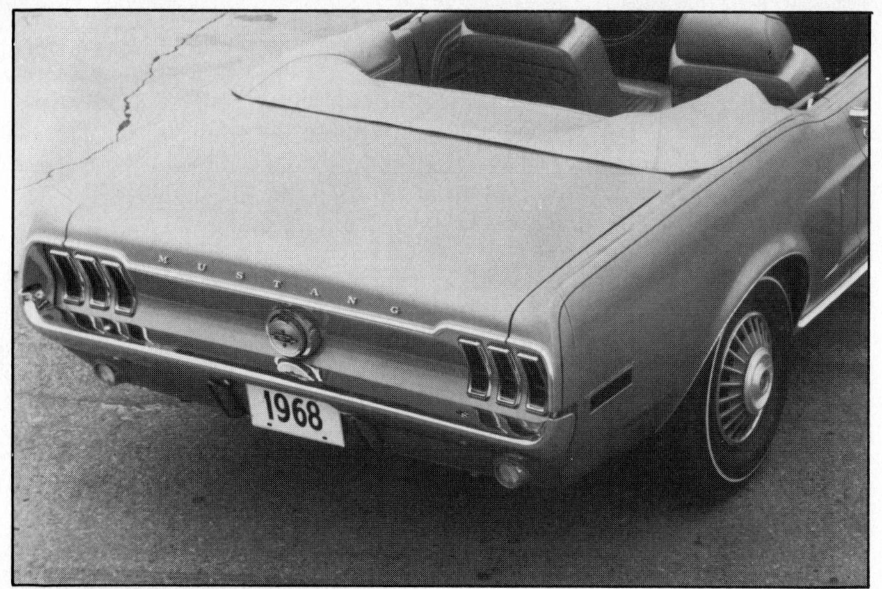

chrome drip moldings around the side windows. The 12-louver vent on the side of the fastback roof is unchanged, and the convertible color selections remains 2 only — black and parchment. However, the convertible top boot, color-keyed to the interior, uses new hidden fasteners: retaining buttons are used at each inside forward corner, but the remainder of the boot attaches to a groove across the top of the rear seat back with a tongue that is stitched to the edge of the boot. The stiff tongue is pushed into the groove, holding the boot in place.

REAR EXTERIOR: The rear exterior of the 1968 Mustang is virtually unchanged, identical to the '67 with the exception of a few cosmetic updates. A new gas cap is the most readily apparent difference. Again, it is a chrome and plastic screw-on type with a retainer wire, but the "knock-off" blades are reduced to 2 (the '67 had 3), one on each side. The center is decorated with the Mustang corral, shaped identically to the one on the front grille — only smaller — with a short bar extending from each side. The inside of the corral is black with a bright running horse in the center.

The concave rear panel contains '67-type taillights. Three separate lens fit into each end of the panel, and each lens is trimmed by a chrome bezel. However, the '68 style bezels contain a black paint insert in the center, rather than the 100% chrome finish used on the '67s.

CONVERTIBLE OPTIONS

1968 Mustang convertibles were available with a power top. The switch is mounted on the instrument panel.

The folding glass rear window was again an extra-cost Mustang option. Made from tempered glass and hinged at the center with transparent silicone rubber, the folding rear window is much easier to maintain than the standard zip-out plastic window.

VINYL ROOF

The vinyl roof was available for the hardtop only. Black and parchment were the only 2 colors offered. A metal trim covers the edge of the vinyl at the base of the roof.

GT EQUIPMENT GROUP

The GT Equipment Group was available for 1968 Mustangs equipped with one of the 4-barrel V-8 engines. It was not available with the 289 2-barrel.

- GT ornamentation - In 1968, the GT emblem is mounted on the lower front fender, just behind the front wheelwell. The emblem is rectangular, with black inside, trimmed with a bright edge. The initials GT stand out in large bright block letters within the black center.
- GT pop-open fuel filler cap - with the G stacked on top of the T. The inside of the block letters is painted red.
- Low restriction dual exhaust with chrome quad outlets.

- 4 inch fog lights - similar to the '67 type, but without the fog light bars. The '68 lights mount directly to the mesh grille with special hidden brackets. A fog light toggle switch mounts under the dash beneath the ignition switch.
- GT "C" stripes - The 1968 GT stripes differ entirely from the rocker panel stripes used on previous GT Mustangs. The new stripes begin on the front fender and follow the sculptured body line around the simulated quarter panel scoop (GT rocker panel stripes, '67 style, were available for the 1968 GT upon request).
- GT chrome styled steel wheels (with Reflective Group option, the wheels are painted with a special reflective paint) — the hub cap is round, with a brushed aluminum finish. The block GT letters, with the G on top of the T, is fastened to the center. The letters are painted red.
- F70x14 Wide Oval white sidewall tires.
- Heavy-duty suspension
- Chrome engine components[1]

[1] - 390 and 427 engines only

DECK LID: The shape of the 1968 rear deck lid is identical to the 1967. Like before, the embossed line on the rear of the fastback curves upward in the area between the taillights with chrome M-U-S-T-A-N-G lettering above. However, in 1968, the chrome rear deck and quarter panel molding became standard for all models (in '67, the molding was standard only on the fastback — optional on the hardtop and convertible).

REAR VALANCE PANEL: The rear valance panel continues to contain the standard back-up lights and license plate bracket. Bumper guards, with black rubber inserts, are color-keyed to the exterior (bumper guards are not included on cars equipped with F70x14 tires).

REFLECTIVE GROUP

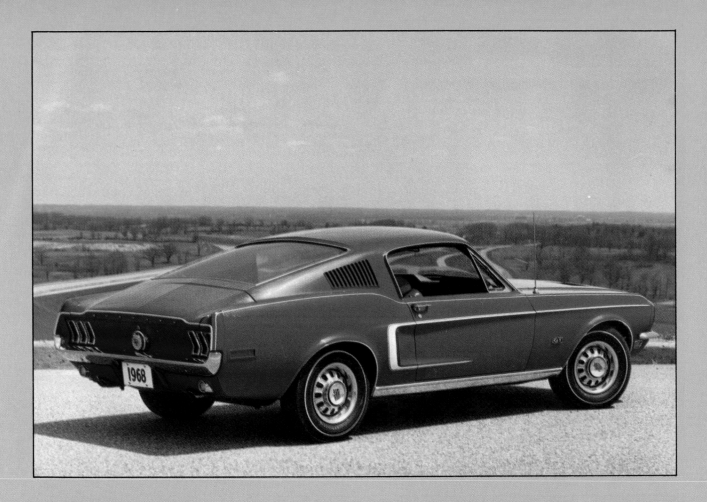

The Reflective Group was available only on 1968 Mustang equipped with GT Equipment Group. It included special reflective GT stripes and reflective paint on the styled steel wheels.

SPORTS TRIM GROUP

The Sports Trim Group is a new-for-'68 option that consists of both interior and exterior trim options. Two packages were available: one for 6 cylinder cars and the other for V-8 models.

- Woodgrain instrument panel applique
- Knitted vinyl inserts in bucket seats (hardtop and fastback only)
- Bright wheel lip moldings
- Two-Tone hood (requires louvered hood; includes low gloss black paint stripes on the hood and the cowl - the stripes end inside the hood louvers)
- Argent painted styled steel wheels*
- E70x14 Wide Oval white sidewall tires*

*V-8 Models Only

PROTECTION GROUP

- Front and rear color-keyed rubber floor mats.
- Bright metal door edge guards.
- Chrome license plate frames.

OTHER EXTERIOR, OPTIONS

- Tinted glass (all windows with a tinted band at the top of the windshield.
- Left-hand remote mirror
- Front and Rear Bumper Guards/Wheel Lip Moldings

INTERIOR

The interior of the 1968 Mustang differs very little from the previous 1967 interior. And the reasoning for most of the minor changes that did occur can be traced back to new and stricter government-imposed safety regulations.

INSTRUMENT PANEL: The configuration of the 1968 instrument panel is identical to the '67. The crash pad retains the same "twin eyebrow" look, and the instrument bezels parallel the '67 layout with a 2 large, 3 small arrangement. The large pod on the left side of the steering wheel continues to house the 120 mph speedometer with a red warning band beginning at the 70 mph marker. The right hand pod incorporates 2 gauges, like the '67, but the upper gauge becomes a fuel dial (the upper gauge in '67 was oil pressure). The lower gauge remains as the alternator charge indicator. In the upper 3 smaller gauges, the oil pressure gauge that was displaced in the lower right pod is transfered to the upper left pod. The center pod is a blank dial intended for the optional electric clock. The right hand pod continues as a water temperature gauge.

A pair of rectangular slots, arrow-shaped on the outside ends, replaces the smaller 1967 slots in the areas above the large instrument pods. The slot above the speedometer, on the left, contains the 2-speed windshield wiper switch. The right hand slot includes a red lens for the seat belt reminder light (with the optional deluxe seat belts only) and the brake warning light. Each slot contains a small green lens within the arrow-shape outside ends for the turn signal indicator lights. A small running horse shaped hi-beam headlight indicator is mounted between the 2 larger pods.

The standard instrument panel finish is once again camera case black. A small padded safety strip along the width of the dash continues as a standard item. On the passenger side instrument panel, a small rectangular emblem with M-U-S-T-A-N-G lettering and a bright running horse is attached to the lower right corner.

INSTRUMENT CONTROLS: The heater/defroster control panel, located on the extreme lower left side of the instrument panel, retains its 1967-type configuration; 3 vertical slots contain (from left to right) the heat, temperature, and defroster switches. A horizontal slot, above, houses the 3-speed fan switch. The knobs, however, are a new, safer flat design with brushed aluminum inserts. The light switch, with a

TACHOMETER

The large dial 8000 rpm tachometer mounts in the lower right hand pod on the instrument panel, displacing the fuel and alternator gauges. The fuel gauges move to the upper left instrument pod (which houses the oil pressure gauge in standard form), and the oil pressure and alternator gauges become warning lights at the bottom of the tachometer. The tach option also includes a trip odometer mounted in the speedometer face.

CONVENIENCE CONTROL PANEL

Like 1967, the 1968 Convenience Control Panel includes 4 red warning lights mounted in the center of the instrument panel (without air conditioning). With air conditioning, the console was a mandatory requirement for the Convenience Control Panel - the warning lights are integrated within the console, 2 lights on either side of the storage compartment.

1967-type knob, is mounted just below the speedometer on the left side of the dash panel. On the right side of the steering column, the ignition switch is inserted into the metal instrument panel below the large fuel/alternator pod. Mounted just to the right of the ignition switch is the flip-open ash tray. When closed, the ash tray exterior forms part of the instrument panel. The cigarette lighter is enclosed within the ash tray. A radio blanking plate is furnished for the radio housing in the lower center of the instrument panel unless an optional radio was ordered (and, in the huge majority of Mustangs, it was). A glove compartment is located on the right side of the instrument panel, equipped with a non-locking push button release.

Below the instrument panel, a foot-operated lever controls the windshield washers. A headlight dimmer switch is mounted directly below the windshield washer lever. A pull-type emergency brake handle is attached under the dash, just to the left of the steering column. An air vent knob mounts directly under the steering column.

STEERING WHEEL: The completely new style steering wheel in the 1968 Mustang replaces the large round padded wheel used in the '67 models. The '68 wheel is a 2-spoke design, wider at the center than at the ends. The heavily padded spoke is color-keyed to the interior. A similarly shaped insert is also color-keyed and contains 7 recesses designed to simulate holes. The center recess mounts a Mustang running horse/tri-color bar emblem; this emblem is flanked on either side by 3 holes that decrease in size as they reach the outer ends of the spoke. A bright semi-circular ring below the steering wheel spoke serves as the horn ring. The steering wheel itself is molded in heavy plastic and is color-keyed to the interior.

The emergency flasher switch remains on the right side of the

steering column. The chrome turn signal stalk, with its 2 position lane changing feature, continues as before on the left of the steering column. The steering column itself is a new "energy absorbing" type that will collapse upon impact.

SHIFTER: With the standard (except 427 equipped models) 3-speed manual transmission, the 1968 Mustang is equipped with a round Ford-made shifter that curves rearward toward the driver. A black rubber shifter boot attaches to the floor with a chrome bezel. The chrome shifter is topped by a screw-on round knob that is inscribed with the transmission shift pattern.

BUCKET SEATS: The 1968 Mustang's standard bucket seats are similar to the 1967 seats, yet quite different. The textured vinyl insert pleats are vertical, as opposed to the '67 horizontal pleats. In addition, the inserts in the '68 seats are completely

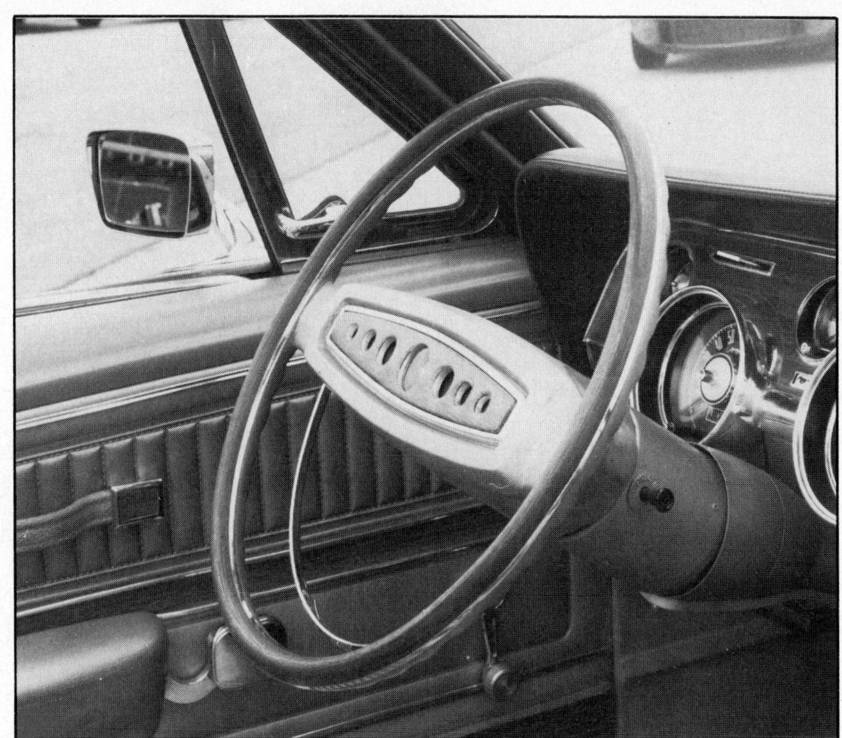

STEERING WHEEL OPTIONS

TILT-STEERING: The tilt-away steering column remained the same in 1968 as it was in 1967. The wheel tilted to 9 different positions by pressing in on the turn signal stalk. In addition, the steering wheel swings up and over when the driver's door is opened, signaled by a switch mounted in the driver's side door jamb. The engine will not start until the wheel is pulled down into the driving position.

DELUXE STEERING WHEEL: The Deluxe steering wheel is a woodgrain unit with a woodgrain applique in the center pad.

SHIFTERS WITH OPTIONAL TRANSMISSIONS

FOUR-SPEED: The 1968 Mustang 4-speed shifter differs from previous models. Instead of the finger-grip reverse lock-out trigger, the '68 used a chrome ring. The shifter knob is round, black plastic with standard interiors and woodgrain with the Decor Interior Option.

AUTOMATIC: The automatic shifter is identical to 1967. The T-handle design is equipped with a push button on the driver's side that releases the handle for shift selection. A dummy button on the passenger side of the handle matches the functional button. The shifter mounting plate is square with a domed selector indicator. The T-handle is chrome with standard interiors, or covered with vinyl with the Interior Decor Group.

COURTESY LIGHT GROUP

The Courtesy Light Group includes underhood, luggage compartment, and glove box lights, plus underdash courtesy lights (hardtops) and a glove box lock.

enclosed by the padding around the outside of both the seat cushion and the seat back (the '67's bottom cushion insert extended over the front edge of the seat). The bracket that attaches the seat back to the seat bottom on the exterior sides of the seats is concealed with a simple color-keyed plastic cover, replacing the chrome trim found on the '65-67 models.

Standard bucket seats and door panel.

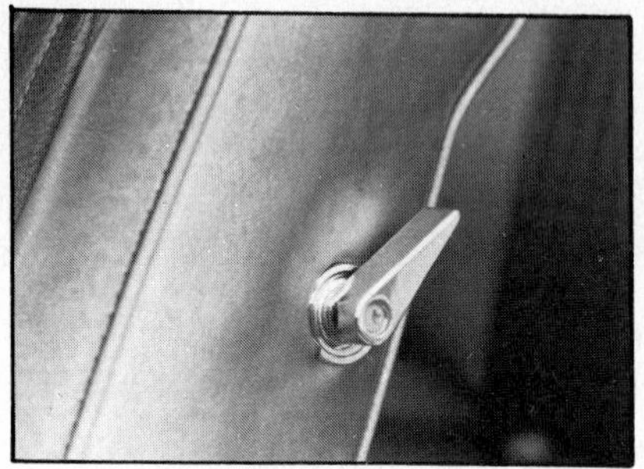

A new-for-'68 safety addition to the seats is the locking seat backs. A chrome lever is attached near the top of the exterior-facing side of each seat back. This lever releases the latch mechanism at the bottom of the seat back, allowing the seat back to fold over to gain passenger access to the rear seat.

Seat belts are furnished as standard equipment on every model. The belts feature a retractor mounted beside the door sill and standard push-button release buckles. Fastbacks and hardtops are equipped with an extra pair of buckles for the new-for-'68 shoulder harnesses. The shoulder harness belt is stored above the side window with a metal bracket that attaches to the roof through the headliner.

Standard bench seat.

REAR SEAT: The 1968 rear seat is a bucket-styled bench type with vertical pleats to match the front buckets. The fastback seat is fixed, and includes a spacious package shelf at the rear. The fastback quarter panel trim continues to house courtesy lights and a sliding knob that operates the functional side vents.

Decor bucket seats and door panel.

INTERIOR DECOR GROUP

The Interior Decor Group is the 1968 Mustang's luxury interior. Included in the package are:

- Woodgrain instrument panel appliques
- Luxury two-toned door panels, shaped identical to the standard panels, but the top portion includes short, horizontal pleats and a door pull. A woodgrain strip is fastened to the center, and a molded arm rest attaches at the lower rear. The bottom of the door is covered with a grille that includes a red/white courtesy light in the center.
- Bright trim on the pedals
- Woodgrain steering wheel with woodgrain applique in the center pad.
- A pair of bright rectangular buttons in the seat backs.
- Roof console with twin map lights and switches, covered with woodgrain (hardtops and fastbacks only).
- Padded quarter trim panels on hardtops only.
- Vinyl grip on T-handle shift lever with automatic transmission; Woodgrain knob on manual transmissions.

The quarter trim panels in both the hardtop and convertible contain cranks for the retractable rear quarter windows. Convertibles also feature padded armrests on either side with ash trays.

DOOR PANEL: The standard 1968 Mustang door panel fits into a textured metal interior door frame and is shaped identically to the '67. However, the '68 vinyl-covered door panel contains wide horizontal pleats, in contrast to the '67's thin band of pleats. The '68 arm rest is longer than the '67 version. The door handles are hinged paddle type, mounted in front of the arm rest. These new door handles are a result of stricter safety standards for American cars. Window cranks differ from the '67's: the 1968 window cranks are shorter, and feature a rounded base with a brushed aluminum circular insert that conceals the attaching screw. The round grip is color-keyed plastic for the first time; earlier 1965-67 knobs were chrome.

The door lock knob changed to a round-top design in '68.

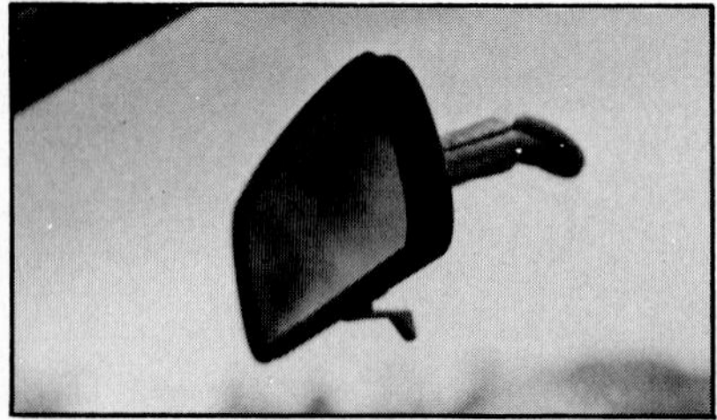

REAR VIEW MIRROR: In 1968, the rear view mirror was attached to the windshield for the first time in a Mustang. The mirror is a day-night type, backed with plastic.

INTERIOR LIGHTS: The 1968 Mustang interior is lighted identically to the '67. The hardtop features a round roof-mounted courtesy light. Convertible lights are attached under the dash at either end. Fastbacks utilize the under-dash lights also, but add an additional pair of lights in the rear quarter panel trim.

TRUNK
LUGGAGE COMPARTMENT

MAT: The luggage compartment floor in all 1968 Mustangs is covered with a patterned rubber mat.

SPARE TIRE: The spare tire, furnished with all 1968 Mustangs, is mounted on the right side of the luggage compartment with a threaded hook and large wing nut. A scissors jack and handle is supplied, stored under the spare tire. The socket end of the handle is the same size as the lug nuts, so the handle serves as both a jack handle and a lug wrench.

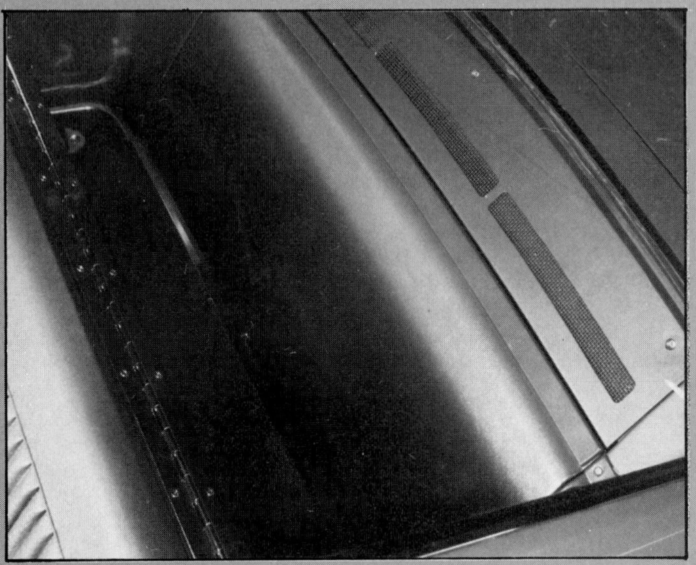

REAR WINDOW DEFOGGER

The 1968 Mustang was the first to offer a rear window defogger, hardtops and fastbacks only. The hardtop blower grille mounted in the rear package tray, but the fastback grilles (3 of them) mounted in the panel just below the rear window.

CONSOLE

The 1968 Mustang optional console is very similar to the one used in 1967. The front of the console attaches to the center of the instrument panel in place of the radio housing. From there, it drops down to the floorboard, then runs aftward between the required bucket seats. The instrument panel portion of the console requires one of the 3 Mustang optional radios, which mounts in the standard radio position. Directly below is the storage compartment with its sliding door. Automatic transmission cars have a set of special shift indicator lights mounted in the console behind the T-handled shifter. The lights are marked P-R-N-D-2-1, all red except for the green "D" marker. A pair of seat belt holsters store the seat belt buckles beside the seats. The rear of the console contains an ash tray for rear seat passengers and a courtesy light. The 1968 console is heavily padded, and covered with color-keyed vinyl.

RADIOS

The 3 available 1968 Mustang radios continue to mount in a housing that attaches below the center of the instrument panel (unless equipped with the optional console - the upper portion of the console replaces the radio housing).

- AM - includes a speaker under the instrument panel crash pad.
- AM-FM STEREO - includes a pair of stereo speakers, one in each door.
- AM-8 TRACK TAPE - The 1968 AM-tape is improved with push button selectors. Earlier tape units did not include the push buttons. Door speakers are included.

OTHER 1968 INTERIOR OPTIONS

- Electric clock - mounts in the center of the instrument cluster.
- Knitted vinyl bucket seats - for hardtops and fastbacks only.
- SelectAire air conditioning - Air conditioned models have a different heater control panel than the standard version. All functions are controlled with 3 knobs, marked AIR, TEMP, and FAN, that slide up and down within vertical slots. A round air outlet vent mounts below the control panel and an identical vent is positioned at the opposite end of the instrument panel. Two additional rectangular vents are mounted side by side in the center of the instrument panel.
- Speed control - A push button in the tip of the turn signal stalk operates the automatic speed control. An on/off switch is attached below the dash.
- Sport Deck Rear Seat (fastbacks only) - fold-down rear seat.
- Front headrest - a new option for 1968.
- Shoulder Harnesses - Additional shoulder harnesses were available for the 1968 Mustang (they were standard with hardtop and fastback models). The shoulder harness option included special front seat harnesses for the convertible and rear seat harnesses for the hardtop and fastback.
- Deluxe Seat and Shoulder Belt - includes a seat belt reminder light mounted in the dash.

COLLAPSIBLE SPARE TIRE

The collapsible space saver tire became a Mustang factory production option for the first time in 1968. With this option, a can of pressurized air was stored under the wheel and used to inflate the tire when needed. By ordering the space saver, the usable trunk space increased substantially.

WHEELS

STANDARD TIRE AND WHEEL: The standard 1968 Mustang wheel is a 14x5" stamped steel ventilated disc with safety type rims. Six cylinder cars are equipped with 4 studs; V-8s with 5. The standard tire for both sixes and V-8s is a 6.95x14.

Standard model Mustangs with the 390 engine are equipped with larger wheels and tires. These models received 14x6 wheels and 7.35x14 tires.

'68 standard hubcap w/optional whitewall trim ring.

WHEELCOVER: The base 1968 Mustang is equipped with a 10½" hubcap. Some of these hubcaps have a Mustang running horse/vertical bar emblem in the center, while others have a Ford crest. However, most '68 Mustangs were delivered with a radial spoke 14" wheelcover with a large brushed aluminum center with M-U-S-T-A-N-G block letters positioned mirror-imaged around the center.

WHEEL/WHEELCOVER OPTIONS

WHEEL: For 1968, the Styled Steel wheel (upper left) became a slotted type. It was available either argent painted or chrome with a chrome trim ring and hub cap. With the GT option, the letters GT are included on the hub cap.

WHEELCOVERS: Most 1968 Mustangs were equipped with an optional "radial spoke" (upper right) wheelcover. It features short bright spokes with rectangular slots cut into the grey areas between the spokes. The center is brushed aluminum with the block letters M-U-S-T-A-N-G stamped mirror-imaged along the outside.

DELUXE WHEELCOVER: The Deluxe wheelcover (lower left) is very similar to the base wheelcover. However, its center protrudes outward to form a base for a red center. A Mustang running horse/vertical bar is positioned in the center.

WIRE WHEELCOVER: The 1968 wire wheelcover (lower right) features a red center with the Mustang running horse/vertical bar. F-O-R-D also appears above the horse and M-U-S-T-A-N-G below.

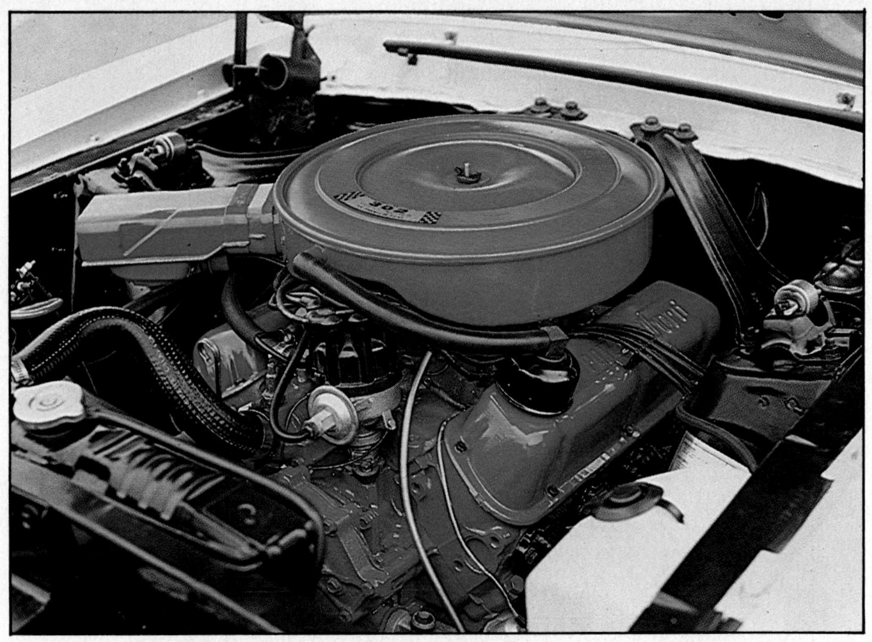

POWERTEAMS

ENGINE: A total of 9 engines were available in 1968, but not all at the same time. The 200 cubic inch 6 cylinder remained as the standard powerplant. At the beginning of the 1968 production year, the 289 4-barrel and the 289 High Performance were dropped from the Mustang powerteam selection, and replaced with a brand new 302 4-barrel. The 289 2-barrel lasted until mid-year before being replaced by the 302 2-barrel. Two high performance engines were offered for the 1968 Mustang: a 302 High Performance and a 390 horsepower 427 — both were very limited production. In November of 1967, Ford added the 250 cubic inch 6 cylinder, and, in January 1968, Ford introduced the new 428 Cobra Jet.

TRANSMISSION: The fully synchronized 3-speed manual transmission was standard equipment with all 1968 Mustang engines except the 427. The 390 3-speed, however, was a special heavy-duty version. The high-performance 427, oddly enough, was available only with the Select Shift Cruise-O-Matic C-6.

SUSPENSION: The 1968 Mustang front suspension uses the same basic design as previous models. However, the '68 model includes a new, curved "hockey stick" lower arm strut, with softer front rubber bushings to cushion road shocks. Also, new precompressed strut insulator bushings provide better caster alignment.

POWER ASSIST OPTIONS

- Power brakes - Power front disc brakes were the only power-assisted brakes available on the 1968 Mustang. With this option, the brake pedal includes a round chrome plate in the center with "DISC BRAKE" stamped in it.
- Power steering.

PERFORMANCE EQUIPMENT

- Rear Axle Ratios
- 55 amp. battery (standard with 390 and 427 V-8s with automatic transmission).
- Extra Cooling Package (standard with air conditioning)
- Heavy Duty Suspension (V-8s only) - Includes increased rate front and rear springs, larger front stabilizer bar, and larger front and rear shock absorbers.
- Limited Slip Differential.

POWER TEAM SELECTION

ENGINES	TRANSMISSIONS			REAR AXLE RATIOS					
	3-Speed Manual	4-Speed Manual	Cruise-O-Matic	3-Speed Manual		4-Speed Manual		Cruise-O-Matic	
				Std.	Opt.	Std.	Opt.	Std.	Opt.
Std. – 200 Six – 115 HP	Std.	N/A	Opt.	3.20	–	–	–	2.83	3.20
Opt. – 289 2v V-8 – 195 HP	Std.	Opt.	Opt.	2.79	3.00[3] 3.25	2.79	[1]3.00[3] 3.25	2.79	3.00[3]
Opt. – 302 4v V-8 – 230 HP	Std.	Opt.	Opt.	3.00[3]	2.79	3.00[3]	2.79	3.00[3]	2.79
Opt. – 390 4v GT V-8 – 325 HP	[2]	Opt.	Opt.	3.00	[4]3.25[3]	3.00	[4]3.25[3]	3.00	[4]3.25[3]
Opt. – 427 4v V-8 – 390 HP	N/A	N/A	Opt.	–	–	–	–	3.50[3]	–

[1] Mandatory ratio with F70-14 Wide-Oval tires.
[2] Requires HD 3-speed manual at extra cost.
[3] Also available with optional limited slip differential.
[4] Mandatory ratio with air conditioning.

REAR: The familiar Hotchkiss type rear suspension is continued in the 1968 Mustangs, which includes 4-leaf springs and angle-mounted shock absorbers. In addition, the '68 shocks including both the front and rear, are filled with a new, more constant viscosity fluid.

STEERING: The 1968 steering system is the same Parallelogram type, with polyethylene filled ball joints, like those used in the 1967 Mustang. The standard steering ratio continues at 25.3 to 1.

OTHER MECHANICAL COMPONENTS

COOLING SYSTEM: The engine cooling system for 1968 requires 9 quarts of coolant for 6-cylinder cars and 13½ quarts for V-8 models. The standard fan is a 5 blade unit.

BRAKES: The 1968 Mustang uses a dual hydraulic brake system with a dual master cylinder. The brakes themselves are duo-servo design with a self-adjusting feature.

The 200 cubic inch 6-cylinder, 289 and 302 2-barrel, and 302 4-barrel use a single exhaust system with the muffler mounted in front of the rear axle. Larger V-8 engines are equipped with a dual exhaust system, using a pair of bullet-shaped resonators in front of the rear axle and a transverse mounted cross-flow dual inlet/outlet muffler positioned between the rear axle and the fuel tank.

1968½ COBRA JET

On April 1st, 1968, Ford introduced the Cobra Jet Mustang fastback, equipped with the brand new 428 Cobra Jet engine. It was the largest powerplant ever stuffed into the production line Mustang, and it officially launched the Mustang into the performance war of the late sixties.

The base Mustang for the Cobra Jet package is the GT fastback, equipping the CJ with grille fog lights, GT side stripes, Styled Steel wheels, and the Heavy Duty Handling package. In addition, the '68½ Cobra Jet is the premier assembly line Mustang to feature a functional hood scoop. A wide, non-glare black stripe stretches from the leading edge of the hood, over the scoop, to the base of the windshield.

1968½ COBRA JET IDENTIFICATION

- R engine code in the serial number
- GT Equipment Group
- Lower shock tower bracing
- Ram Air scoop, functional, without turn signal indicators
- Black stripe on hood and cowl
- 9'' rear end
- Staggered rear shocks on 4-speed cars
- Power front disc brakes
- 8,000 rpm tachometer with all 4-speed cars, optional with automatics

SPRINT

During the spring and summer months of 1968, Ford advertised a "See-The-Light Sale" for 2 versions of the Mustang Sprint. One package was offered for 6 cylinder models, while the V-8s received a couple of additional items.

SIX CYLINDER SPRINT

- GT stripes
- Pop-open gas cap
- Full wheel covers.

V-8 SPRINTS

- Six cylinder Sprint items plus:
- Wide Oval tires
- Styled Steel wheels
- GT fog lamps

CALIFORNIA SPECIAL

The limited production California Special was a promotional Shelby-ized Mustang marketed by the Southern California Ford Dealers. It was available in hardtop form only, and the base model was a standard 6 cylinder version. Of course, most Mustang options, including V-8 engines and other performance items, were optional.

California Special body features:

- Blacked-out grille - The California Special grille deletes the standard Mustang chrome running horse and corral.
- Lucas fog lamps - These lamps are mounted on brackets that position the lights in either end of the grille. Some of the very early California Specials used Marchal lamps.
- Fiberglass side scoops - non-functional, mounted in the rear quarter panels in place of the standard Mustang ornamentation.
- Fiberglass rear deck lid and quarter panel caps - Identical to the 1968 Shelby convertible, forming an integral spoiler. Mustang script lettering appears in the upper right corner of the spoiler.
- Fiberglass rear panel with Shelby taillights.
- Side stripes - The California Special side stripes extend down the center of the body from the leading edge of the front fender to the rear edge of the side scoop. The letters GT/CS (for GT/California Special) are cut out of the stripe on the side scoop.
- Rear deck stripes - extends around the top edge of the rear spoiler.
- California Special script lettering on the rear quarter panel.
- Twist type hood locks - The Mustang optional louvered hood is standard equipment on the California Special. It fastens via the standard Mustang latch mechanism, and is secured by twist type hood locks.

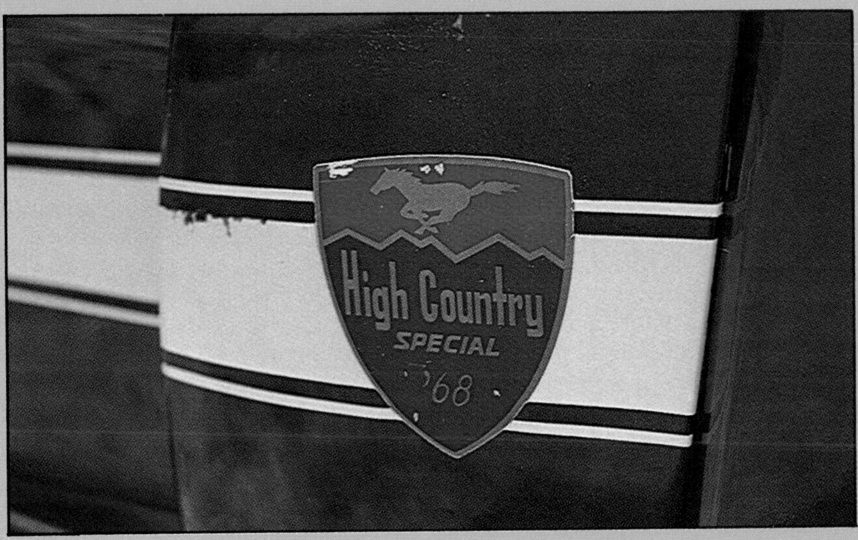

HIGH COUNTRY SPECIAL

The 1968 High Country Special was a spin-off from the California Special, sold as a promotional "limited edition" by the Colorado Ford Dealers. The High Country Special is identical to the California Special. However, the GT/CS cut-out on the side scoop stripe is replaced by a triangular "High Country Special" decal that features a running horse in a blue "sky" background over a "mountain" horizon. Also, the California Special script lettering on the rear quarter panel is eliminated.

Like the California Special, the High Country Special was available only as a hardtop. In standard form, the car was sold as a base Mustang with plain hubcaps and 6 cylinder engine, but most Mustang options were offered.

High Country Specials have a 51 DSO number on their data plate, representing a Denver delivery.

'68 SHELBY

Production of the Shelby Mustangs moved from the Shelby American facility in Los Angeles to the A.O. Smith Company in Livonia, Michigan in 1968, a switch forced by the lack of enough high quality fiberglass in the L.A. area and an expiring lease at Shelby's airport plant. The name of the Shelby Mustangs also changed in 1968 — to Shelby Cobra GT350 or 500.

Since the 1968 Mustang changed very little, the Shelby also required few modifications. However, it can be recognized very easily by the new front end treatment.

The new models entered the shelby line-up in 1968. The first was a convertible, available both as a GT350 or GT500. The second model, the GT500KR, was introduced at mid-year, coinciding with the Ford introduction of the Cobra Jet engine for the Mustang.

EXTERIOR

The 1968 Shelby's fiberglass front nosepiece forms the wide grille opening, unlike the standard Mustang, which uses the leading edge of the hood to border the top of the grille opening. The nosepiece also forms the headlight housing, sweeping back toward the fender much like the production Mustang. A chrome headlight bezel replaces the Mustang's color-keyed bezel. Block letters S-H-E-L-B-Y stretch across the top of the nosepiece in front of the hood. The valance panel, also fiberglass, forms another opening below the bumper. A chrome molding borders both the nosepiece opening and the valance opening, creating the visual appearance of a single wide mouth.

A wire-mesh grille is set deeply within the grille cavity, and a pair of Lucas fog lamps are positioned in either end of the grille, mounted on brackets that attach to the lower nosepiece opening. Some early Shelbys were equipped with Marchal fog lamps.

The 1968 Shelby hood is again formed from fiberglass, but with new wider scoops that appear at the very front edge, just behind the grille nosepiece. A wide "wind-splitter" separates the opening into twin scoops. A pair of functional louvers, positioned on either side of the hood about ¾ of the way back, allows air to escape from the engine compartment. The standard Mustang hood latch mechanism is retained, but additional twist-type hood fasteners are employed.

The Shelby side exterior, per government regulations, received side marker lights and reflectors, like the production Mustang. However, the rear reflectors on the early Shelbys were bordered with chrome, in place of the Mustang's color-keyed trim. After February 15, 1968, when Mustangs began using the chrome oval reflector, Shelby changed over to an identical unit.

Shelby rear quarter panels carry the '67-type rear brake air-scoops, as well as the roof vent scoop. Side rocker panel stripes included either GT350, GT500, or GT500KR on the front fender.

The '68 Shelby's rear deck lid is fiberglass, and, with the fiberglass quarter panel caps, forms an integral spoiler across the rear of the car. Block S-H-E-L-B-Y letters are positioned in the center of the spoiler. The rear panel is also fiberglass, but is painted silver in '68. 1965 Thunderbird sequential taillights replace the '67's Cougar assemblies. A pop-open gas cap, with the Shelby snake and "SHELBY COBRA", mounts in the center. The rear valance panel is from the standard Mustang GT, with exhaust cutouts. Chrome exhaust tips are large diameter "pipe within a pipe" type on GT350s and 500s; later model GT500KRs use the GT quad tips.

A new coiled snake emblem is used on the 1968 Shelbys. The newer snake stands alone (the '67 snake was mounted in a rectangular emblem) and has a rectangular bar positioned below stamped with the word "COBRA".

1968 SHELBY INTERIOR

Shelby interiors in 1968 are Deluxe Mustang. A console is standard equipment, but it differs substantially from the Mustang unit. The Shelby console features a pair of Stewart Warner gauges - oil pressure and amperes - mounted side by side in the center just below the radio. The padded arm rest top, which also serves as the lid for the storage compartment, is embossed with a Cobra insignia. A special GT350 or GT500 snake emblem appears on the passenger side of the instrument panel as well as the door panels. A "SHELBY COBRA" rectangular emblem is centered on the padded steering wheel spoke.

The padded roll bar and inertia reel shoulder harnesses are standard, as is the fold-down rear seat.

1968 SHELBY ENGINES

GT350: The small-block GT350 received a new engine in 1968 - the 302 4-barrel rated at 250 horsepower. It features a Cobra aluminum intake and 600 cfm Holley carburetor in place of the standard cast iron/Autolite setup (early GT350s did have the standard Ford intake and carburetor, but were recalled for updating when the Shelby items became available). The engines were dressed-up with "SHELBY-POWERED by FORD" valve covers and oval "COBRA" air cleaners.

GT500: The GT500 Shelbys were equipped with a 360 horsepower version 428 Ford Police Interceptor. A "COBRA" aluminum intake with a 715 cfm Holley carburetor is standard. "COBRA LEMANS" finned aluminum valve covers and an oval "COBRA" air cleaner are also regular 1968 Shelby features.

A very small number of 1968 Shelbys — probably less than 50 were produced with the 400 horse 427 medium riser. These cars were built on special order and came with C-6 automatic transmission.

GT500KR: The Shelby GT500KR (the KR stands for "King of the Road") was the Cobra Jet version of the GT500. Actually, the GT500KR replaced the standard GT500 which was discontinued. The KRs were introduced around mid-year when Ford released the 428 Cobra Jet engine.

The GT500KRs are updated with "COBRA JET 428" emblems affixed behind the Cobra snake emblem on the front fenders, "COBRA JET" emblem on the dash, and a "COBRA JET" gas cap applique. In addition, the side stripes included "GT500KR" on the bottom of the fenders.

KRs feature a functional Ram-Air hood. A fiberglass chamber mounted under the hood channels cold outside air into a rubber-sealed air cleaner.

1968 SHELBY CONVERTIBLE

The new-for-'68 Shelby convertible includes all the items that made a Shelby a Shelby (except the upper side scoop and fold down rear seat). It even includes a padded roll bar that, unlike the fastback's round bar, is flatter in appearance. Two small rectangular hinged rings mounted on top of the roll bar were reportedly included for securing surfboards.

1968 SHELBY WHEELS

The 1968 Shelby standard wheel is a 15" stamped unit with a Mag-style 5-spoke wheelcover. A "SHELBY COBRA" applique is placed in the round center. The 15" aluminum 10-spoke wheel was offered as optional equipment.

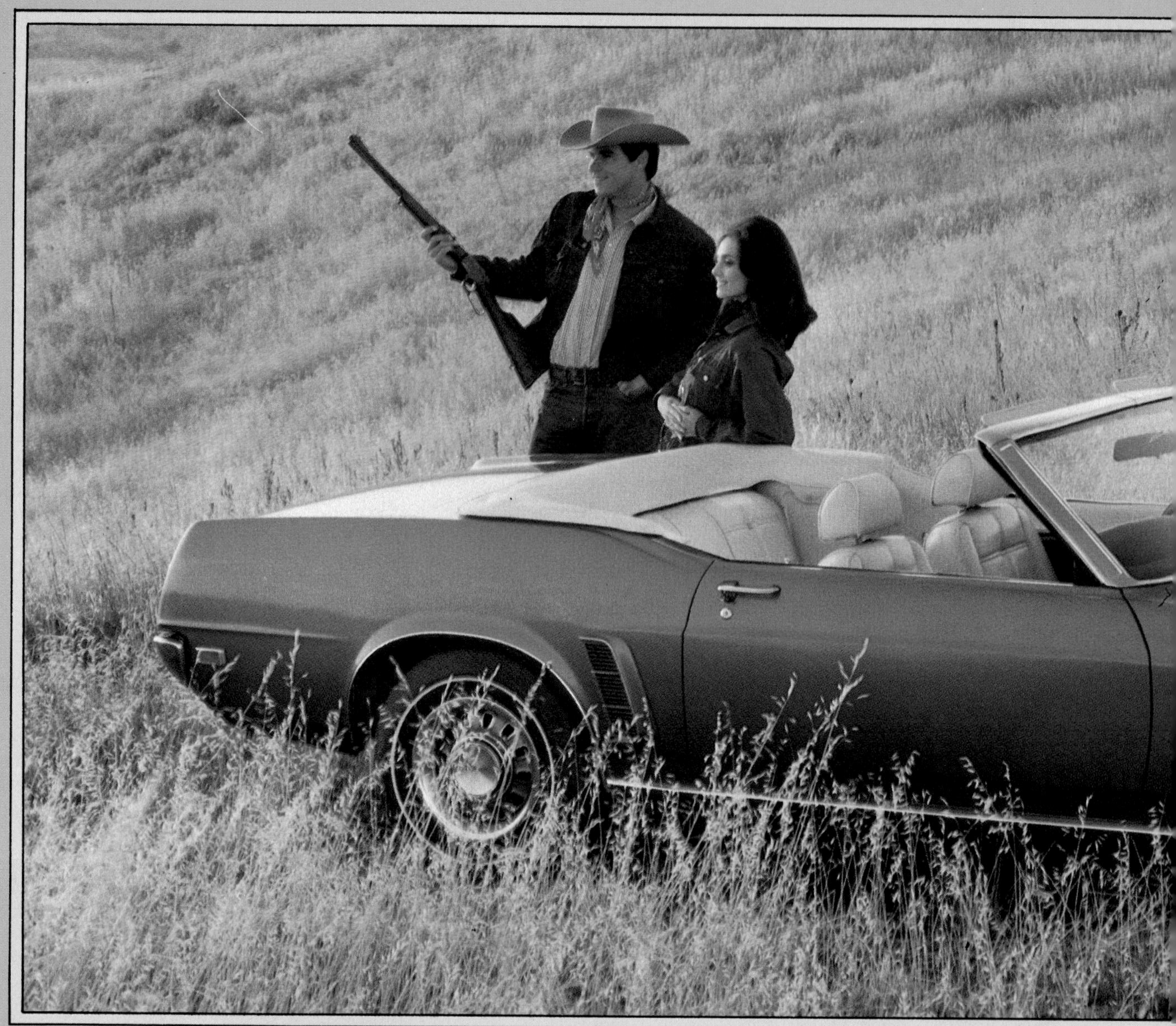

1969

Ford pulled off another major restyling of the Mustang in 1969, the most dramatic to date. The three body styles now had an even longer, lower, meaner look, which helped showcase the many high performance engines of that wild era.

Still, the six cylinder was standard in each body style, and the Mustang continued to appeal to a wide range of buyers — from economy seekers clear to hot rodders wanting factory super cars. Even the rakish fastback was a favorite, despite its radical, chopped-top look. In fact, fastback sales totaled 134,438, or an astounding 44.8% of 1969 model year production! More fastbacks were sold in 1969, than in any previous model year! Looks like Ford had designed another Mustang with a broad-based eye appeal. Of course, performance was a major key to selling cars in 1969, and extra performance looks were very popular, even with the buyer who chose to hide a six cylinder under that long Mustang hood.

Mustang interiors took-on a fresh look, with a "dual cockpit" style padded dash, plush bucket seats, and a host of other luxury features — many standard.

Specialty models were added this year — the Mach 1, the Boss 429, Boss 302, and the luxury Grande. The GT was in its last season.

Through 1968, the Shelbys had been easily recognized as racier looking Mustangs with higher output V-8's. But in 1969, the Shelbys used their own unique fiberglass front end pieces, taking on a unique look apart from the Mustang. However, a "duplication of effort" was beginning, as Ford Boss fastbacks and Mach 1's competed against the higher priced Shelbys.

BODY STYLES

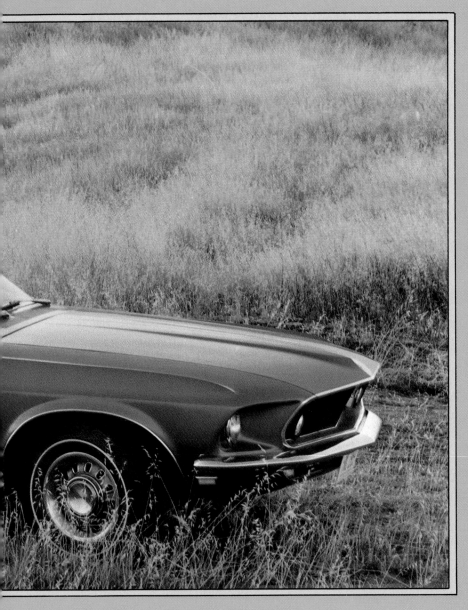

The new styling of the 1969 Mustang effected all three body styles. Each model — hardtop, convertible, and fastback - grew nearly 4 inches in length to 187.4'' — the largest Mustang to date. The basic body style of the hardtop and convertible is almost identical, but the SportsRoof (Ford's new term for the fastback body style) differs considerably with a bold new quarter panel scoop and built-in rear spoiler.

Two new models entered the Mustang line-up at the September, 1968 introduction, but both were actually standard body styles equipped with option packages. The Grande was a luxury version of the hardtop and the Mach 1 improved the performance image of the already sporty SportsRoof.

EXTERIOR

GRILLE: The rectangular mesh Mustang grille is molded in heavy-duty plastic for the first time in 1969, instead of the metal grille used in previous years. The top edge of the V-shaped grille tips forward to blend the front edge of the hood with the bumper. A headlight mounts at either end of the grille, part of the '69's new quad headlight system. The inner headlights are shrouded with a plastic hood that matches the dark gray grille color. The chrome Mustang running horse/bar is placed off-center on the driver's side, replacing the large chrome horse and corral that was employed from 1965 through 1968.

The somewhat larger grille opening is formed by the chrome-bordered hood, outside headlight housings, and lower grille trim.

HEADLIGHTS: The outboard headlights are mounted in a swept back housing similar to previous years. A chrome bezel surrounds each light, replacing the color-keyed 1968 bezel.

VALANCE PANEL: The new 1969 valance panel forms an air intake below the bumper. Parking/turn signal lights are mounted at either end of this intake. The center of the valance panel has protruding holes for attaching the license plate bracket, no longer built-in. The panel wraps under the front of the car and meets the front fender just below the bumper. A side marker light mounts on either side of the car below the wrap-around bumper.

HOOD: The 1969 hood is smoother than the '68, but has a much more pronounced "wind-splitter" in the center. The front edge is trimmed with a chrome molding. A new latch mechanism is required with a longer release lever at the center of the hood.

SIDE EXTERIOR: The new 1969 side exterior includes a body line that continues from the upper lip of the headlight housing. The line stretches back to the rear quarter panel, blending into the sheetmetal on hardtops and convertibles and forming the bottom of the SportsRoof's new scoop. A restyled MUSTANG script emblem

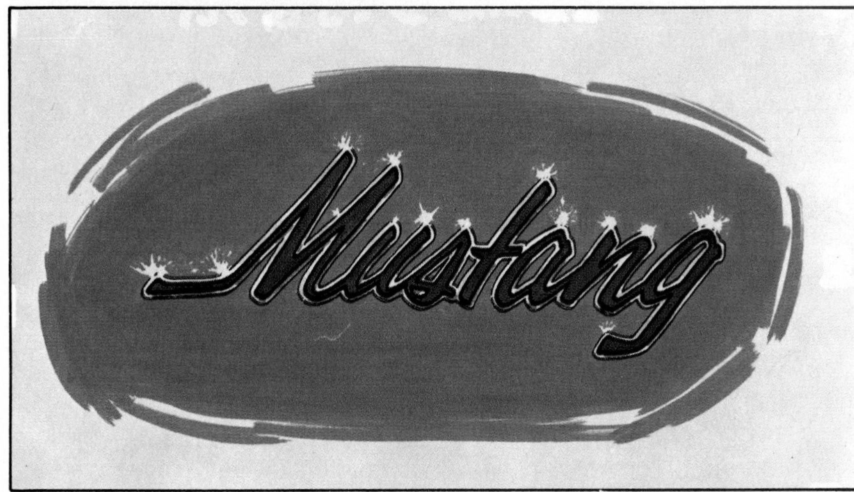

replaces the old '68 script. A chrome non-remote rectangular rear view mirror is standard on the driver's door. Scoops decorate the rear quarter panel on all models: the hardtops and convertibles have a simulated finned air exhaust vent and the SportsRoofs include a non-functional scoop in the quarter panel behind the door handle. All models received a new red side marker light on the rear quarter panel in place of the '68's reflector. On hardtops and convertibles, another smaller body line extends from the rear of the quarter panel, just above the bumper, to a point just behind the rear wheelwell where the line blends into the sheetmetal.

WINDOWS: The 1969 Mustang windshield is slightly larger than before, and features an increased rearward slope. The side vent window is eliminated in 1969. Rear quarter windows on the hardtop and convertible continue to retract as before. And, for the first time in a Mustang, the fastback has a rear quarter window, a pivot-open type attached to a rubber-encased wire that limits its outward travel.

Rear windows are all-new necessitated by the restyled body designs. The hardtop rear window mounts in a "tunnel" roof C pillar and the convertible keeps its standard plastic window. All SportsRoof rear windows are tinted.

Dual stream windshield washers remain from the '68 model year. The nozzles continue to mount in the cowl vents.

ROOF: All three 1969 Mustang roofs are restyled. The hardtop is equipped with wider C pillars on the side that form a "tunnel" for the rear window. The SportsRoof roof eliminates the side louvers and replaces them with a simple, round Mustang running horse emblem. Convertible top color selections remains at 2 — black, or white.

REAR EXTERIOR: The Mustang rear appearance changes substantially in 1969. The rear panel is still concave, but the '69's taillight lens, 3 at each end of the panel, protrude outward nearly 1½

inches. A new gas cap loses the "knock-off" blades from the '67-68 period; it is simply round with a bright Mustang running horse centered in a black background. A wire retains the gas cap during fill-ups.

DECK LID: The rear deck lid on all 3 models became flush above the rear panel in 1969, unlike the '67-68 models that had a downward curve on the hardtops and convertibles and an upward line on the fastback. The SportsRoof deck lid, combined with the quarter panel caps, forms an integral spoiler. M-U-S-T-A-N-G block letters stretch across the rear of the deck lid on all models.

REAR VALANCE PANEL: Rear valance panels on the 1969 Mustang contain standard back-up lights and the rear license plate bracket. Bumpers guards, which were used on the previous 1967-68 Mustangs, are eliminated.

EXTERIOR DECOR GROUP

The Exterior Decor Group returned to the Mustang option list in 1969 after a year's absence. The option package wasn't quite as complete as before; for 1969, it included only 4 options. The Exterior Decor Group was not available for the Mach 1 or Grande.

- Wheel lip moldings
- Rocker panel moldings
- Rear end moldings
- Base 5-spoke wheelcovers

TWO-TONE PAINT

A low-gloss black hood and cowl treatment was available for any 1969 Mustang. This paint option was standard on Mach 1s.

OTHER EXTERIOR OPTIONS

- Front bumper guards
- Rocker panel moldings
- Vinyl roof (hardtop only, black or white)
- Dual racing mirrors (color-keyed)
- Left-hand remote control outside mirror
- Tinted glass
- Tinted windshield only

GT EQUIPMENT GROUP

Nineteen Sixty-Nine was the final year for the Mustang GT Equipment Group option. Ford's new option selling technique ''packaged'' options together as separate models, like the Mach 1 and Grande. In addition, the Mach 1 package itself offered the buyer a much better choice of standard equipment, including a special interior. So, in 1969, the GT faded from existence because of meager sales, which makes the '69 GT one of the rarest of Mustangs.

The GT Equipment Group was available for all 3 Mustang body styles, but only with one of the 5 larger engines — either of the 351s (2 barrel or 4 barrel), the 390, or one of the 428s.

- GT racing stripe - mounted along the rocker panel i

:andard GT style, but without any GT or
IUSTANG emblems. The stripe was available in 4 olors — black, white, red or gold — depending pon the body and interior colors.
'op-open gas cap — with the letters GT in the center.
Iood scoop — non-functional, with integral (rear acing) turn signal indicators. The Shaker scoop is tandard with the 428 Cobra Jet Ram-Air, but does ot have turn signal indicators.
Pin-type hood latches
Styled steel wheels — with E70x14 white sidewall tires. GT letters are included in the hubcap centers.
Dual exhaust — with 4-barrel engines only. Chrome quad exhaust tips mount under valance panel cutouts.
Heavy-duty suspension — heavy-purpose springs and shocks, beefier front stabilizer bar.

INTERIOR

A totally new Mustang interior debuted in 1969. The new instrument panel and crash pad design reiterates the performance image of the exterior, forming a separate "cockpit" effect for the driver and passenger.

INSTRUMENT PANEL: The Mustang instrument panel was completely redesigned in 1969. The crash pad forms an instrument panel "hood" on each side, and the center drops down to blend into a radio/heater control housing that protrudes from the metal lower instrument panel. The recessed gauges are mounted in 4 pods in a camera-case black plastic housing. The 2 inner pods are

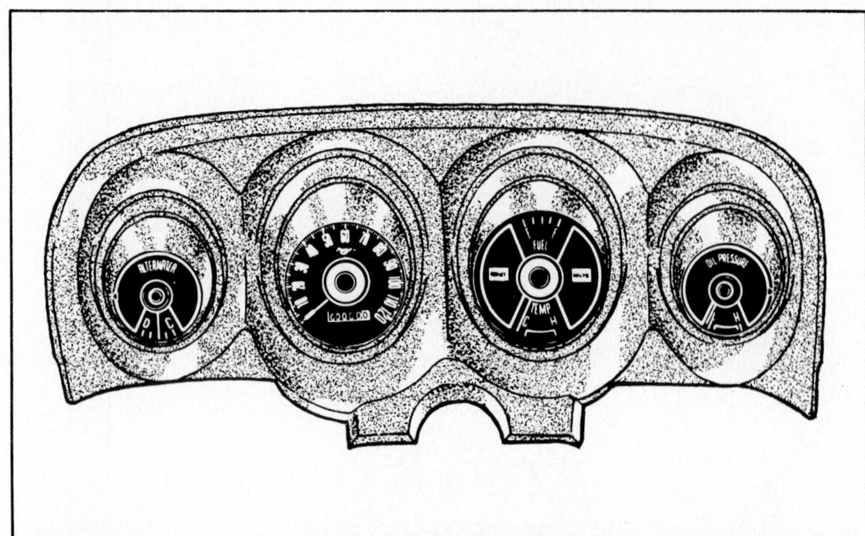

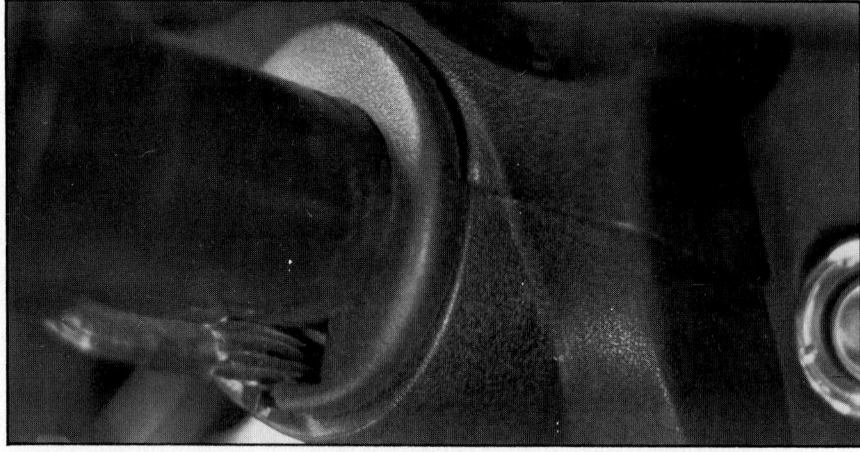

In 1969, a rubber seal covers the gap between the steering column and the instrument panel.

larger than the outside pair. The small pod on the extreme left contains the alternator gauge. The left-hand, large pod houses the speedometer as well as the running horse-shaped high beam indicator and mileage odometer. The adjacent pod to the right indicates both the fuel level (upper gauge) and the engine coolant temperature (lower gauge). A rectangular red brake warning light sits to the left of the pod center, and a seat belt warning light, also rectangular, mounts on the right. The smaller right side pod contains the oil pressure gauge. Arrow-shaped turn indicator lights are located in the outside smaller pods, to the left of the alternator gauge and the right of the oil pressure gauge.

The passenger side "cockpit" features a plain camera-case black panel to match the instrument panel. A glove compartment, with the latch button off-centered to the left, mounts in the lower passenger-side panel.

INSTRUMENT CONTROLS: All of the 1969 Mustang controls are located on the metal lower dash panel. Knobs are new, recognized by the round camera-case black inserts in their centers. The headlight switch mounts on the left side of the steering wheel, while the ignition and windshield wiper switches are located to the right of the steering column. Windshield washers are activated by pushing the wiper switch, which also activates the wipers.

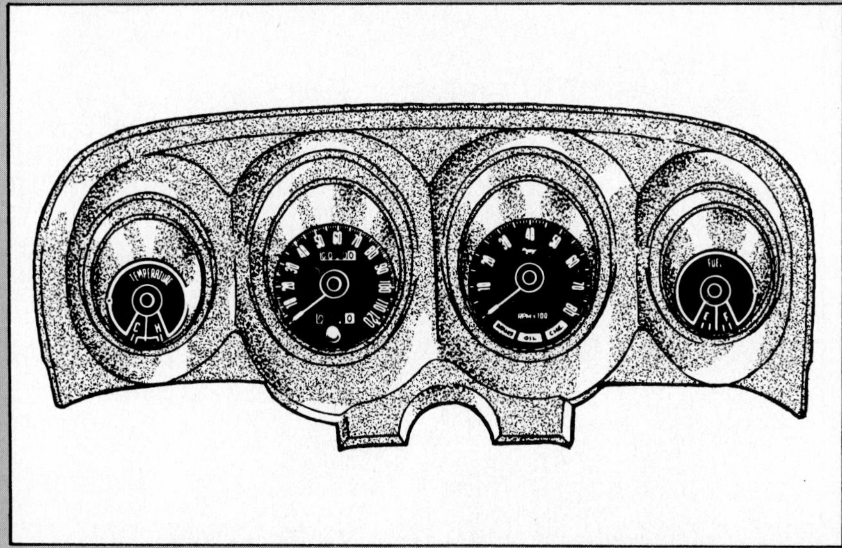

TACHOMETER

The optional tachometer displaces both the temperature and fuel gauges in the large right-hand instrument panel pod. The temperature gauge moves into the alternator spot in the extreme left-hand pod, and the fuel gauge replaces the oil pressure gauge n the extreme right-hand pod. Both the oil pressure and alternator functions are relegated to warning lights at the bottom of the tachometer face. A brake system warning light is also included.

With standard interior, the tachometer face is black and contains large white numerals in increments of 10, up to 80 (8000 rpms). With Deluxe Decor Interior, tach faces are dark gray and contain 2 sets of numbers — outer numbers in increments of 10, and smaller inner numbers that mark the fives: 5, 15, 25, etc. Again calibrated, RPM x 100.

A trip odometer mounts at the bottom of the speedometer face with the tachometer option, while the mileage odometer moves to the top, displacing the high beam indicator light. The high beam indicator switches to the top of the tachometer face — a running horse shape with the standard interior, or a small round indicator with the Deluxe (wood-grained) Interior.

RADIOS

- AM — includes a speaker mounted under the center of the crash pad.
- AM-FM — includes a speaker in each door. A sliding bar at the bottom of the radio dial changes the am-fm selection.
- AM-8 TRACK TAPE - also includes stereo speakers, one in each door.

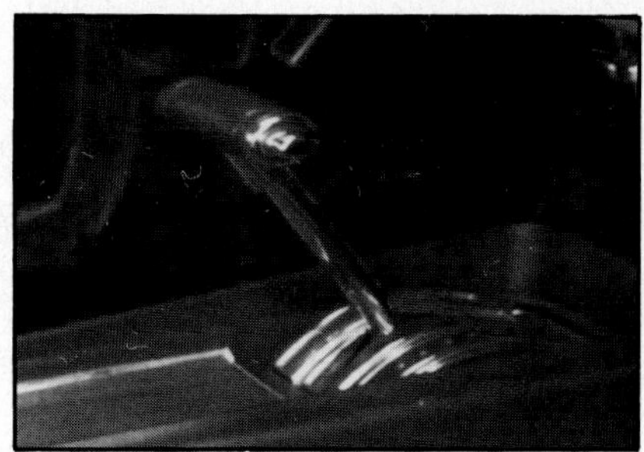

Under the instrument panel, a new foot-operated emergency brake lever takes the place of the '65-'68 Mustang pull handle. A small chrome handle, stamped brake, releases the emergency brake when pulled. Also new are the sliding-type air vent handles recessed into each kick panel.

The center of the instrument panel houses the optional radio, (a blanking plate is supplied if a radio is not included), and heater/defroster switches. Both are covered by a camera-case black panel trimmed with bright mylar.

The heater/defroster controls are configured of three sliding lever-knobs. At left is the vertically sliding fan-speed knob. The two knobs at right are horizontal sliding — the upper knob is the heater/defroster functions — the lower knob regulates the temperature.

STEERING WHEEL: The 1969 Mustang standard steering wheel is a 2 spoke design. The center padding contains a new for '69, red rectangular emblem with a small Mustang running horse in the center. A bright horn ring forms a semi-circle below the spoke. Both the wheel and the spoke are color-keyed to the interior.

The emergency flasher switch remains on the right side of the steering column, but it is a new type — made from black plastic instead of the chrome metal switch used in 1968. A wide black bezel, embossed with the word "emergency flasher" surrounds the switch. The chrome turn signal handle is located in the conventional position on the left side of the collapsible steering column.

SHIFTER: A round chrome Ford-made shifter is supplied as standard equipment with all 1969 Mustang engines except the 390 and 428s. Road noise and dirt is blocked out by a black rubber boot that attaches to the floor with a chrome bezel. The shifter knob is round and inscribed with the transmission shift pattern.

INTERIOR DECOR GROUPS

The 1969 Mustang's optional interior selection can be quite confusing. There were 2 optional interiors offered — the Interior Decor Group and the Deluxe Interior Decor Group. To add to the confusion, the Deluxe Group was available only on SportsRoofs and convertibles. And high back buckets could have been ordered at an additional cost for either Decor interior.

Neither Decor Group was available for the Grande and Mach 1, since those models carried the Decor items as standard equipment.

INTERIOR DECOR GROUP:

- Deluxe seat trim with "Comfortweave" knitted vinyl inserts — the Deluxe bucket seats differ substantially from the standard buckets. The vertical pleats on the seat cushions extends over the front edge of the seat with vinyl bolsters on either side. The seat backs are more rounded at the top, and only the bottom third of the seat insert contains pleats. The top two-thirds of the seat back is separated into a series of 6 vinyl-covered rectangles, with 2 small wood-grained buttons in the center. Inserts are knitted vinyl in hardtops and SportsRoofs; textured vinyl in convertibles. The squeeze-type door handle is buried in the arm rest, and a red/white courtesy light mounts on the arm rest. The lower portion of the door handle is covered with carpet, color-keyed to the interior.

- Deluxe 3-spoke steering wheel - with Rim-Blow horn.
- Driver's side remote rear view mirror — rectangular, chrome finished. Mirror position is controlled by a multi-directional lever mounted inside a chrome, rectangular bezel in the door panel.

DELUXE INTERIOR DECOR GROUP:
(SportsRoof and hardtop only)

- Simulated wood-grain instrument panel appliques — to match the wood-grain panel in the Decor Interior door panel. The color of the instrument faces changes to a dark gray, instead of the standard interior's black. Also, the speedometer (and tachometer, if equipped) numbers are smaller than the standard speedometer, and a second, even smaller, set of numbers mark the speed in multiples of 5. The smaller numbers are positioned inside a marked ring; the larger numbers outside. A small, round high beam headlight indicator replaces the running horse light from the standard speedometer. On the passenger side instrument panel, a large, round rally-type clock mounts into the center of the wood-grain panel.

DELUXE 3-SPOKE STEERING WHEEL

The 3-spoke Rim-Blow steering wheel was offered for the Mustang for the first time in 1969. It features a horn switch built into the inner rim; when the rubber strip is pressed, a hidden metal contact sounds the horn. The rim is simulated wood-grain, and the spokes are heavily padded. The round, black emblem in the steering wheel center corrals a Mustang running horse/tri-color bar, and each spoke contains 3 recesses to simulate holes.

Standard bucket seats and door panel.

Deluxe bucket seats and door panels.

BUCKET SEATS: The standard 1969 Mustang bucket seats are nearly identical to the 1968 buckets — the vinyl-covered bolsters enclose the vertically pleated vinyl inserts on both the seat cushion and back. The 1969 seats, however, include an adjustable headrest at the top of the seat back. A chrome lever on the exterior-facing side of the seats releases the latch mechanism that locks the seat back in the upright position.

Again, seat belts are standard equipment on every model. A retractor, mounted to the door sill at the rear of the seats, stores the short belt section when not in use. Four push button buckles are furnished on hardtop and SportsRoof models — 2 for the seat belts and another pair for the standard shoulder harnesses. Convertibles, however, contain only 2 buckles for the seat belts.

REAR SEAT: A bucket-style bench seat with vertical pleats to match the front buckets is supplied with every 1969 Mustang. The standard SportsRoof rear seat continues to be fixed, including a spacious package shelf at the rear. With the deletion of the SportsRoof's side louvers, the rear seat courtesy light moves upward into the plastic trim panel above the quarter panel trim (in 1968, the lights were mounted in the quarter-trim panels).

BENCH SEATS

A front bench seat, with center arm rest, was available optionally for the hardtop only, in either standard or deluxe trim level. Upholstery is identical to bucket seats with vertical pleats.

HIGH BACK BUCKET SEATS

High back bucket seats were offered for the first time in 1969, in both standard and deluxe configurations. They were optional in all models except Grande, and standard with the Mach 1.

SHIFTERS WITH OPTIONAL TRANSMISSIONS

FOUR-SPEED: The 1969 Mustang 4-speed shifter is a Ford built unit, similar to earlier Mustang shifters but without the reverse lock-out. A new knob is flat on top with a blue racing stripe through the center. The shift pattern is also indicated.

AUTOMATIC: The automatic shifter base is changed in 1969. The new version is wider than before. The shifter T-handle is centered in the base with the shift positions P-R-N-D-2-1 on the left and a new matching panel on the right with bright dots.

Decor bench seat.

Mach 1 only.

CONSOLE

The 1969 Mustang console is completely redesigned. As usual, it mounts atop the transmission tunnel, but the front section that blended into the 1968 instrument panel is gone. The 1969 console fits under the center instrument panel just below the heater/defroster controls, in place of the standard ash tray and cigarette lighter. A unique flip-top ash tray is inserted into the front of the console. A pair of seat belt holsters mount into the top of the console. The back portion of the console serves as an arm rest/glove compartment. The compartment lid is hinged on the passenger side and raises to allow access to the compartment interior. A cigarette lighter is inserted into the front exterior of the compartment, at the rear of the seat belt holsters. With standard interiors, the console center is black; with Decor interiors, the center is wood-grain to match the door appliques.

The quarter panel trim in the convertible includes an arm rest with ash tray, while the hardtop is not furnished with an arm rest at all for the rear seat. Both the hardtop and convertible rear quarter panel trim contains the window crank for the fully retractable rear quarter window.

DOOR PANEL: Door panel design changed completely in 1969. In previous years, the door panel did not extend the entire length of the door; it was rounded off at the rear of the door. In '69, however, the door panel is rectangular and covers the entire center portion of the interior door. An arm rest mounts in the lower center of the vinyl-covered panel, and includes a door pull handle and new-for-'69 recessed door handles. A small Mustang running horse/tri-color bar fastens at the top center of the door panel. New window cranks include an open groove along the handle stem.

INTERIOR LIGHTS: 1969 Mustang hardtops feature a round courtesy light mounted to the headliner. Convertibles and SportsRoofs utilize under-dash lights, and the SportsRoof alone mounts round lights in the rear seat area above the quarter panel trim. All courtesy lights operate through door jamb switches, as well as the headlight switch on the instrument panel.

ELECTRIC CLOCK OPTION

Optional clocks in 1969 are mounted on the passenger side instrument panel. With the standard or Decor Interior (non-Deluxe), the clock is rectangular. Mustangs equipped with the Deluxe Decor Interior (with the wood-grained panel) get the rally-type round clock. (The round clock is a standard item with the Grande and Mach 1.)

VISIBILITY GROUP OPTION

- Left-hand remote mirror - rectangular, chrome
- Glove box lock
- Lights in the luggage compartment, glove box, and ash tray. The glove box light, oddly enough, does not mount inside the glove box. With the standard interior (non-woodgrain), it is molded into the passenger side instrument panel, just above the glove box, in the same housing used by the optional electric clock. A blanking plate is supplied if the clock was not ordered. On models with the Deluxe Decor Interior Group, the glove box light is mounted under the wood-grain instrument panel applique on the passenger side. Every wood-grain panel has the slotted holes for the glove box light, but very few were actually installed. With both type lights, a switch in the glove box opening actuates the light when the door is opened. A manual switch is supplied also, which converts the light into a dual purpose glove box/map light.
- Parking brake warning light — a small red light mounted on the instrument control panel to the lower right of the ignition switch. The light will glow for a few seconds after the ignition switch is turned on.
- Under dash courtesy light (hardtop only)
- Lighted ignition switch

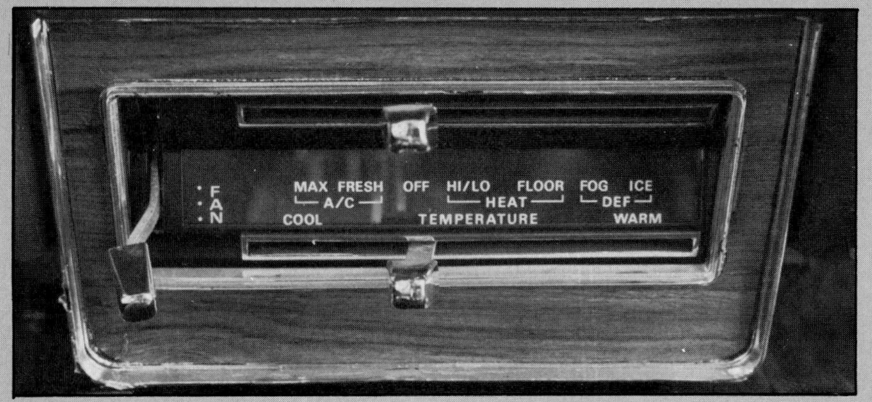

OTHER 1969 INTERIOR OPTIONS

- SelectAire air conditioning — Models equipped with the optional air conditioning received a different heater/defroster control panel below the radio. The same control levers are used, but their function positions change to provide for the air conditioning. A round outlet vent is located in each outside corner of the instrument control panel. Two more vents mount in the center of the crash pad, above the radio. (Air conditioning was not available with the 200 6 cylinder or the 428 with 4-speed manual transmission).
- Power Ventilation — The Power Ventilation system is a new-for-'69 option. With this system, the heater blower is utilized to direct cool air from the cowl vents through a pair of outlet vents mounted in the center of the crash pad (identical to the air conditioning outlets; however, the round vents at the instrument panel corners are not included). The heater control panel is modified slightly to include a ''power vent'' setting at the extreme right.
- Intermittent windshield wipers — controlled by the windshield wiper switch.
- Deluxe seat and shoulder belts — includes a small round reminder light located on the instrument control panel to the upper right of the ignition switch.
- Sport Deck rear seat — fold-down rear seat for SportsRoof models only.
- Tilt-Away steering wheel
- Rear seat speaker (hardtop only)
- Speed Control — operated by a switch located in the end of the turn signal stalk and a second on-off switch mounted in the center instrument panel just above the radio.

TRUNK

LUGGAGE COMPARTMENT

MAT: All 1969 Mustangs received a patterned rubber mat on the luggage compartment floor.

SPARE TIRE: The standard spare tire in all 1969 Mustangs (except Boss 429s) is located in the conventional luggage compartment position. The spare mounts on the right side of the compartment with a threaded hook and large wing nut. A scissors jack and handle is stored under the tire.

WHEELS

STANDARD TIRE AND WHEEL: The standard 1969 Mustang wheel is a 14''x5'' stamped steel ventilated disc type with safety rims. Six cylinder cars are equipped with 4 studs, while V-8 models get 5. Wheel size increases to 14''x6'' on 428 equipped Mustangs.

The base tire for the '69 Mustang is a C78x14.

WHEELCOVER: Standard model Mustangs were all originally to be equipped with a small 10½'' hubcap with a Ford crest in the center, yet most were fitted with the above spoke-type full wheel cover at no extra cost.

STYLED STEEL WHEEL (Color)
Optional All Except GT
With All Body Colors

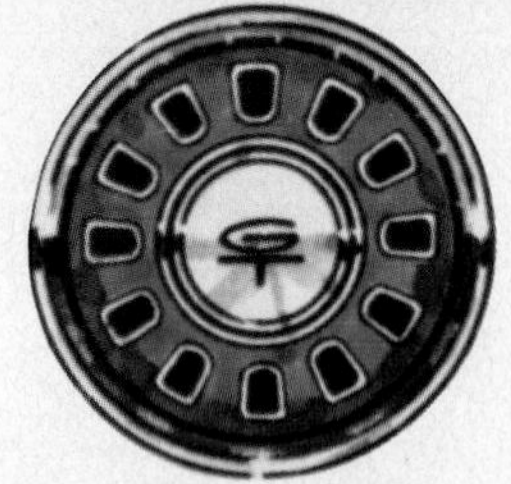

STYLED STEEL WHEEL (Color)
Optional GT With All
Body Colors

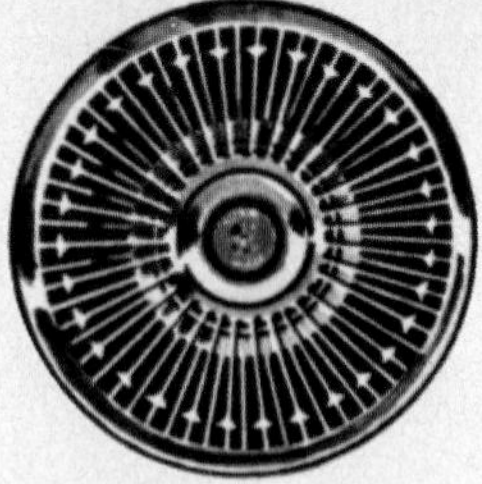

WIRE STYLE WHEEL COVER
Optional All Models

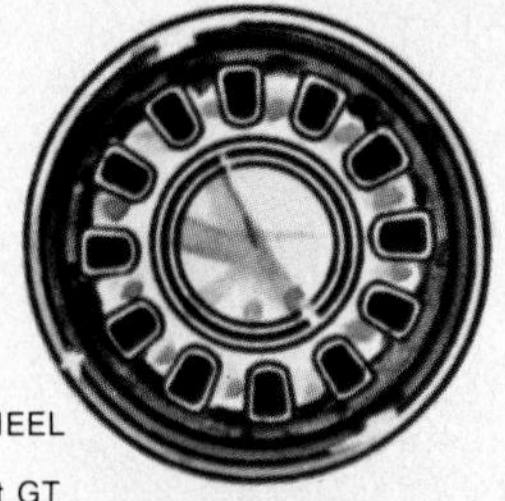

STYLED STEEL WHEEL
(Chrome)
Optional All Except GT

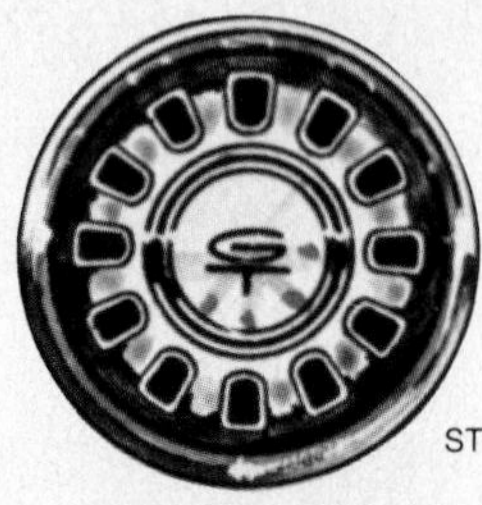

STYLED STEEL WHEEL
(Chrome)
Optional GT

STYLED STEEL WHEEL
(Argent)
Optional All Except GT

STYLED STEEL WHEEL
(Argent)
Standard GT

OPTIONAL WHEELS/WHEELCOVERS

WHEEL: The 1969 Styled Steel Wheel is identical to the 1968 version. In addition to the chrome and argent-painted Styled Steels, a color-keyed version was added in 1969. The styled-steel option included a bright hubcap/trim ring, (with the letters GT only on cars equipped with that option).

Mustangs built after October 15, 1968 and equipped with the color-keyed Styled Steel wheels also have chrome inserts in the wheel slots.

WIRE WHEELCOVER: The 1969 wire wheelcover is identical to the one used on the '67 and '68 Mustangs. It features a red center with the Mustang running horse/tri-color bar.

TIRE SPECIFICATIONS

	C78 x 14	E78 x 14	E70-14 Wide-Oval Fiberglass-Belted, WSW	F70-14 Wide-Oval Fiberglass-Belted, WSW	FR70-14 Wide-Oval Radial Ply	F70-14 Fiberglass-Belted
Six-Cylinder Models	Std.	Opt.	—	—	—	—
302 V-8 Models	Std.	Opt.	Opt.	Opt.	Opt.	—
351 & 390 V-8	—	Std.	Opt.	Opt.	Opt.	—
428 V-8	—	—	Std.	Opt.	Opt.	—
GT Equipment Group	—	—	Std.	Opt.	Opt.	—
428 Cobra Jet	—	—	—	—	—	Mandatory Option

POWERTEAM

ENGINE/TRANSMISSION/ REAR AXLE

ENGINE: The 302 4-barrel engine was dropped in 1969, leaving a total of 8 engines for the Mustang. The 200 cubic inch six cylinder remained as the standard powerplant.

TRANSMISSION: A fully-synchronized 3-speed manual transmission was supplied as standard equipment for all 1969 Mustangs equipped with 200 cubic inch through 351 cubic inch engines.

POWER TEAM SELECTIONS

ENGINES	TRANSMISSIONS			REAR AXLE RATIOS					
				3-Speed Manual		4-Speed Manual		Cruise-O-Matic	
	3-Speed Manual	4-Speed Manual	Cruise-O-Matic	Std.	Option	Std.	Option	Std.	Option
Std. 200 Six	Std.	N.A.**	Option	3.08	N.A.**	N.A.**	N.A.**	2.83	3.08
Opt. 250 Six	Std.	N.A.**	Option	3.00+	2.79	N.A.**	N.A.**	2.79	3.00+
Opt. 302 2v V-8	Std.	Option	Option	2.79	3.00+	3.00+	2.79	2.79	3.00+
Opt. 351 2v V-8	Std.	Option	Option	2.75	3.00 3.25+	3.00	3.25+	2.75	3.00 3.25+
Opt. 351 4v V-8	Std.	Option	Option	3.00	3.25+	3.00	3.25+ 3.50* 3.91* 4.30*	3.00	3.25+
Opt. 390 4v V-8	N.A.**	Option	Option	N.A.**	N.A.**	3.00	3.25+ 3.50* 3.91* 4.30*	2.75	3.00 3.25+ 3.50* 3.91*
Opt. 428 4v V-8 (Non-Ram-Air)	N.A.**	Option	Option	N.A.**	N.A.**	3.25	3.50+ 3.91* 4.30*	3.25	3.50+ 3.91* 4.30*
428 4v V-8 CJ (Ram-Air)	N.A.**	Option	Option	N.A.**	N.A.**	3.50+	3.25+ 3.91* 4.30*	3.50+	3.25+ 3.91* 4.30*

+ Also available with optional limited-slip differential.
*Available only with limited-slip differential.
**N.A.—Not available.

SUSPENSION

For 1969, Ford made no major changes to the Mustang's suspension system. Like always, the springs and shock absorbers were calibrated to match the weight/ride requirements of each car, depending on the model, engine size, and optional equipment (air conditioning and power steering, or the 2 options together, often required different rate springs and shocks).

STEERING: The Parallelogram linkage steering system, with cross link and idler arm, continued in 1969 as the Mustang's manual steering.

OTHER MECHANICAL COMPONENTS

COOLING SYSTEM: The radiator capacities in 1969 became dependent upon the engine size, unlike previous models that based their capacity on 6 and 8 cylinder engines.

EXHAUST SYSTEM:

A single muffler exhaust system is utilized on 1969 Mustangs with 6-cylinder or V-8 2-barrel engines. Mustangs with a 4-barrel engine are equipped with a dual exhaust system, including a pair of resonators mounted in front of the rear axle and a dual inlet/dual outlet, cross-flow muffler mounted transversely behind the rear axle. Chrome exhaust tips are used with GT or Mach 1 models.

BRAKES: Mustang brakes in 1969 are again a dual hydraulic system with a dual master cylinder. The brakes themselves are duo-servo with a self-adjusting feature.

FUEL TANK: The fuel tank capacity for all Mustangs was increased 4 gallons in 1969, giving the Mustang a total capacity of 20 gallons.

PERFORMANCE OPTIONS

- Limited-Slip differential (with 250 or 302 engines)
- Traction-Lok differential (351 and larger engines)
- Handling suspension (not available on Grandes or models equipped with 200, 250, or 428 engines) — Heavy-purpose springs and shocks, beefier front stabilizer bar.
- Competition suspension (428 engines only, standard with 428 Mach 1s, GTs, and Boss 302) — Adds staggered rear shocks to the Handling suspension package — the left shock absorbers is relocated to the rear of the axle housing, while the right shock remains ahead of the axle.
- Heavy-Duty Batteries — -55 amp. (standard with 351, 390, and Cruise-O-Matic), and 80 amp, (standard with 428)
- Trunk Mounted Battery — 85 amp. (428s only, standard with Boss 429)

POWER ASSISTS OPTIONS

- Power front disc brakes
- Power steering
- Power convertible top

GRANDE

The 1969 Grande is the luxury Mustang. Available in hardtop form only, the Grande features many optional items as standard equipment, plus unique cloth seats.

EXTERIOR TRIM:

- Grande script lettering on "C" pillar.
- Dual racing mirrors.
- Wire wheelcovers.
- Bright wheel lip, rocker panel, and rear deck moldings.
- Two-toned narrow paint stripe below fender line — either black with gold insert, or gold with white insert.

INTERIOR:

The Grande's interior is basically the Mustang Deluxe Decor Interior, including the following items:

- Simulated wood-grain instrument panel appliques.
- Deluxe 3-spoke "Rim-Blow" steering wheel.
- Molded door panels with wood-grain insert and courtesy lights.
- Padded interior quarter trim panels with simulated wood-grain inserts.
- Round electric clock.
- Bright-trimmed pedal pads.
- Unique Grande bucket seats with Hopsack cloth inserts.

SPECIAL INSULATION:

The Grande features a special insulation package that includes 55 additional pounds of sound deadener materials.

UNIQUE REAR SUSPENSION:

Voided rubber bushings are used in the front spring eyes of the Grande's rear leaf springs. These bushings permit a slight rearward movement of the springs to absorb impacts from bumps and uneven road surfaces.

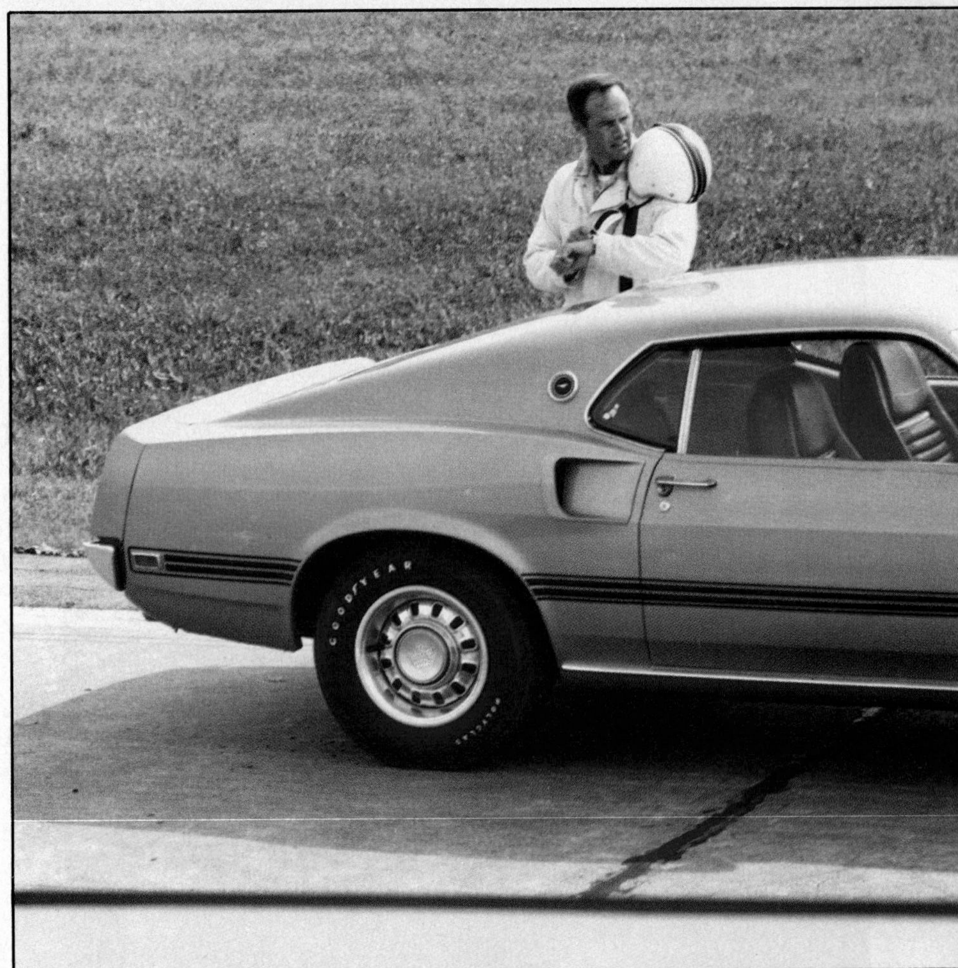

MACH 1

The Mach 1 SportsRoof was introduced in 1969 as the performance-oriented Mustang. It was available with any one of the 5 larger V-8 engines, from the 351, 2-barrel through the 428 Cobra Jet Ram-Air. Unlike the GT option, the Mach 1 model included a special interior that featured many of the Deluxe Decor Group items, plus new high back bucket seats and special carpet.

EXTERIOR:

- Low-gloss black hood and cowl.
- Non-functional hood scoop - with integral turn signal indicators and engine identification. Mach 1s equipped with the 428 Cobra Jet Ram-Air engine get a new-for '69 "Shaker" hood scoop that attaches to the top of the engine air cleaner and protrudes up through a cutout in the hood. The scoop is functional, operating on engine vacuum — a vacuum valve inside the scoop opens the air inlet valve when the engine vacuum drops during acceleration; at idle and low speed operation, the inlet valve remains closed, but opens when the engine is shut off.
- Racing type hood pins - the pins are secured to the car by plastic-encased wires. Upon the original buyer's request, the hood pins were a delete option.
- Dual color-keyed racing mirrors.
- MACH 1 stripe on body side and rear of deck lid - The stripe begins just aft of the front wheel-well, with MACH 1 in the forward section, and stretches to the rear bumper. MACH 1 is also

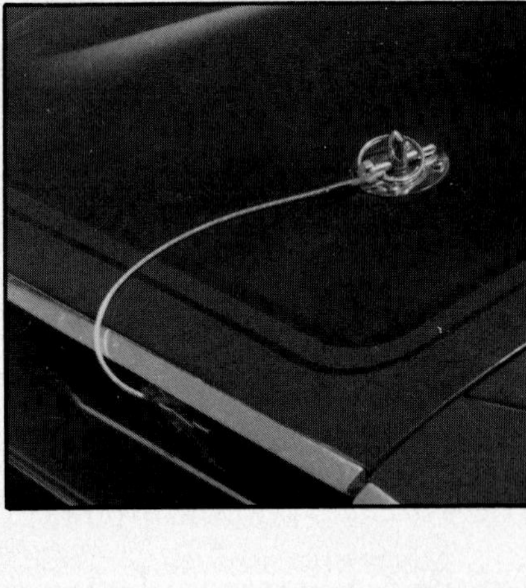

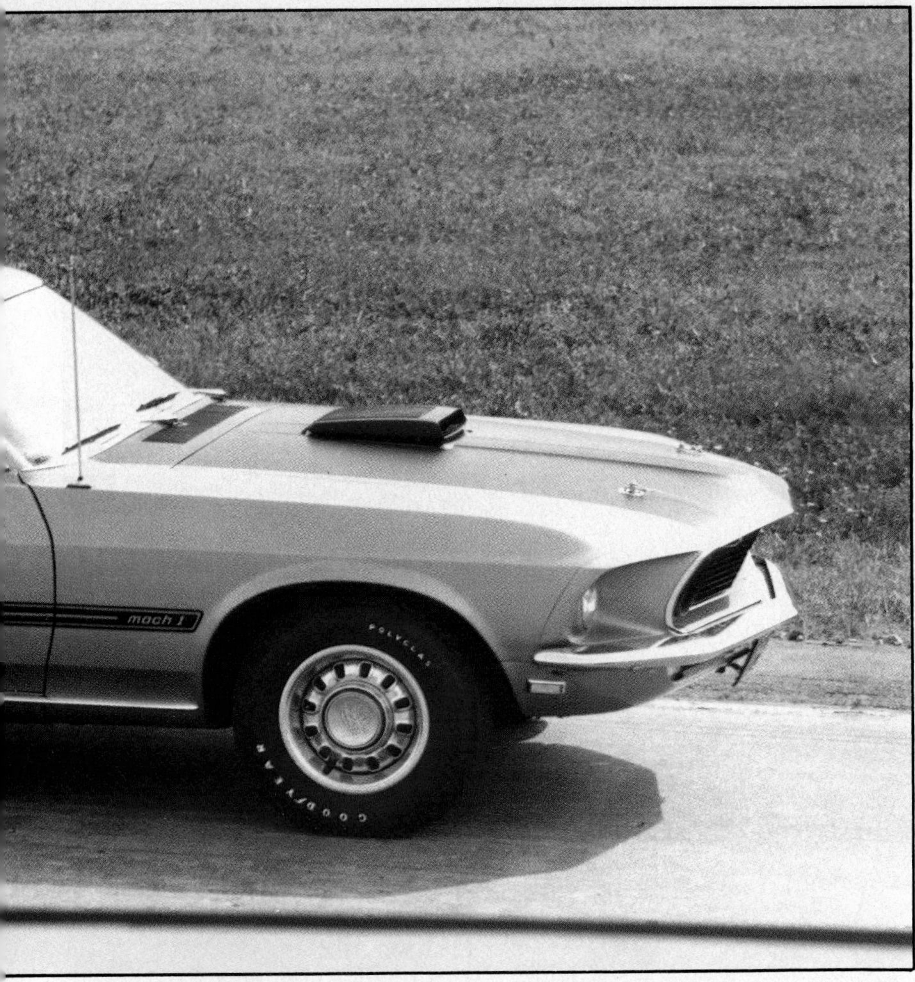

cut out of the rear deck lid-stripe. The stripes were available in 3 color combinations — black w/gold, red w/gold, or gold w/white — depending upon body and interior colors.

- Pop-open gas cap - with a Mustang running horse/tri-color bar in the center.
- Chrome Styled Steel Wheels -with plain hubcap (no GT emblem).
- Dual exhaust with chrome quad outlets (4-barrel engines only)
- E70x14 white sidewall tires.
- Bright rocker panel molding.

INTERIOR:

- High back bucket seats - with "Comfortweave" knitted vinyl inserts and red trim across the top of the insert on the seat back.
- Deluxe 3-spoke Rim-Blow steering wheel.
- Special carpet - with red sewn-in floor mats, front and rear.
- Console - with simulated wood-grain.
- Molded door panels - with simulated wood-grain insert and courtesy lights.
- Simulated wood-grain instrument panel appliques - including a round rally-type electric clock and Mach 1 emblem on the passenger side.
- Bright rocker panel moldings.
- Simulated wood-grain panel around radio and heater controls.

SUSPENSION:

The Handling Suspension is standard on the Mach 1.

SPECIAL INSULATION:

The Mach 1s include a special sound insulation package that adds 55 pounds of sound insulation and deadener materials.

BOSS 302

Ford added the Boss 302 Mustang to its corral of performance cars around the end of March, 1969, a mid-year addition to counter the Chevrolet Z/28 Camaro and qualify the Mustang SportsRoof for the Sports Car Club of America's Trans-Am race series. The Boss 302 was a performance package, available in SportsRoof body style only, with a mandatory 290 horsepower Boss 302 high-output engine, 4-speed transmission, and 3.50:1 rear axle ratio. The staggered-shocked Competition Suspension and quick 16 to 1 steering ratio were standard equipment. No automatic transmission, nor air conditioning was available.

EXTERIOR:

- Low-gloss black paint on hood and cowl.
- Blacked-out headlight housing.
- Front spoiler.
- Reflective "C" stripes on body side - with BOSS 302 in the center of the front fender stripe.

- Low-gloss black paint on deck lid and rear panel.
- Choice of 4 colors - Wimbledon White, Bright Yellow, Calypso Coral, and Acapulco Blue.
- Flared front fenders - The Boss 302's front fenders are rolled under to provide more room for the standard F60x15 tires.
- Magnum 500 wheels - 15 inch, with argent centers and chrome lug nuts.
- Filled in rear quarter panel scoop - The SportsRoof's standard non-functional rear quarter panel scoop is filled in on the Boss 302.

INTERIOR:

All Mustang optional interiors were available for the Boss 302. Most Bosses, however, were equipped with the standard Mustang black interior. The shifter in '69 is the standard Ford, 4-speed type. A choke knob is mounted under the instrument panel, just above the accelerator pedal, to operate the Boss 302's standard manual choke.

HANDLING:

- Competition suspension - heavy-duty springs and shock absorbers, staggered rear shocks, beefier front stabilizer bar.
- 16 to 1 steering ratio.
- Power front disc brakes.

REV LIMITER:

All Boss 302s were originally equipped with an Autolite engine rev limiter. The limiter mounts on the driver's side engine compartment wall, and restricts engine rpms to 6150, maximum. The wiring is attached to the Mustang's standard coil circuitry, being easily disconnected, however, it was often removed by the car's owner.

BOSS 302 OPTIONS:

- Rear spoiler - plastic.
- Sports slats - mount on rear window with chrome hinges at the roof and spring-loaded latches above the deck lid.
- Gear ratios - the standard Boss 302 rear axle is a conventional 3.50; optional Traction-Loc axles were 3.50, 3.91, and 4.30
- Chrome Magnum 500 wheels.

BOSS 429

The Boss 429 Mustangs were produced to satisfy a NASCAR homologation rule for Grand National racing. In effect, the rule stated that for any trick part, or engine to be deemed legal, at least 500 units had to be installed in cars and sold to the public. Ford chose the Mustang SportsRoof for the task - for 2 reasons: to satisfy NASCAR's requirements and to enhance the Mustang's (and Ford's) performance reputation on the street.

To fit the extra-wide semi-Hemi Boss 429 powerplant into the Mustang's engine compartment, the factory spring towers had to be moved outward 1 inch. With such a heavy engine up front, the nose-heavy handling characteristics were compensated by lowering the A arms 1 inch. These modifications were performed by Kar Kraft, a mini-assembly plant in Brighton, Michigan. Ford delivered the Mustang SportsRoof to Kar Kraft partially assembled, and Kar Kraft made the needed modifications and installed the Boss 429 engines.

EXTERIOR:

- Hood scoop - The Boss 429's hood scoop is the largest ever installed on a Mustang. It is manually operated by a driver controlled cable that mounts under the instrument panel.
- Front spoiler - The Boss 429's front spoiler is shallower than the units found on the Boss 302, Mustangs. Due, no doubt, to the 429s lower stance.
- Flared front fenders - The front

fenders on the Boss 429 are rolled under to provide the extra clearance needed for the large F60x15 tires. The Boss 429 was the first Mustang to utilize such huge rubber, since it preceded the Boss 302 by nearly 2 months (the 429 was introduced in January, 1969; the 302 in March).

- BOSS 429, decals - mounted inconspicuously on the front fenders behind the wheel opening.
- Magnum 500 wheels - chrome 15 inch, with large center caps.
- Dual color-keyed racing mirrors.

A Kar Kraft mini-assembly line practically hand-built the Boss 429 Mustangs. Here, Kar Kraft workers perform suspension modifications to Boss 429 Job #1.

INTERIOR:

- Interior Decor Group.
- High back "Comfortweave" knitted vinyl bucket seats.
- Visibility Group - includes parking brake warning light (mounted on the instrument control panel to the lower right of the ignition switch), glove box lock; luggage compartment, ash tray, and glove box light; and lighted ignition switch.
- Deluxe seat belts - includes a seat belt reminder light mounted on the instrument control panel at the upper right of the ignition switch.
- Console
- Ford-built 4-speed shifter.
- Choke and Ram-Air control knobs - mounted in a unique bracket attached below the instrument panel just above the accelerator pedal.
- Optional instrument panel with tachometer.

SUSPENSION:

- Competition suspension - with ultra-heavy-duty Gabriel shocks.
- Rear stabilizer bar.
- A-arms lowered 1 inch.
- Power front disc brakes.
- Power steering - with fluid oil cooler.

OTHER BOSS 429 FEATURES:

- Engine oil cooler - mounted on the left side of the radiator support. The left horn is relocated to the right side, adjacent to the right-hand horn. The oil cooler line passes through a hole in the radiator support to a special oil filter adapter on the engine block.
- 65 amp. alternator
- Trunk-mounted 85 amp. battery.
- Traction-Lok rear axle with 3.91 gears.
- Boss 429 colors - Raven Black, Royal Maroon, Candyapple Red, Wimbleton White, Blue, and Black Jade.

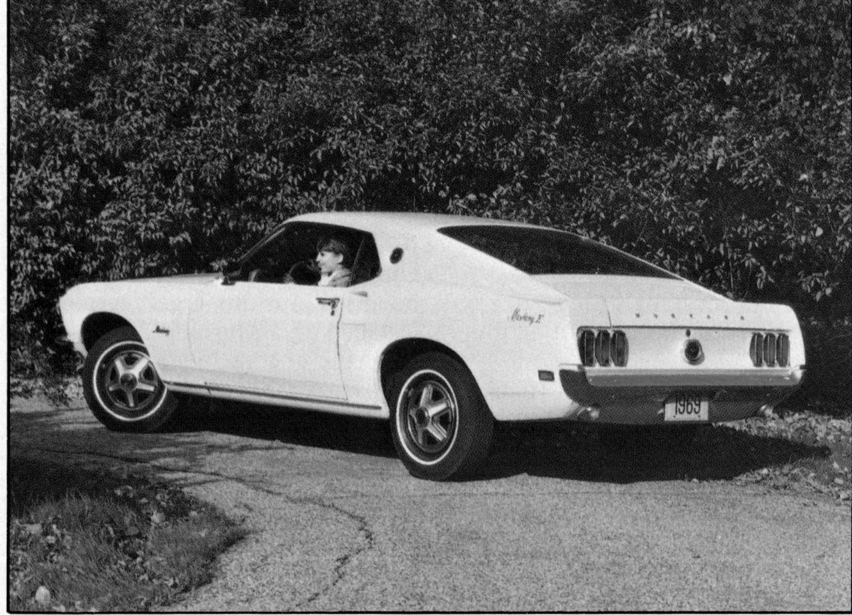

MUSTANG "E"

The 1969 Mustang "E" is an economy version of the standard Mustang SportsRoof. The package included a six cylinder engine, low axle ratio, and an automatic transmission with a special torque converter.

SHELBY

The new 1969 Mustang body style forced yet another styling change for the Shelby. For '69, the Shelby Mustang's appearance looked less like a production Mustang than ever before. The all-fiberglass front end is flat, or chopped off, across the front, a preview of the future '71 Mustang's frontal appearance. A new hood contained no less than 5 NASA scoops, and all 4 brakes were cooled by scoops in the front fenders and rear quarter panels.

Both the GT350 and GT500 were offered; the KR designation was no longer needed since the 428, Cobra Jet engine was standard in the GT500. The GT350's engine became the new-for-'69 351, Windsor.

A convertible model was again offered, either as a GT350 or GT500 model.

EXTERIOR:

The 1969 Shelby utilizes 2 headlights (the '69 Mustang has 4), located at each end of the wide rectangular grille opening. A bright concentric trim ring, attached to the wire-mesh grille, follows the shape of the grille opening. A Shelby snake with a "SHELBY" embossed bar below attaches to the driver's side of the grille within the bright trim. The grille opening is formed by a unique Shelby bumper at the bottom, chrome fender extensions on the sides, and a chrome hood trim at the top. The valance panel, a short fiberglass piece that stretches beneath the front of the car from fender to fender, forms a lower scoop and contains unique parking lights and Lucas rectangular driving lights.

The fiberglass hood contains 5 NASA scoops: 2 toward the leading edge of the hood that introduce cold air to the engine compartment; 1 in the center that supplies cold air to the Ram-Air air cleaner; and 2 at the rear, in line with the front pair, that draw hot air out of the engine compartment. A pair of twist-type hood locks are recessed in the front to secure the hood. The standard Mustang hood latch is also utilized.

The front fenders are also fiberglass. A vertical brake cooling scoop is molded into the front of each fender. For the first time, the stripes are mounted up on the center of the body side, stretching from the leading edge of the front fender to the rear bumper. A GT350 or 500 motif is cut out of the stripe in front of the fender scoop.

The Mustang SportsRoof's recessed non-functional quarter panel scoop is replaced by a bolt-on Shelby scoop. A hose directs cool air from the scoop to the inner fender, which aids in cooling the rear brakes. A Shelby snake is attached to the fastback's side roof in place of the Mustang's round running horse emblem.

On convertible models, a narrower side scoop is mounted lower on the quarter panel.

The Shelby's rear spoiler is similar to the Mustang SportsRoof's, but the Shelby version is more pronounced. The deck lid and quarter panel extensions are fiberglass. A black insert runs the entire width of the car on the rear of the spoiler, with the letters S-H-E-L-B-Y stretched across the deck lid. Taillights are identical to the '68 Shelby ('65 Thunderbird). A hinged license plate bracket mounts between the taillights in the center of the rear panel; the bracket swings up to reveal the fuel filler.

A large aluminum exhaust outlet replaces the Mustang's license plate bracket on the rear valance panel.

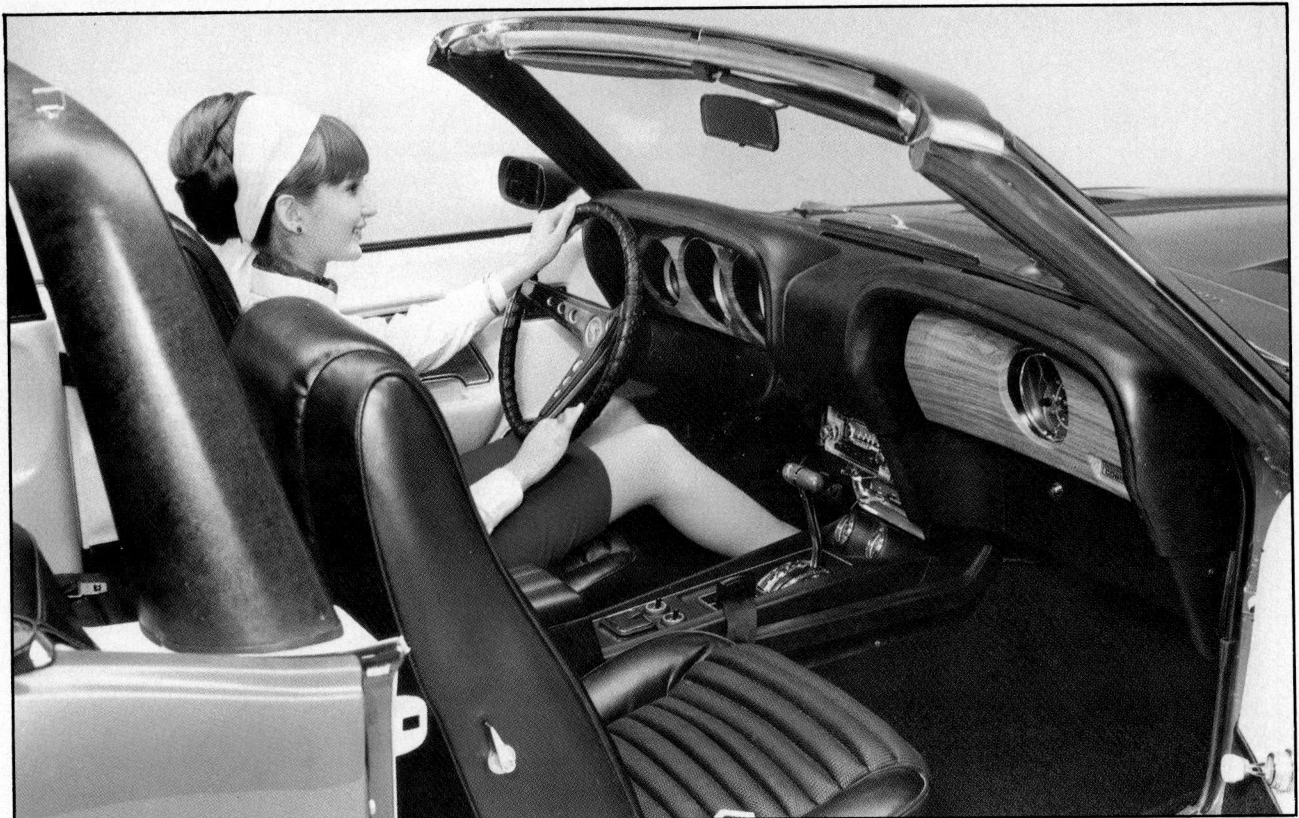

INTERIOR:

The 1969 Shelby interior is Deluxe Decor Mustang, with molded door panels, simulated wood-grain dash appliques, and 3-spoke Rim-Blow steering wheel. The speedometer is a 140 mph unit, and the tachometer reads to 8000 rpms. The center console is identical to the Mustang, except the Shelby unit uses a new top housing with gauges, a pair of toggle switches (one for the driving lights and one for the interior courtesy lights), an ash tray, and seat belt holsters. The gauges - Stewart Warner oil pressure and amps - mount in front of the shifter, angled toward the driver. The door panels contain round Cobra emblems in the wood-grain inserts, and a Shelby rectangular emblem attaches in place of the Mustang emblem on the right bottom corner of the passenger side wood-grained instrument panel.

Both the fastback and convertible models are equipped with a roll bar. The fastback version utilizes inertia-reel shoulder harnesses; the convertible bar, like '68, is flatter and has small rectangular rings on top that are reportedly for securing surf boards. Fold down rear seats are standard in Shelby fastbacks.

WHEELS:

The 1969 Shelbys were equipped with a unique 15x7, 5-spoke mag-style wheel. The centers are cast aluminum with chrome rims and a round "Shelby Cobra" hub cap. The standard tire is an E70x15 wide oval with F60s optional. Both tires are raised white letter.

Because of a defect found in some of the early Shelby wheels, some cars were sold with Boss 302, Magnum 500s. Also, wheels on dealer stock were replaced with the Magnums. However, owners had the option of returning to the dealer at a later date to exchange the Magnums for improved Shelby wheels.

ENGINES:

GT350s feature the 290 horsepower 351 Windsor powerplant as standard equipment. The Shelby version is modified with an aluminum high-rise intake manifold and finned aluminum "Cobra - Powered by Ford" valve covers.

GT500 models received 335 horsepower 428 Cobra Jet engines with a medium-rise aluminum intake and die cast "428 Cobra Jet" valve covers.

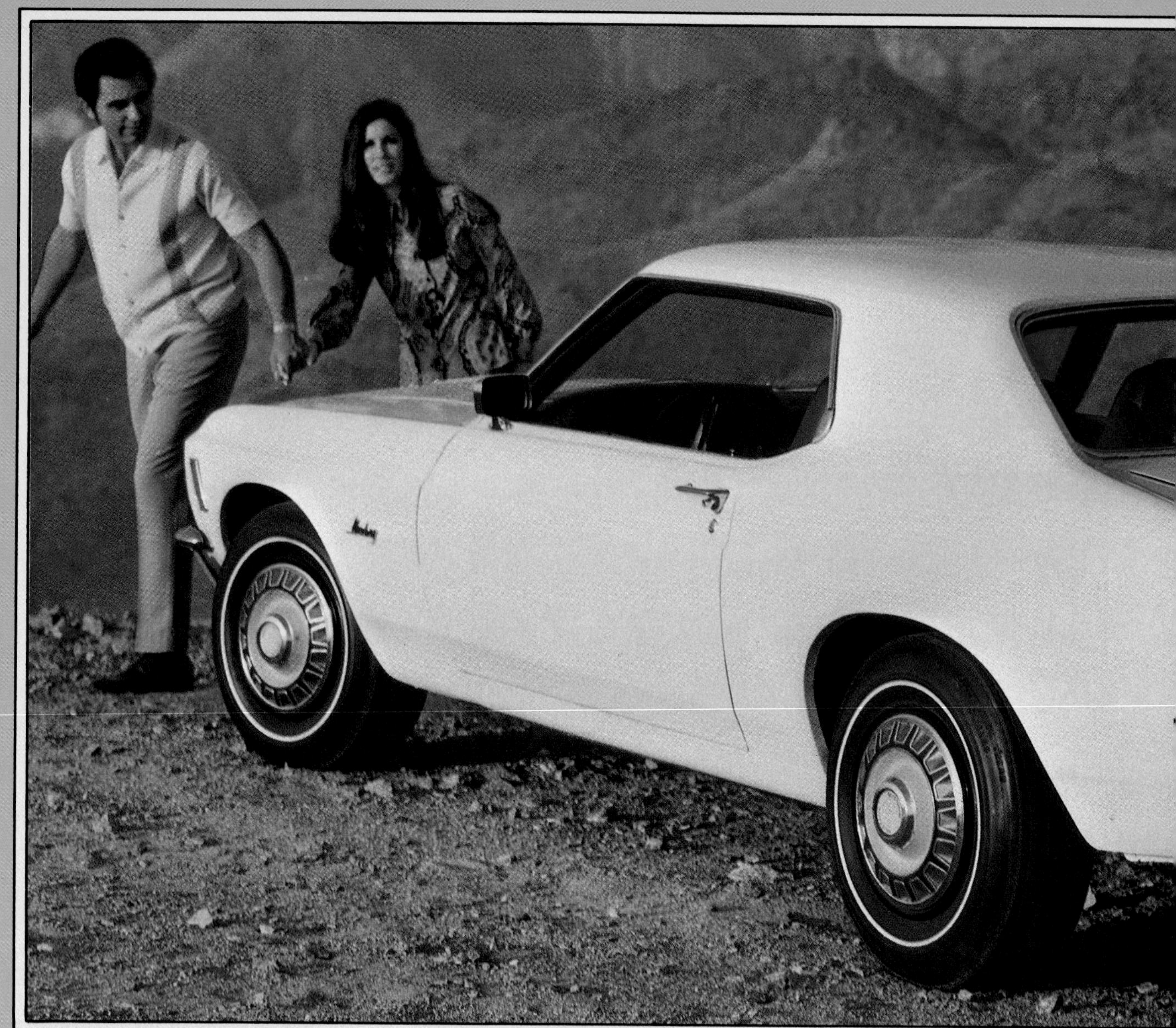

1970

Nineteen seventy was a continuation of 1969. Mustang was still #1 on ponycar sales charts, comfortably ahead of second place Camaro. In fact, throughout the entire first generation, Mustang remained the top selling ponycar. Looks like Ford did stay a step or two ahead of the competition. Of course, styling refinements, rather than major styling revisions, were in schedule for 1970. Ford's major goal with this new model was to continue the success of the 1969's, and stay ahead or perhaps even widen the sales gap between Mustang and Camaro.

Still, the minor changes made were more noticeable than ever. It's easy to tell a '69 from a '70. For example, the four headlamp arrangement was replaced by single headlights. Front fender extensions were given simulated air intake scoops, and the fake scoops on the rear quarters (on the fastback) were deleted.

As far as performance models, the fabulous Boss 302 and Boss 429 remained in the lineup for one last model year. The 428 Cobra Jet was likewise optional through 1970 — a "natural" in the Mach 1 fastback. The luxury Grande was also continued, although the Mustang GT was dropped in 1969.

Nineteen seventy ranks with 1969 as one of the most exciting performance years. Racing prepped Boss 302's successfully won the prestigious Trans Am series, with Parnelli Jones and George Follmer driving to the manufacturer's championship.

As far as Shelbys, the 1970's were really leftover 1969's, updated with a pair of black hood stripes, a front spoiler, and altered serial numbers.

BODYSTYLES

Mustang body styles for 1970 remained about the same — hardtop, convertible, and SportsRoof — however, all 3 received minor styling changes.

The mid-year, 1969 Boss 302 and Boss 429 continued with the Mach 1, Grande, and Shelby as optional models. All 5 were updated with 1970, minor styling changes.

EXTERIOR

GRILLE: The 1970 Mustang grille is similar to the '69, but the rectangular slots are wider and the Mustang running horse/tri-color bar is fastened to the center. Both ends of the grille are shaped around the adjacent headlights.

HEADLIGHTS: The number of headlights is reduced to 2 in 1970, after the 1969, one-year span with 4 lights. A dark gray plastic bezel surrounds the lights. The thin chrome headlight trim ring contains slots for access to the headlight adjusting screws, a first-time feature in 1970.

The front fender extensions that housed the '69 Mustang's outside headlamps are replaced by a new trim piece with a pair of simulated air scoops.

VALANCE PANEL: The 1970 Mustang valance panel is shaped identically like the '69 version. However, the 1970 side marker lights are located on the fenders instead of the valance panel. The parking/turn signal lights are coupled electrically with the headlights in 1970 — the parking lights remain on when the headlights are turned on (in 1969 and previous years, the parking lights went off whenever the headlights were on).

OPTIONAL SPORTS SLATS

The rear window louvers that were first offered on the 1969 Boss 302 Mustangs became an option for all 1970 Mustang SportsRoof models. The black-only slats shade the large rear window and help reduce interior temperature. Chrome hinges that attach the louvers to the roof allow the slats to be raised for window cleaning. A pair of latches below the rear window secure the slats. Dual racing mirrors are a required option with the Sports Slat option.

OPTIONAL REAR DECK SPOILER

The rear spoiler that debuted on the 1969 Boss 302 was an extra cost option for all 1970 Mustang SportsRoofs. the black-only spoiler attaches to 2, trunk-mounted pedestals. The spoiler can be adjusted to various angles by loosening an allen screw on each pedestal.

DUAL ACCENT PAINT STRIPE OPTION

Dual pin stripes that begin on the front fender extension, above the twin simulated scoops, and stretch along the upper body line to a point on the rear quarter panel. The stripes are standard on Grande models, and optional on Mach 1s only.

OPTIONAL VINYL ROOFS

Vinyl roof choices more than doubled for 1970. In addition to black and white, 2, houndstooth vinyl roofs — blue and green and a Saddle Kiwi — were added to the Mustang's option list. Houndstooth tops are a checkered design; the Saddle Kiwi features a leather-look with western-type trim (full tops only).

OTHER EXTERIOR OPTIONS

- Rocker panel molding.
- Front bumper guards.
- Tinted glass.
- Dual racing mirrors — color-keyed to the exterior.
- Shaker hood scoop — with Boss 302, 351 2 or 4-barrel, or 428.

HOOD: The 1970 Mustang hood is identical to the one used on the 1969 Mustang.

SIDE EXTERIOR: The 1970 body design is virtually the same as the 1969 models. A new yellow, vertical side marker light replaces the valance panel unit used in 1969. As a new feature, both the front and rear 1970 side marker lights flash on and off with the turn signals and emergency flashers. The Mustang script lettering on the fenders remains identical to 1969. A chrome non-remote rear view mirror is mounted on the driver's door.

All of the non-functional scoops from the 1969 Mustang are deleted from the '70 models. Both the hardtop and convertible lose their fake air vents from the rear quarter panel, and the SportsRoof scoops are likewise eliminated.

The thin, short body line on the '69's rear quarter panel is deleted in 1970 for a smoother look.

WINDOWS: No major changes were made to the Mustang's windows in 1970. One non-visable, but important modification was added sometime during early production: the glue-in 1969 Mustang side windows were found to be inadequate, so a switch was made to more durable bolt-in glass.

ROOF: Mustang roof design remained the same for 1970. The round Mustang running horse emblem on the SportsRoof's "C" pillar are deleted. On the hardtop, the wide, black trim that surrounded the '69's rear window is replaced by a standard chrome molding.

REAR EXTERIOR: The 1970 rear panel is flat, in place of the previous 1969's concave shaped panel. Taillights still feature the traditional Mustang 3 lens arrangement, but the 1970 lamp is recessed into the rear panel instead of protruding like before. The new taillight bezel is chrome trimmed with a camera-case black insert that surrounds the 3 recessed lens. The area between the bezel and lens is painted argent. The 1970 gas cap is unchanged from 1969.

DECK LID: The 1970 rear luggage compartment deck lids remain the same as the previous 1969s. Chrome M-U-S-T-A-N-G block lettering stretches across the rear of the deck lid on all 3 models.

REAR VALANCE PANEL: The rear valance panel on all standard 1970 Mustangs contains the chrome-bezeled back-up lights, one on each end of the panel, and the rear license plate bracket.

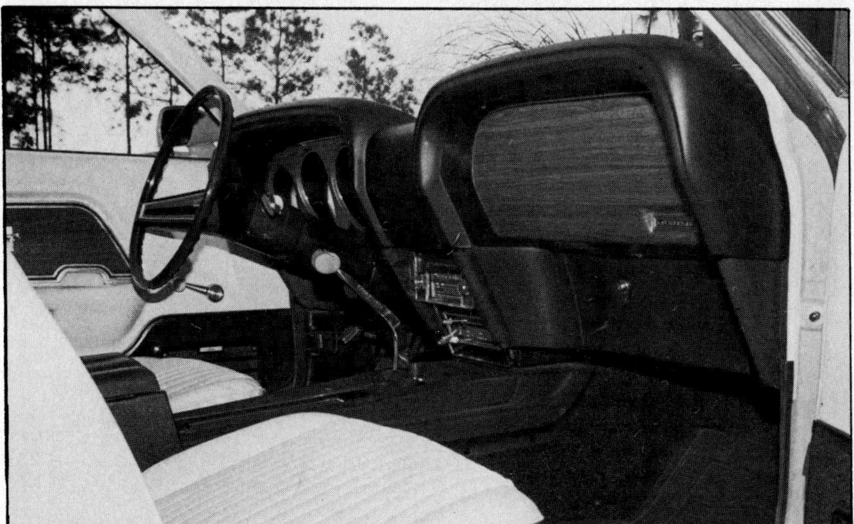

INTERIOR

The 1970 Mustang interior is basically the same design as the 1969 interior. The 1969 Mustang's optional high-back bucket seats became standard for 1970, and a newly shaped steering wheel mounted on a new steering column that locked when the ignition switch, located on the column for the first time, was moved to the off position.

INSTRUMENT PANEL: The 1970 Mustang's instrument panel design stays the same as 1969. The crash pad is unchanged, retaining the twin cockpit theme with a center section that drops down to blend into the radio heater control housing on the metal lower instrument control panel. On the driver's side, 4 instrument pods are recessed into a camera-case black panel. The 2 larger pods house the speedometer (on the left) and the combined fuel/temperature gauges. A running horse shaped high beam indicator light is located in the

DECOR GROUP

In 1970, the number of optional interiors was reduced to 1, and called, simply, the Decor Group. It is basically the old 1969 Deluxe Interior Decor Group with special seats and wood-grain appliques. The Decor Group was not available on Mach 1 or Grande models.

- Choice of high-back bucket seats — either knitted vinyl or "Blazer Stripe". The 1970 knitted vinyl seat has vertical pleats that end at the forward edge of the seat bottom. The knitted pleats form the bottom of the seat back, while the upper portion is divided into eight padded sections. The "Blazer Stripe" seats are designed like the Mach 1 seats, but the knitted vinyl inserts are replaced by brightly striped cloth inserts. The inserts contain 3 pairs of horizontal pleats, both on the seat cushion and back. "Blazer Stripe" cloth seats were not available with the convertible.
- Simulated wood-grain instrument panel appliques — with MUSTANG applique on the passenger side (except Grande & Mach 1). Instrument gauges became dark gray instead of the standard black. Also, the speedometer is marked in increments of 5 instead of the standard 10.
- Deluxe 2-spoke steering wheel — the deluxe steering wheel is identical to the standard wheel, but wood-grain spoke trim is added.
- Molded door trim panels — The molded door panels, like the 1969 deluxe panels, are one-piece. The upper portion is vinyl-covered with an integral arm rest. The door handle is buried in the arm rest, and the door-pull grip is shorter than the '69 version. A simulated wood-grain panel fits in the recessed area above the arm rest with a small Mustang running horse/tri-color bar at front center. A rectangular red/white courtesy light mounts on the arm rest. The lower portion of the door panel is covered with color-keyed carpet.
- Dual racing mirrors — color-keyed to the exterior. (Not available with special order paint.) The driver's side mirror is remote, with a door panel-mounted lever. The 1970 lever fits inside a chrome, round bezel, instead of the large rectangular bezel used in 1969.
- Bright rocker panel and wheel lip moldings (except F60x15 tires).

upper portion of the speedometer face; the odometer is positioned below the speedometer center. In the larger right hand pod, a rectangular brake warning light sits to the left of the pod center, and a matching rectangular seat belt warning light mounts on the right. The smaller extreme left-hand instrument pod contains the alternator gauge, and the right-hand pod houses the oil pressure. Arrow-shaped turn signal indicators are located at either side of the smaller outside gauges.

On the passenger side, a plain camera-case black panel attaches below the crash pad.

INSTRUMENT CONTROLS: The 1970 instrument controls, are located on the lower instrument panel. The headlight switch remains on the left side of the panel. To the right of the steering column, the windshield wiper/washer switch moves into the position previously occupied by the 1969 ignition switch, which moves to the steering column in 1970. A cigarette lighter mounts to the adjacent right.

Under the driver's side panel, the foot-operated emergency brake lever mounts above the headlight high beam switch, with a chrome pull-type brake release handle - stamped brake. Sliding-type air vent knobs are recessed into the kick panels. A new "Flow-Thru" air vent system is employed for the first time in 1970. With the new system, air entering the interior through the kick panel air vents circulates around the interior and exits via one-way vents mounted in the rear door jambs, below the latch. The center of the instrument

TACHOMETER

Like 1969, the optional tachometer displaces both the temperature and fuel gauges in the large right-hand instrument panel pod. The temperature gauge moves into the alternator spot in the extreme left-hand pod, and the fuel gauge replaces the oil pressure gauge in the extreme right-hand pod. Both the oil pressure and alternator functions are relegated to warning lights at the bottom of the tachometer face. A brake system warning light is also included.

With the tachometer option, a trip odometer mounts at the bottom of the speedometer face, and the mileage odometer moves to the top, displacing the high beam indicator light which moves to the top of the tachometer face in the form of a running horse (standard interior) or round (Decor Group).

The tachometer was available only with the V-8 engines.

TILT STEERING WHEEL

The tilt steering system in 1970 is a 5 position unit. The tilt-away feature is discontinued. As always, the tilt mechanism is operated by the turn signal lever.

CONSOLE

The 1970 Mustang console is nearly identical to the 1969 unit. The need for seat belt holsters is eliminated with the shorter 1970 belts, and the cigarette lighter, moved to the instrument panel for '70, is deleted. A wood-grain applique is included with the Decor Group option.

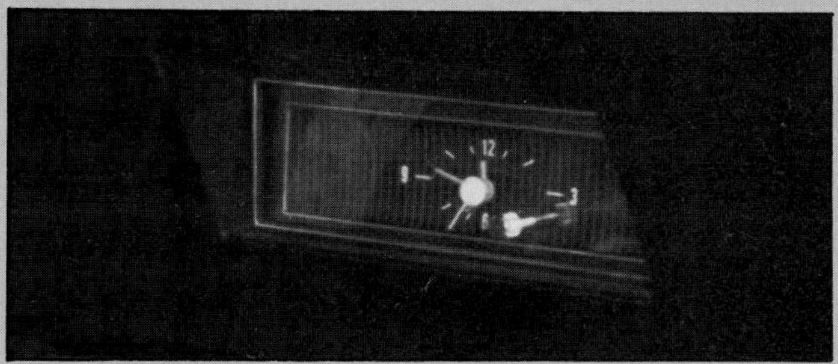

RADIOS

- AM — Includes a single speaker mounted under the center of the crash pad.
- AM-FM — Includes a speaker and grille mounted in each door. A sliding bar at the bottom of the radio dial changes the AM-FM selection.
- AM-8 TRACK TAPE — Includes stereo door speakers, one in each door with grilles. The tape door is marked "MUSTANG".

SELECTAIRE AIR CONDITIONING

A different heater/defroster control panel was supplied with air conditioned 1970 Mustangs. The same levers are used, but the positions change to provide for the air conditioning functions. Like 1969, a round vent is located at either end of the instrument control panel. Two additional vents mount in the crash pad center section. (Air conditioning was not available with 200 cubic inch 6 cylinder or Boss 302 and Boss 429 models.)

ELECTRIC CLOCKS

Two electric clocks were offered in 1970; both mount on the passenger side instrument panel. With the standard interior, the clock is rectangular. Mustangs equipped with the Decor Group get a round Rally-type clock mounted in the simulated wood-grain panel. (The round clock is standard equipment on Mach 1 and Grande models.)

panel contains the optional radio (a radio blanking plate is supplied if the radio is not ordered) and heater/defroster control panel. Both are covered by a single camera-case black panel trimmed with bright mylar. An ash tray, wider than 1969 because of the relocated cigarette lighter, mounts below the center panel.

STEERING WHEEL: All 1970 steering wheels are reconfigured in a semi-oval design to add extra leg room for the driver when sliding under the wheel. The standard 2-spoke wheel features a horn switch under the spoke padding, eliminating the need for a separate horn ring. A red rectangular emblem with a centered Mustang running horse mounts in the center of the steering wheel pad. Both the wheel and the padding are color-keyed to the interior color.

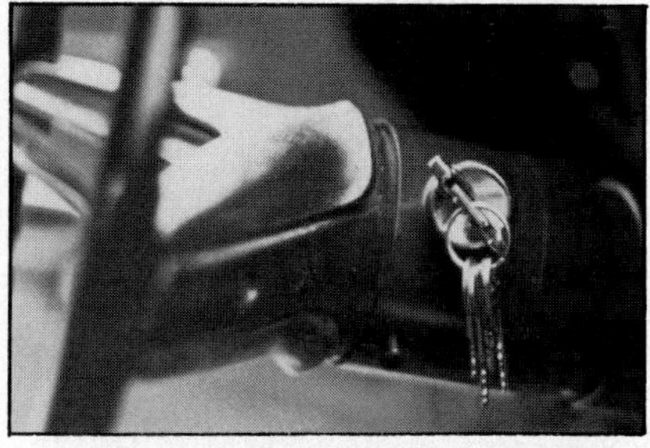

For the first time, the steering column is a locking type with a 5 position ignition switch located on the right side. With the switch in the "lock" position, the ignition switch, transmission linkage, and steering wheel are locked to prevent theft. Locking can only be accomplished with the manual transmission in reverse or the automatic in park. The emergency flasher switch is also positioned on the right side of the steering column. The chrome turn signal lever is located in the traditional position on the left-hand side of the column.

Mustangs built after January 1, 1970 have an ignition switch warning signal that buzzes when the key is left in the switch and the door is opened.

Standard bucket seats and door panel.

Decor bucket seats and door panel.

SHIFTER: A floor-mounted 3-speed shifter is supplied with all standard Mustangs except the Boss 302, Boss 429, and 428 Cobra Jet models. A rubber boot, with a chrome floor plate, blocks out dirt and road noise. The shifter knob is round with the shift pattern inscribed on top.

BUCKET SEATS: High back bucket seats are standard equipment for the first time in 1970. Standard seats are all vinyl, with horizontal pleats. The chrome seat back latch lever is moved to a lower position on the side of the seat backs (the '69 lever is located near the center).

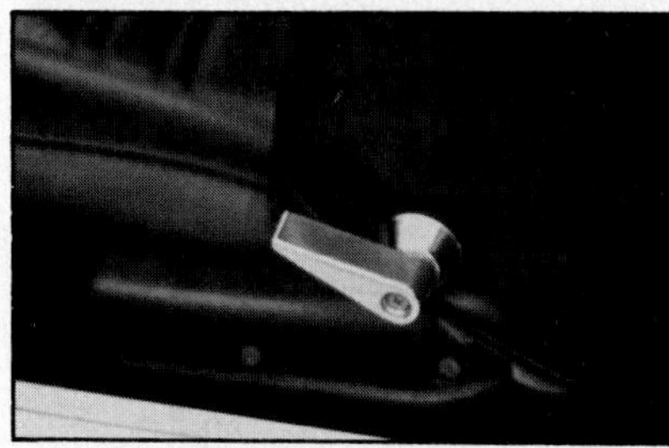

Seat belts are standard on every Mustang model; however, the 1970 belts are different from the '69s. The seat belt buckles are attached to a shorter belt that bolts to the transmission hump behind the seats. The retractor belt, located to the outside of each seat, is longer than before and automatically adjusts seat belt length to each individual. A new latch, located on the retractor belt on hardtop and SportsRoof models only, features a

CONVENIENCE GROUP

- Left-hand remote control mirror — chrome, with door panel control lever mounted in a chrome, round bezel.
- Automatic seat back release — A switch in each door jamb releases the latch in the respective seat back when the door is opened.
- Trunk light — hidden in the luggage compartment lid.
- Glove compartment light — With the standard interior, the glove compartment light is located in the passenger side instrument panel, just above the glove box, in the same housing used by the rectangular clock. A clock blanking plate is supplied if the clock was not ordered. With the Decor Group, the glove compartment light is mounted under the passenger side wood-grain

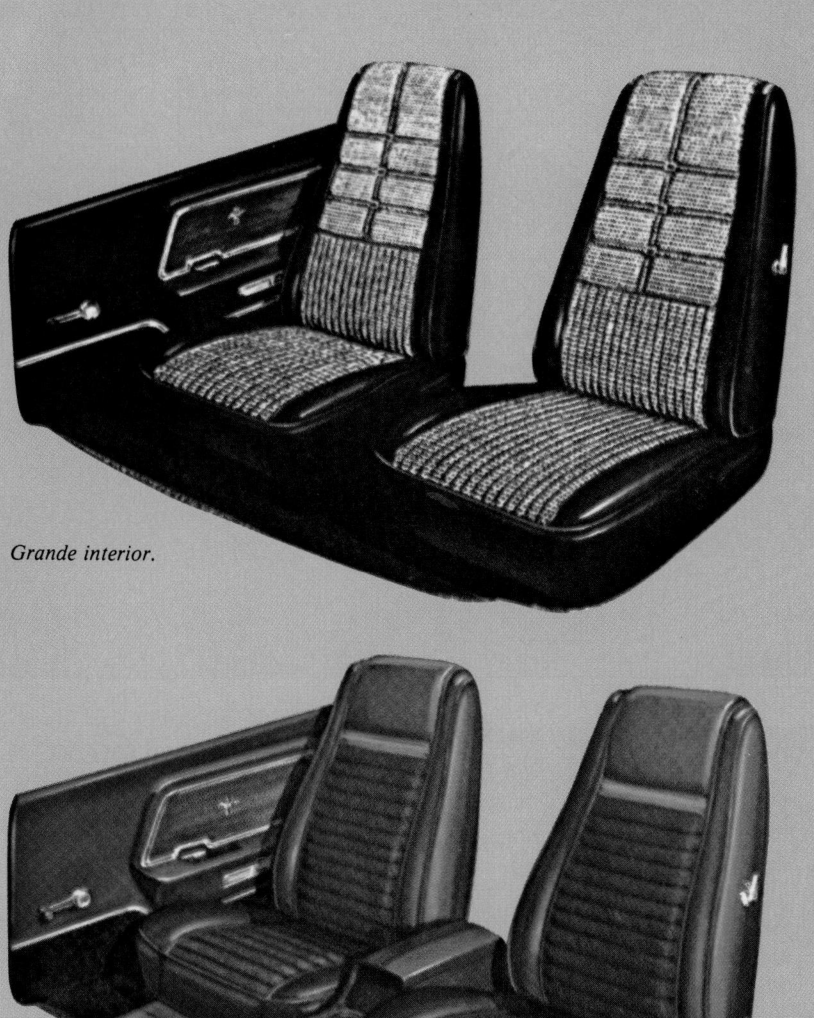

Grande interior.

Mach 1 interior.

applique. A switch in the glove compartment opening actuates the light when the door is opened. A manual switch is also supplied.

- Headlights-on warning buzzer.
- Parking brake warning light — mounted on the instrument panel to the lower left of the windshield wiper switch.

OTHER INTERIOR OPTIONS

- Rear window defogger — hardtops only.
- Deluxe seat belts — with reminder light located to the upper right of the windshield wiper switch on the instrument control panel.
- Rear sport deck seat — a fold-down rear seat for SportsRoof models only.
- Rim-Blow 3-spoke steering wheel.
- Intermittent windshield wipers.

slot for the new "Uni-Lock" shoulder harness, eliminating the need for separate shoulder harness buckles.

REAR SEAT: A bucket-style rear bench seat with horizontal pleats to match the front seats is supplied with every 1970 Mustang. A rear seat courtesy light is located in the SportsRoof's plastic trim panel above the quarter panel.

Convertible quarter panel trim includes an arm rest with ash tray. Both the hardtop and convertible quarter panel trim includes window cranks for the fully retractible rear windows. The SportsRoof windows are a "flipper-type" push out design, limited in outward travel by a plastic wire.

DOOR PANEL: The 1970 Mustang standard door panel features a different pleat design than the 1969 models. The shape of the panel itself remains the same, but the pleats in the center form a leaning rectangular design. An arm rest mounts on the lower center of the panel, and includes the recessed door handles and a door pull grip. Window cranks are mounted at a forward position on the panel.

INTERIOR LIGHTS: The 1970 Mustang hardtops feature a round interior courtesy light attached to their roof. Both the convertible and SportsRoof utilize under-dash lights, and only the SportsRoof has rear seat courtesy lights.

TRUNK

LUGGAGE COMPARTMENT

MAT: All 1970 Mustangs received a speckled design rubber mat on the luggage compartment floor.

SPARE TIRE: The standard spare tire in all 1970 Mustangs (except Boss 429) is located in the conventional position on the right side of the luggage compartment with a threaded hook and large wing-nut. A scissors jack and handle are stored under the tire.

WHEELS

STANDARD TIRE AND WHEEL: Standard wheel for the 1970 Mustang is a stamped steel type with a ventilated disc and safety rims. Wheels on 6 cylinder models have 4 stud holes; V-8s have 5.

The standard Mustang tire in 1970 is an E78x14 black sidewall.

WHEELCOVER: Standard model 1970 Mustangs are equipped with a 10½" hubcap with "FORD MOTOR COMPANY" stamped in a circular pattern in the center. However, most standard 1970 Mustangs were equipped with a base wheelcover — a brushed aluminum type with a bright, protruding center. The outside edge of the wheelcover is trimmed with black, and features 16 simulated air slots.

Sport Wheel Covers
Standard Mach 1
Optional All Models
Except 200 CID 1V Engine

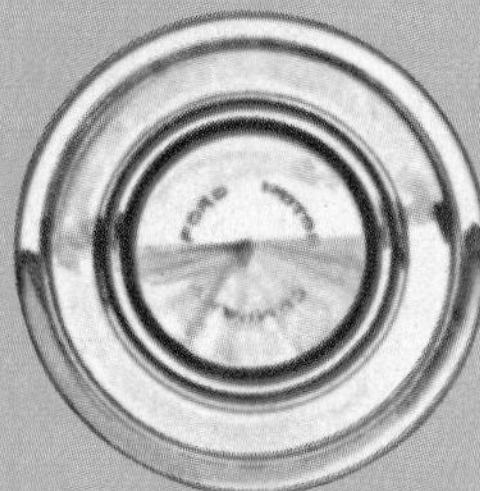

Hub Caps With Trim Rings
Standard Boss 302
Optional Other Models

Wire Wheel Covers
Not Available Boss 302
Optional Other Models

Argent Styled Steel Wheels
Not Available 200 CID Engine or Boss 302
Optional Other Models

Chrome "Magnum 500" Wheels
Optional Boss 302 Only

WHEELS/WHEELCOVERS

STYLED STEEL WHEEL: The 1970 Mustang styled steel wheel is completely changed from 1969. The '70 version is simpler, with only 5 slots. It is painted argent with bright trim rings and hub cap.

HUB CAPS WITH TRIM RINGS: A dish-type flat hub cap with trim rings was available for all Mustang models. The hubcap has FORD MOTOR COMPANY around the center. Both 14 and 15 inch sizes were available.

SPORT WHEELCOVERS: The Sport wheelcover is a 5-spoke simulated mag, argent in the center with bright trim. Chrome lug nuts are simulated and the center is red with a Mustang running horse/bar. They were available in 14 and 15 inch sizes.

WIRE WHEELCOVERS: The 1970 wire wheelcover is identical to the covers used in 1969. It features a red center with the Mustang running horse/tri-color bar.

SPACE SAVER SPARE

A space saver spare tire was available as an extra cost option in 1970. It mounted in the traditional location on the right side of the luggage compartment, with a spring-mounted air canister beneath. The space saver is standard with the Boss 302, not available with the 200 cubic inch 6 cylinder.

POWERTEAMS

ENGINE: The 200 cubic inch 6 cylinder engine is standard for all 1970 Mustang hardtop, convertible, and SportsRoof models (except Mach 1, Boss 302, and Boss 429). A new 351 Cleveland 4-barrel engine entered the Mustang line-up in 1970, featuring canted valves (like the Boss 302) and 300 horsepower, replacing the deleted 351 Windsor 4-barrel.

TRANSMISSION: A fully-synchronized 3-speed manual transmission was supplied as standard equipment on all 1970 Mustangs with 200 through 351 4-barrel engines (except Boss 302). With 428 engines, the buyer had a selection of 4-speed manual or automatic. Boss 302s and Boss 429s were equipped with the 4-speed only.

POWER TEAM SELECTIONS

ENGINES		TRANSMISSIONS			REAR AXLE RATIOS					
					3-Speed Manual		4-Speed Manual		Cruise-O-Matic	
Description	Horse-power	3-Speed Manual	4-Speed Manual	Cruise-O-Matic	Std.	Option	Std.	Option	Std.	Option
Std. 200 Six	120	Std.	NA	Option	3.08	NA	NA	NA	2.83	3.08
Opt. 250 Six	155	Std.	NA	Option	3.00 +	2.79	NA	NA	2.79	3.00 +
Opt. 302 2v V-8	220	Std.	Option	Option	2.79	3.00 +	3.00 +	NA	2.79	3.00 +
Opt. 351 2v V-8	250	Std.	Option	Option	2.75	3.00 + 3.25 +	3.00 +	3.25 +	2.75	3.00 + 3.25 +
Opt. 351 2v V-8 Mach I and Ram-Air	250	Std.	Option	Option	3.00 +	2.75 3.25 +	3.25 +	3.00 +	3.00 +	2.75 3.25 +
Opt. 351 4v V-8	300	Std.	Option	Option	3.25 +	3.00 +	3.25 +	3.00 + 3.50*	3.00 +	3.25 + 3.50*
Opt. 351 4v V-8 Mach 1 and Ram-Air	300	Std.	Option	Option	3.25 +	3.00 +	3.25 +	3.00 + 3.50*	3.25 +	3.00 + 3.50*
Opt. 302 Boss	290	NA	Std.	NA	NA	NA	3.50 +	3.91* 4.30**	NA	NA
Opt. 428 4v Cobra V-8 (Non-Ram-Air)	335	NA	Option	Option	NA	NA	3.25	3.50 +	3.25	3.00* 3.50 +
Opt. 428 4v Cobra Jet V-8 (Ram-Air)	335	NA	Option	Option	NA	NA	3.50 +	3.25 +	3.50 +	3.00 + 3.25 +
Opt. 429 Boss	375	NA	Std.	NA	NA	NA	3.91*	NA	NA	NA
Opt. Drag Pack		NA	Option	Option	NA	NA	3.91*	4.30**	3.91*	4.30**

+ Also available with optional "Traction-Lok" differential.
* Available only with "Traction-Lok" differential.
** Available only with Detroit Automotive "No-Spin" differential.
NA Not available.

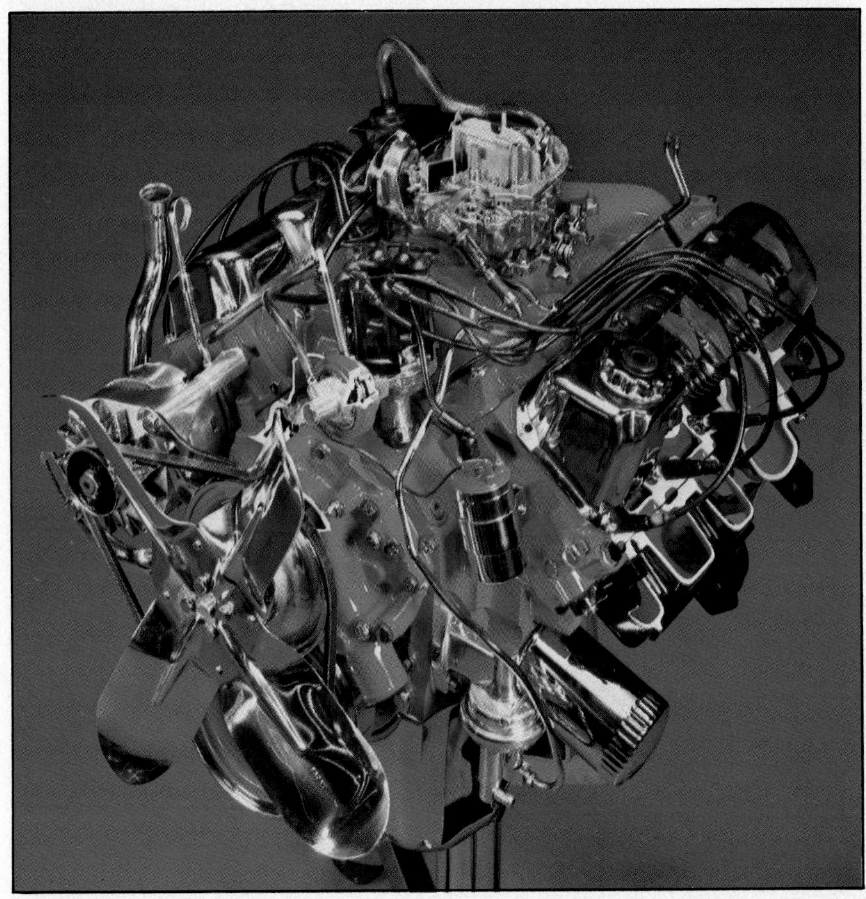

SUSPENSION

No major changes were made to the standard Mustang suspension or steering in 1970.

OTHER MECHANICAL COMPONENTS

COOLING SYSTEM: Radiator capacities in 1970, like 1969, were dependent upon the engine size.

EXHAUST SYSTEM:

In 1970, Mustangs with 4-barrel engines use a new dual exhaust system with a pair of mufflers mounted ahead of the rear axle. The '69 dual exhaust system used a single cross-flow muffler behind the axle.

BRAKES: The standard 1970 Mustang brakes are an expanding drum type on all 4 wheels, identical to the 1969 system. Self-adjusters are again incorporated.

FUEL TANK: Fuel capacity in 1970 was upped 2 gallons (except cars destined for California), bringing the total capacity to 22 gallons.

POWER ASSISTS

- Power front disc brakes (not available with 200 cubic inch 6 cylinder)
- Power steering
- Power convertible top

PERFORMANCE OPTIONS

- Drag Pack — (428 engines only). Includes Traction-Lok differential with 3.91 axle ratio or "Detroit Locker" 4.30 ratio. An engine oil cooler is mounted on the radiator support, and the 428 engine receives heavier cap screw connecting rods and specially balanced crankshaft, flywheel, and damper.
- Traction-Lok differential
- Quick ratio steering.
- Heavy-duty batteries — 55 amp (standard with 200 cubic inch 6 cylinder with automatic and 351 V-8s. Available optionally only with the 250 cubic inch 6 cylinder or 302.) 70 amp (available only with 200 cubic inch 6 cylinder with automatic and 351 V-8s).
- Extra cooling package (standard with SelectAire and 428 engines)

COMPETITION SUSPENSION

- Extra-heavy-duty springs and shocks.
- Heavier front stabilizer bar.
- Rear stabilizer bar.
- Staggered rear shocks with 4-speed models.

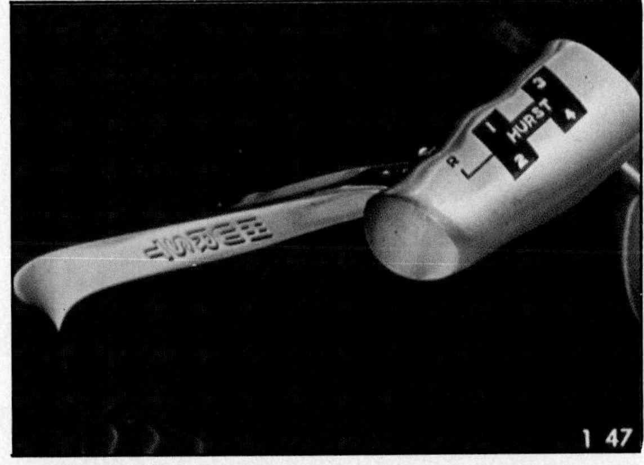

SHIFTERS WITH OPTIONAL TRANSMISSIONS

FOUR-SPEED: In 1970, all Ford 4-speed transmissions received the Hurst shifter. The shifter handle is an aluminum T-type with the shift pattern inscribed on top. The shifter itself is chrome with HURST on the sides. A rubber boot is included, attached to the floor with a chrome bezel.

AUTOMATIC: The 1970 automatic shifter is unchanged from 1969.

MACH 1

The Mach 1 SportsRoof underwent a considerable updating in 1970. No longer the top performance model because of the mid-1969 introduction of the Boss 302 and 429, the Mach 1 exterior appearance was toned down somewhat. The 1969's bold side stripes and blacked out hood were discontinued, and the chrome Styled Steel wheels were replaced by mag-style wheelcovers.

The 351 2-barrel remained as the standard Mach 1 powerplant, with the new 351 Cleveland 4-barrel and both 428 Cobra Jets as more powerful options.

EXTERIOR:

- Special grille with unique driving lamps.
- Mach 1 hood treatments — The 1970 Mach 1 hood features a wide, paint stripe down the center of the hood, either low-gloss black or white depending upon the body color. A thinner tape

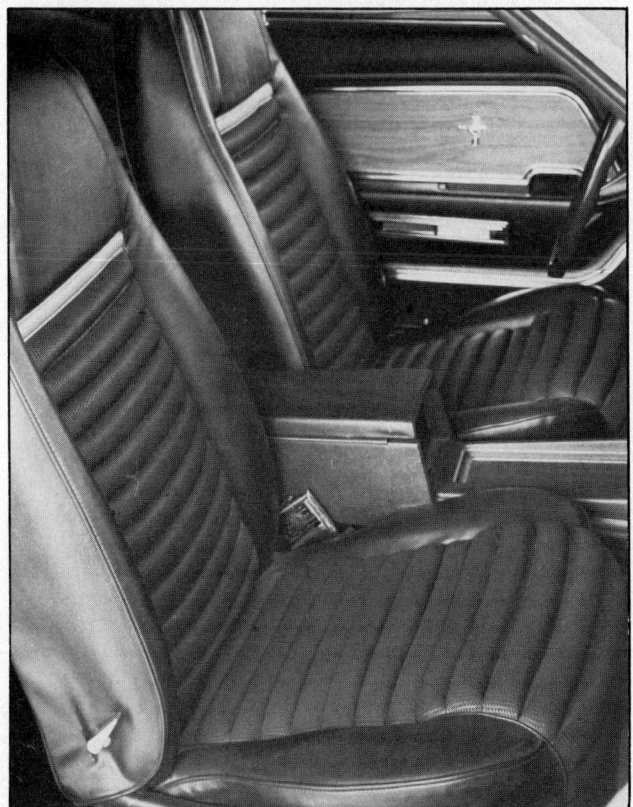

stripe surrounds the large stripe. The engine size is inserted into the stripe on each side of the standard hood scoop (bolt on, non-functional — the functional Shaker is standard with the 428 Cobra Jet Ram-Air, optional with all other engines). Twist-type hood latches are standard.

- Dual color-keyed racing mirrors.
- Aluminum rocker panel molding — unique to the 1970 Mach 1. The dark moldings are finned and feature die-cast "MACH 1" lettering on the front fender.
- Wide deck lid tape stripe, either black or white depending upon the body color, with die-cast "MACH 1" centered on the rear of the spoiler.
- Black honeycomb rear panel applique.
- Pop-open gas cap.
- Chrome oval exhaust extensions — with the 351 Cleveland 4-barrel or 428 only.
- E70x14 fiberglass-belted tires.
- Sports wheelcovers — simulated mag-type.

MACH 1 INTERIOR:

- Special Mach 1 bucket seats — Mach 1 seats are knitted vinyl with horizontal pleats like the 1969 Mach 1 buckets. However, the stripe at the top of the seat back insert is color-keyed to the interior instead of the '69 red stripe.
- Deluxe 3-spoke Rim-Blow steering wheel — with simulated wood-grain rim.
- Special color-keyed carpet — with built-in floor mats color-keyed to the interior.
- Console — with simulated wood-grain trim.
- Molded door panels.
- Simulated wood-grain instrument panel appliques — with Mach 1 emblem on the passenger side.
- Round electric clock — mounted in the passenger side instrument panel.
- Bright-trimmed pedal pads.

SUSPENSION:

- Higher rate front and rear springs.
- High capacity shock absorbers.
- Large diameter front stabilizer bar.
- Rear stabilizer bar.

GRANDE

The Grande hardtop remained as the luxury Mustang in 1970. New Houndstooth cloth seats were added to the interior and the exterior was updated with a new Landau vinyl roof.

EXTERIOR TRIM:

- Landau vinyl roof — covered with black or white "Levant" vinyl (a full vinyl roof was available at extra cost).
- "Grande" "C" pillar script lettering.
- Dual color-keyed racing mirrors.
- Bright rocker panel moldings — with vinyl insert.
- Dual body side pin stripes.
- Camera-case textured rear panel applique.
- Base wheelcovers.

INTERIOR:

- High back bucket seats — with Houndstooth cloth and vinyl trim. The Houndstooth cloth covers the entire seat except for the side bolsters.
- Simulated wood-grain instrument panel appliques — with Grande emblem on the passenger side.
- Deluxe 2-spoke steering wheel — includes simulated wood-grain trim in the spoke padding.
- Round electric clock — mounted in the passenger side instrument panel.
- Molded door panels.
- Bright-trimmed pedal pads.

SPECIAL INSULATION:

The 1970 Grande features a special sound insulation package with 55 additional pounds of sound insulation and deadener materials.

BOSS 302

The Boss 302 Mustang SportsRoof continued into 1970 with few mechanical changes, but numerous external appearance differences. Under the hood, the valve size was reduced from 2.23 inches to 2.19, and the chrome valve covers were replaced by aluminum covers. The exterior features a new, bolder side stripe.

EXTERIOR:

- Front spoiler.
- Boss 302 hood treatment — A wide, low-gloss black stripe stretches the length of the Boss 302 hood. Triple tape stripes flank each side of the wide stripe to the rear of the hood before branching off towards and over the fender, stopping at the fender edge.
- Side stripes — The 1970 Boss 302 reflective side stripes begin at the top of the front fenders, continuing the hood stripe that terminated at the top of the fender. The word "BOSS" sits on top of the stripe with "302" cut into the stripe immediately below. The stripe continues down the fender to the lower body line

where it streaks back toward the rear of the car.

- Dual color-keyed racing mirrors.
- Low-gloss black rear panel and taillight bezels.
- F60x15 raised white letter tires.
- 15 inch wheels with flat hub caps and trim rings (Magnum 500 chrome wheels were available optionally for the Boss 302 only).
- Special flared under front fenders — for additional clearance for the F60x15 tires.

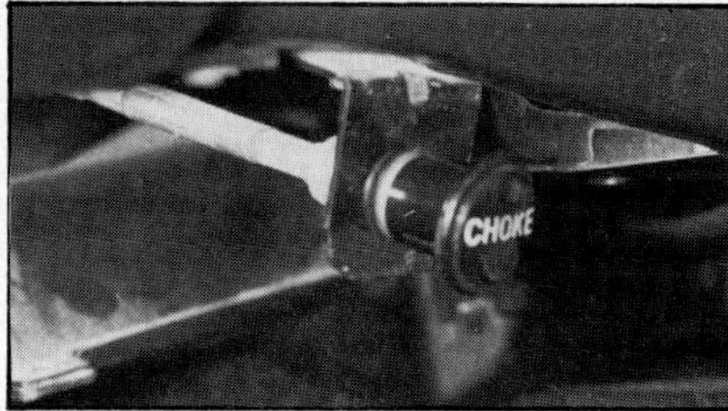

INTERIOR:

Most Boss 302s were originally equipped with the standard black interior. However, the Decor Group was available optionally.

The Boss 302 4-speed shifter is a Hurst unit. A small choke knob is mounted under the instrument panel, just above the accelerator pedal, to operate the Boss 302's standard manual choke.

HANDLING:

Boss 302 cornering is handled by the Competition Suspension with heavy-duty springs, higher capacity shocks (staggered in the rear), heavier front stabilizer bar, and rear stabilizer bar.

REV LIMITER:

Like 1969, all Boss 302s were originally equipped with an Autolite rev limiter that restricted engine rpms to 6150.

BOSS 429

The Boss 429 Mustang SportsRoof continued as a very limited production performance car in 1970. Other than the regular 1970 sheetmetal and interior changes, the Boss 429 equipment remained the same as 1969, with the addition of the Convenience Group as standard equipment. As a minor update, the '70 hood scoop was painted black.

EXTERIOR:
- Hood scoop — The 1970 Boss 429 hood scoop is identical to 1969, except painted black. It continues to be manually operated by an interior-mounted knob.
- Front spoiler — shallower than the Boss 302 spoiler.
- Boss 429 decals on front fenders.
- Chrome 15 inch Magnum 500 wheels — with small, Boss 302 type hub caps.
- F60x15 raised white letter tires.
- Flared under front fender wheel openings — to provide clearance for the wide F60 tires.
- Dual color-keyed racing mirrors.

INTERIOR:
- Decor Group — Knitted vinyl "Comfortweave" seats, simulated wood-grain instrument panel appliques.
- Round electric clock.
- Console — with wood-grain applique.
- Convenience Group — trunk light, glove compartment light, headlights-on warning buzzer, automatic seat back release, and parking brake-on warning light.
- Deluxe seat belts — with seat belt warning light.
- AM radio.
- Deluxe 3-spoke Rim-Blow steering wheel.
- 8000 rpm tachometer and trip odometer.
- Hurst 4-speed shifter.
- Special under-instrument panel bracket with choke and hood scoop knobs.

PERFORMANCE FEATURES:
- Boss 429 engine — with special "semi-hemi" aluminum heads, aluminum valve covers.
- Ford 4-speed transmission.
- Drag-Pack axle — with 3.91 Traction-Lok differential.
- Power steering.
- Power front disc brakes.
- Special suspension — extra-heavy-duty front and rear springs, rear stabilizer bar, staggered rear shocks.
- Engine oil cooler — mounted on the driver's side radiator support, displacing one of the horns, which moves next to the other horn on the passenger side.
- 65 amp alternator.
- 85 amp. trunk-mounted battery (mounted on the right side of the luggage compartment, displacing the spare tire). The spare moves to the left side.
- Space saver spare tire.

1970 SHELBY

The year 1970 was the final year of Shelby production. The 1970s were actually 1969 cars (in some cases, unsold 1969s that were updated by individual dealers under Shelby's guidelines). The only changes were the addition of a unique black chin spoiler and two black stripes on the hood. The serial numbers were also changed: the "9" was changed to "0" as the first VIN digit.

1970 GRABBER SPORTSROOF

During 1970, Ford offered a unique Grabber SportsRoof Mustang with reflective side "C" stripes and 14" flat hub caps and trim rings. A second version features Boss-type non-reflective stripes with either a "302" or "351" engine designation at the top.

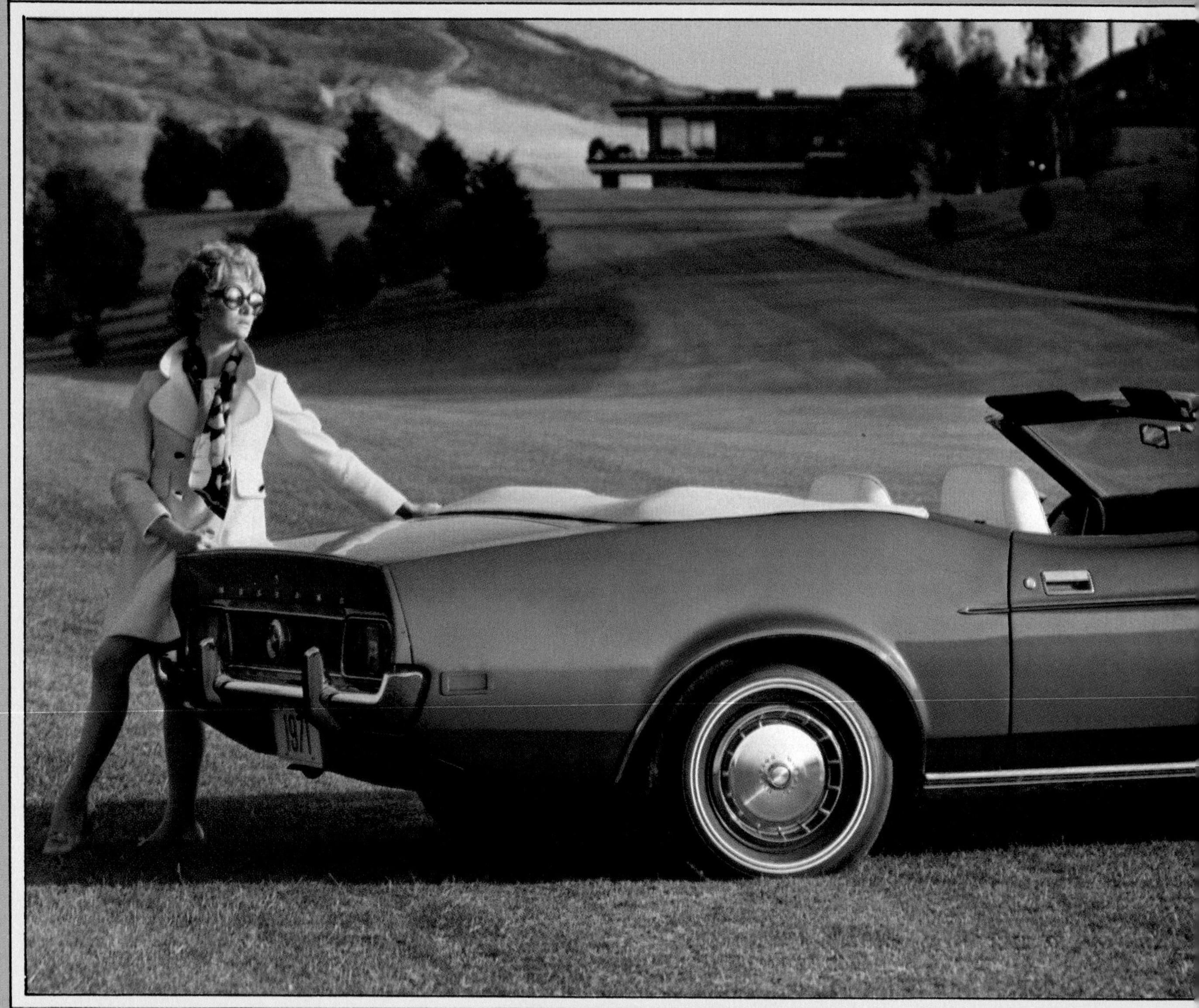

1971

Nineteen seventy-one was the first year of the "big" Mustangs — longer, lower, and wider than ever before, with a one inch longer wheelbase. This last major restyling created a Mustang that looked more like a mid-sized Ford Torino, rather than a pony-sized Mustang of old. What was Ford trying to do?

Obviously, they were aiming for even more performance! The 428 was dropped completely from production after 1970, replaced by a more modern, race-bred big block — the 429. To hold this huge powerplant required a larger engine compartment, and a car with a wider stance. Unlike the 428 (developed originally for big passenger cars), the 429 was "race-bred", incorporating canted valves and thin-wall casting, more like the small block 221/260/289/302/351 series engines. Once the 429 was developed, and had the right speed equipment, the Mustang would really have a super car or two in its lineup!

Specialty models included a Mach 1, a Grande, and a new Boss 351 SportsRoof. Imagine a fully equipped Mach 1 — 429 SCJ (solid lifters), four speed, digger rear axle ("Drag Pack" option), plus air conditioning, power windows (first available this year), AM/FM tape player, etc. Ford made such cars!

For one last year, Ford offered a "Boss" Mustang, this time a unique Boss 351 SportsRoof — a true factory super car with a high compression, high output 351 "Cleveland" engine.

The Shelbys were gone, but you could still see their 1969-1970 styling in these new Mustangs, and Ford was still going for top performance! Despite the larger look, 1971 turned into one of the most exciting years ever for the Ford Mustang.

BODYSTYLES

The major Mustang restyling growth affected all three 1971 body styles — hardtop, convertible, and SportsRoof — including the hardtop-based Grande and the SportsRoof-based Mach 1 and new-for-'71 Boss 351. The 1971 Mustang grew in all directions except height — the wheelbase increased for the first time since 1964, up one inch to 109; the width increased 2.4 inches to 74.1; and the length stretched to 189.5", 2.1 inches longer than the '70 Mustang. The height shrank a full inch on the convertible, slightly less on hardtops and SportsRoofs.

By 1971, safety had become a large factor in automobile styling. Several 1971 Mustang features can be attributed to the new government safety regulations, including the exterior recessed door handles, steel beam guards in the doors, and extra-visibility hidden windshield wipers.

EXTERIOR

GRILLE: The front end of the 1971 Mustang was obviously influenced by the 1969 Shelby. The new grille cavity extends the entire width of the car, surrounded on standard models by a chrome wraparound bumper and chrome hood and fender trim. The grille opening itself is formed in a one-piece housing that extends the width of the front end, incorporating headlight openings on either end. The grille mesh is hexagonal, molded plastic. A molded bar extends horizontally across the center of the grille opening, forming a corral in the grille center with a chrome Mustang running horse in the middle.

HEADLIGHTS: The 1971 headlights are mounted at either end of the grille opening in the one-piece grille housing. The area around the lamps is argent.

VALANCE PANEL: The 1971 Mustang's front valance panel is much slimmer than the panel used in '69-70. Parking/turn signal lights, with clear lens, mount at either end of an air slot below the

bumper. A bolt-on license plate bracket attaches to the center of the valance.

HOOD: The 1971 hood is newly designed. The front edge, trimmed with chrome, is nearly straight. A wide, recessed "windsplitter" is molded into the center. The '71's hood is longer than previous Mustang hoods, stretching all the way back to the windshield where it turns up to cover the new-for-'71 concealed windshield wipers and cowl vent. The cowl panel is eliminated completely. The back edge of the hood is trimmed with chrome.

SIDE EXTERIOR: The side exterior of all 3 1971 Mustang models — hardtop, convertible, and SportsRoof — is basically the same, featuring a sloping front end and a prominent rear "hop-up" The leading edge of the front fenders is trimmed with a chrome strip that blends in with the leading edge of the hood. The upper rear corner of the fenders, also trimmed with chrome, blends the back edge of the hood with the tops of the doors. A side marker light, with color-keyed bezel, mounts in the front of the fenders, just aft of the bumper. The Mustang script lettering, identical to 1969-70, attaches in the conventional location behind the wheelwell.

New Mustang exterior door handles debuted in 1971 as a standard safety feature. The '71 handles mount flush in the door, and must be pulled outward to release the door latch. A round lock cylinder mounts directly behind the handle. One step locking is a new 1971 feature — the doors can be locked from the outside by simply depressing the inside door lock knob, then closing the door. A door-mounted, chrome rectangular non-remote mirror is standard equipment on the driver's door.

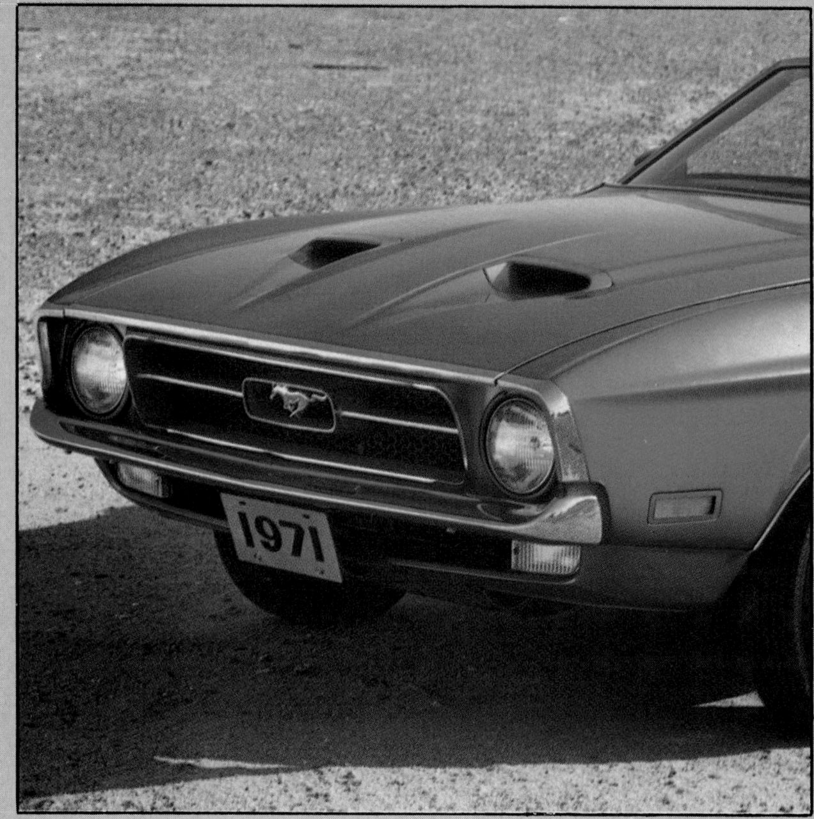

Another standard safety feature added to the '71 Mustang is steel "Guard Rail" side impact protection bars inside the doors. Combined with new, stronger door hinges and latches, the 1971 Mustang doors provide greater protection in the event of a side impact.

The 1971 rear quarter panels are wider than previous Mustangs, giving the '71s much of their larger appearance. Side marker lights, with color-keyed bezels, are mounted at the rear of the quarter panel.

WINDOWS: All 1971 Mustang windows are reshaped to blend with the new Mustang styling. Side windows remain ventless, and all 3 models include rear quarter windows — SportsRoof quarter windows are fixed in 1971, replacing the "flipper-type" used in 1970. The large rear window in the SportsRoof is tinted.

ROOF: Roof design for all 3 Mustang models is changed completely for '71. The hardtop's side roof ("C" pillar) is wider than before, stretching all the way back to the rear of the car in a semi-fastback fashion. The rear window is deeply recessed into the roof.

DUAL RAM INDUCTION

The 1970 Shaker hood scoop option was discontinued in 1971, replaced by a new Dual Ram Induction hood that features a pair of functional NASA scoops. A unique plastic housing fits under the hood, funneling the cool outside air into a rubber-sealed air cleaner assembly. Flaps mounted inside each scoop operate via a vacuum diaphram — at idle or low speeds, engine vacuum holds the flap shut; at full throttle when engine vacuum drops to zero, the flaps open to allow fresh air into the carburetor. The flaps also open when the engine is shut off.

Also included with the Dual Ram Induction hood are twist-type hood lock pins, Ram-Air decal (placed on the outboard side of each scoop), and black or argent two-tone paint (depending upon body color).

REAR DECK SPOILER

The rear spoiler continued as a Mustang SportsRoof option in 1971. Because of the '71's new shape, the spoiler pedestals are redesigned to mount the spoiler in the correct position. As before, the spoiler is adjustable, secured in position by an allen screw in each pedestal.

OTHER EXTERIOR OPTIONS

- Dual color-keyed racing mirrors — standard on Grande, Mach 1, Boss 351, and models with the Decor Group.
- Tinted glass — recommended with air conditioning, but not required as in previous years.

The 1971 convertible top gets new linkage, providing more room in the rear seat area. All convertible tops are power-operated in 1971, and feature a new one-piece semi-flexible rear window. The top can be lowered without unfastening the window.

SportsRoof models are "flatbacks" in 1971. The new roof is nearly horizontal as it stretches to the rear of the car. The 1970 molded-in spoiler is eliminated.

REAR EXTERIOR: The '71 rear panel is flat, with newly designed tail lights positioned at each end. For the first time, the triple lens configuration contains back-up lights in the center lens, eliminating the valance panel lights. The outer edges of the tail-lights are rounded to blend with the contour of the rear sheetmetal. As always, the fuel filler is located in the center of the rear panel. The 1971 gas cap, externally identical to the 1970 version, is no longer attached to the car.

The rear panel on SportsRoof models is painted the same color as the car, but hardtops and convertibles get a new black rear panel applique with chrome trim on the top and bottom.

BUMPER GUARDS

Rear bumper guards return to the Mustang option list in 1971 as a front/rear combination. Rear guards are chrome with a black rubber insert, and bolt to the rear bumper. Unlike previous Mustang bumper guards, the '71 versions extend upward, protecting both the bumper and the rear panel. Front guards on most '71s are similar, however, some models are equipped with low protection front bumper guards that bolt to the bumper at the top and the valance panel below, similar to the guards found on earlier Mustangs. Bumper guards were not available for Mach 1 models.

VINYL ROOFS

A SportsRoof vinyl roof became available for the first time in 1971. The partial vinyl covering extends from the windshield to a point three quarters of the way back on the roof. A chrome trim borders the back edge. The only color is black.

The optional hardtop vinyl roof (standard on Grande) is recessed slightly away from the window edges in 1971. A chrome strip borders the entire covering. The hardtop vinyl roof was available in several colors — black, white, blue, green, or brown.

PROTECTION PACKAGE

- Body side protective molding with color-keyed vinyl insert.
- Front bumper guards with rubber insert.

The Protection Package was not available on Mach 1 or Boss 351 models.

DECK LID: The new Mustang deck lids are wider at the rear of the car, blending with the rear of the quarter panels (the rear quarter panel extensions are eliminated in 1971). The luggage compartment lock moves up from the rear panel to the rear of the deck lid. On hardtops and convertibles, M-U-S-T-A-N-G block letters stretch widely spaced across the rear of the deck lid. SportsRoof models have a new tape stripe across the lid and rear quarter panels, including M-U-S-T-A-N-G in the center.

REAR VALANCE PANEL: The rear valance panel in 1971 is thinner than previous panels. Back-up lights are no longer included, having moved to within the tail lights.

INTERIOR

The Mustang interior, like the exterior, was completely redesigned for 1971. The instrument panel is larger than ever, and a mini-console is added as standard equipment.

INSTRUMENT PANEL: From top to bottom, the 1971 Mustang instrument panel is much wider than ever before. In all previous years, the crash pad formed separate "cockpits" for the driver and passenger with a lower center section. In '71, however, the center of the crash pad rises and juts outward toward the interior.

On the driver's side, the instrument gauge layout is redesigned. A 3 pod arrangement in a camera-case black panel replaces the 4 pods from '69-70. Two large, round pods sit on each side of the steering column, with a smaller pod mounted slightly higher in the center. The left-hand pod contains oil pressure, temperature, alternator, and brake warning lights around a circular lay-out. A new design speedometer fits in the right-hand pod, with 2 sets of numbers — the larger, outside numbers are marked in increments of 10; the smaller, inner figures in fives. The odometer sits just below the speedometer center, and the running horse shaped headlight high beam indicator is positioned at the bottom of the speedometer face. The small, center pod contains the fuel gauge. Arrow-

shaped turn signal indicators mount to the left and right of the fuel gauge.

A new-for-'71 Directaire ventilation system adds rectangular vents, mounted vertically, at each end of the instrument panel.

On the passenger side, a large, flat camera-case black panel attaches below the crash pad.

INSTRUMENT CONTROLS: The headlight switch is located in the conventional position to the left of the steering column on the lower instrument panel. The windshield wiper/washer switch mounts to the right of the steering column, adjacent to the cigarette lighter.

Below the instrument panel, a foot-operated emergency brake lever mounts just above the high beam headlight switch. A chrome brake release is positioned under the instrument panel, just below and to the left of the headlight switch. Kick panel-mounted air vents are eliminated, and push-pull knobs added below the driver and passenger side instrument panels to operate the DirectAire ventilation system.

The center section of the instrument panel contains, from top to bottom, a small storage compartment, a rectangular Mustang and running horse emblem, the radio, and the heater control panel. The storage compartment at the top is lined with a felt material to prevent items from sliding. The rectangular emblem below is recessed into the camera-case black. panel and includes MUSTANG in the left 3/4 section and a running horse at the right. A blanking plate is supplied with models not equipped with the optional radio. The heater control panel is very similar to the one used in 1969-70. Fan speeds are operated by a vertically sliding knob on the left; temperature and heater/defroster functions are controlled by a pair of horizontal sliding knobs to the right. The '70-type ash tray is no longer mounted beneath the center panel — it moves to the new mini-console on the transmission tunnel.

STEERING WHEEL: The standard 1971 Mustang steering wheel is a new 2-spoke design with a round center horn cap. The entire unit is molded plastic, color-keyed to the interior. A small round emblem, with the Mustang running horse/tri-color bar, fits in the center of the horn cap.

The steering column continues as a locking type with the 5 position ignition switch located on the right side. With the switch in the "lock" position, the ignition switch, steering wheel, and transmission are locked to prevent theft. The emergency flasher switch continues to mount on the lower right-hand side of the steering column.

SHIFTER: The floor-mounted 3-speed shifter is standard in all models with the 250, 302, and 351 2V engines. The handle is chrome,

CONVENIENCE GROUP

- Trunk light.
- Under hood light.
- Map light — mounted just above the center instrument panel storage compartment, or air conditioner registers (if equipped).
- Glove compartment light.
- Glove compartment lock.
- Front "lights on" warning buzzer.
- Automatic seat back release — includes a switch mounted in the door jambs.
- Under instrument panel courtesy lights (standard on convertibles).
- Parking brake warning light — mounted in the lower instrument panel to the left of the headlight switch.

CONSOLE

The optional full-length center console replaces the standard mini-console. It is a completely new design, shaped to fit the '71 Mustang's new instrument panel and interior. The front of the console is wider than the rear, shaped to blend in below the center instrument panel. A rectangular clock mounts in a leaning position in the forward section, between the shifter and the heater/defroster control panel. The recessed area around the shifter is camera-case black with bright mylar trim. An ash tray mounts between the shifter and the arm rest/storage compartment. The top arm rest padding is secured with a latch, and can be opened by depressing a button on the side. The console is color-keyed to the interior.

INSTRUMENTATION GROUP

The Instrumentation Group features an 8000 rpm tachometer in the left-hand instrument panel pod, displacing the oil pressure, temperature, alternator, and brake warning lights. Three of the functions — oil pressure, alternator, and temperature — move into a brand new 3-pod gauge panel located on the center instrument panel in place of the rectangular Mustang/running horse emblem. The gauges are mounted facing the driver. Also, the speedometer includes a trip odometer mounted in the lower portion of the face, including a reset button. The standard odometer moves upward to the top of the speedometer face. The displaced high beam indicator moves to the top of the tachometer face, and the rectangular brake warning light mounts at the bottom. The Instrumentation Group is standard on the Boss 351, not available with 250 6 cylinders.

REAR WINDOW DEFROSTER

The 1971 Mustang rear window defroster is completely different from the blower units used in previous years. With the new defroster, the rear window contains a silver-filled, ceramic, high-resistance printed circuit silk-screened into the inside of the glass. The circuit is visible as a series of 1/32 inch horizontal lines across the rear window on both hardtops and SportsRoofs. The defroster toggle switch is mounted on the extreme left side of the lower instrument panel. A small indicator light to the left of the switch indicates when the defroster unit is operating. The rear window defroster is available only with V-8 models, not available on convertibles.

STEERING WHEELS

THREE-SPOKE RIM-BLOW: The 1971 Mustang 3-spoke Rim-Blow steering wheel is very similar to the unit used during 1969-70. The '71 wheel, however, uses a new center pad with long rectangular simulated slots in the spokes in place of the earlier round simulated holes. A rubber contact strip in the steering wheel rim continues to operate the horn.

TILT STEERING: The 1971 tilt steering features 5 positions, 2 above and 2 below the center position. The tilt feature operates by pushing the turn signal stalk toward the instrument panel, releasing the tilt latch. Power steering is required at extra cost.

with a round shifter knob.

A plastic mini-console, color-keyed to the interior, is standard equipment in all 1971 Mustangs. The console fits around the shifter (all shifters — either standard or optional) and includes an ash tray in the rear facing section.

BUCKET SEATS: The '71 Mustang's high-back bucket seats are completely redesigned. The seat is thinner and trimmer than previous Mustang bucket seats, the result of a new seat frame. Standard seats are all-vinyl with 3 rows of double pleats on both the seat cushion and the seat back.

The seat back release handle moves to the rear of the seat back in 1971. The handle is square, and must be lifted upward to release the seat back for access to the rear seat area.

REAR SEAT: A rear bench seat with horizontal pleats to match the front buckets is standard in all models.

DOOR PANEL: The standard 1971 Mustang door panel is an all-new design. The pleat design in the center of the vinyl-covered panel is rectangular shaped. Vertical and horizontal pleats divide the rectangle into 8 separate sections, with 3 circular pleats in the center. A separate arm rest attaches to the panel at the middle. A pull-type door handle fits just forward of the arm rest.

INTERIOR LIGHTS: Overhead dome interior lights are standard on hardtop and, for the first time, SportsRoof models. The SportsRoof's rear quarter panel courtesy lights are eliminated. Courtesy lights are located under the instrument panel on convertibles.

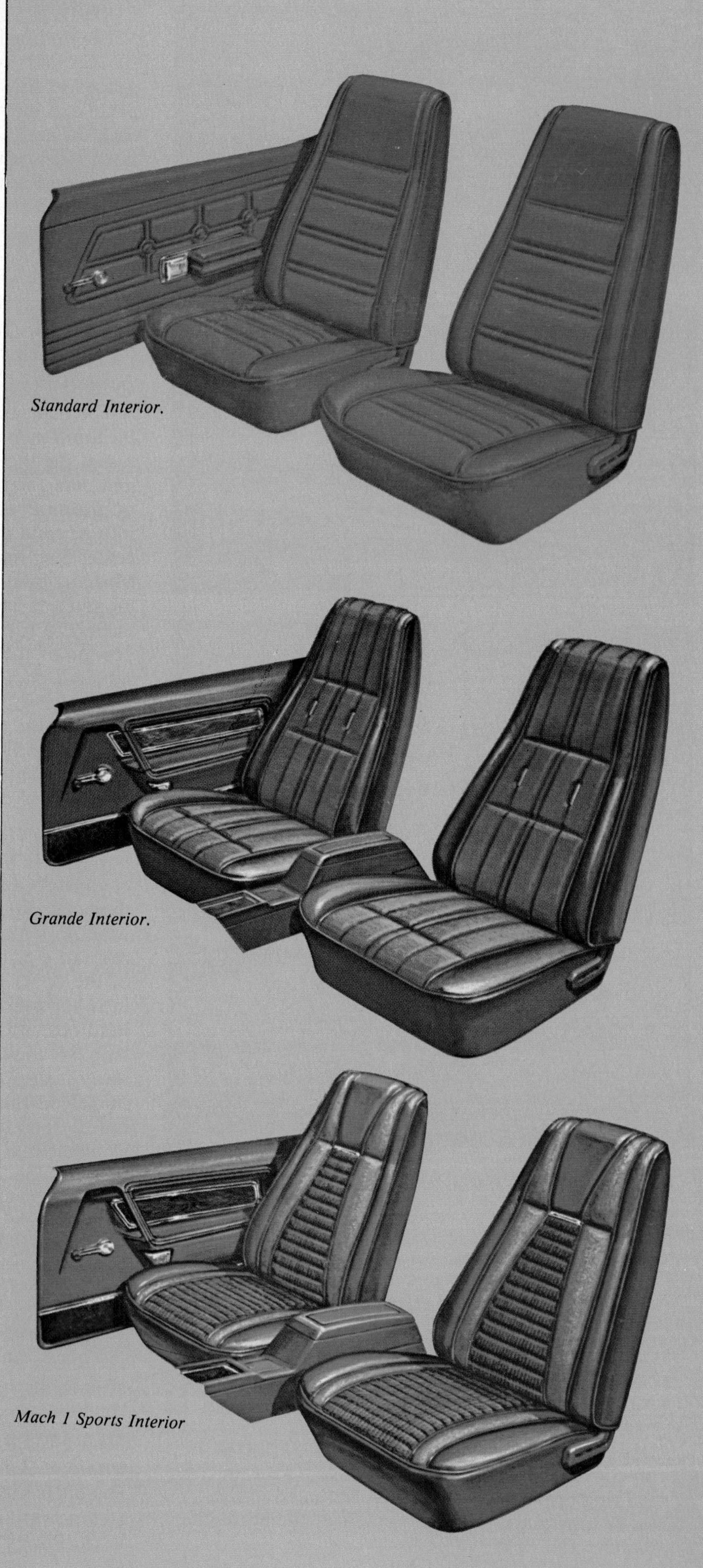

Standard Interior.

Grande Interior.

Mach 1 Sports Interior

DECOR GROUP

- Choice of knitted vinyl or cloth bucket seats — Like the standard seats, the Decor buckets are a new thin-shell design. With the Decor Group, the knitted vinyl or cloth inserts cover the entire seating area, from the top of the seat back to the front edge of the seat cushion. Vinyl-covered bolsters border the inserts on the outside. The inserts contain 4 vertical pleats, and 2 horizontal pleats on the seat back, 1 at the front of the seat cushion.
- Deluxe right- and left-hand black instrument panel appliques.
- Deluxe 2-spoke steering wheel — identical to the Deluxe 2-spoke used in 1970. Includes a wood-grained strip in the spoke padding.
- Rear ash tray in right quarter trim.
- Molded door panels — (convertible and Boss 351 only). The new 1971 molded door panel features an integral arm rest with a pull-type door handle mounted in the lower front. A rectangular wood-grained panel fits in the recessed area above the arm rest. Door pulls are no longer recessed into the top of the arm rest; the 1971 door pulls are a handle-type that bridge the recess in the panel center. The lower portion of the Decor molded panel is covered with color-keyed carpet.
- Outside dual color-keyed racing mirrors.
- Rocker panel and wheel lip moldings — chrome, deleted on Boss 351. The Decor Group is not available on Mach 1 or Grande models.

MACH 1 SPORTS INTERIOR

The Mach 1 Sports Interior is a new 1971 option. It was not restricted to Mach 1s, however; it was available for any SportsRoof model.

- Knitted vinyl bucket seats with accent stripe — the Sports Interior seats, like all 1971 seats, are thin-shelled. The cloth inserts contain horizontal pleats. The seat back insert does not stretch to the top of the seat — it covers only the lower three quarters. Special color-keyed vinyl stripes stretch the entire length of the seat, from the front edge of the seat cushion to the top of the seat back, between the inserts and the vinyl-covered side bolsters.
- Deluxe 2-spoke steering wheel.
- Molded door panels.
- Bright pedal pads.
- Deluxe instrument panel black applique.
- Wood-grained center instrument panel applique.
- Oil pressure, alternator, and temperature gauges — mounted in the center instrument panel, facing the driver.
- Rear seat ash tray — mounted in the passenger side quarter panel trim.
- Embossed carpet runners — The Sports Interior carpet features unique rubber floor mats, color-keyed, stitched into the carpet on both the driver and passenger floors.
- Electric clock — mounted in the left-hand instrument panel pod. If a console is also included, the console-mounted clock is deleted and the hole is covered with a special panel — marked either "Mach 1" or "Mustang".

RADIOS

- AM — includes a single speaker mounted under the center of the crash pad.
- AM-FM — stereo, deletes the crash pad mounted speaker and, instead, includes a pair of door mounted speakers, one in the front lower corner of each door with grilles.
- AM-8-TRACK TAPE — includes stereo door speakers.

POWER SIDE WINDOWS

For the first time ever in a Mustang, the '71 models offered power side windows as optional equipment. A brushed aluminum rectangular master control panel, with 5 switches, mounts on the driver's door, and a smaller, square panel with a single switch mounts on the passenger side door and rear quarter panel trims. The driver can control all windows using 4 of the switches on the master control panel. The fifth switch permits the driver to override the entire system.

With the Power Window option, the rear quarter windows in the SportsRoof become fully retractable.

OTHER INTERIOR OPTIONS

- Rear Sport Deck Seat — for SportsRoof models only. For the first time in 1971, the fold-down rear seat option includes a special spare tire — the F78x14 space saver.
- Intermittent windshield wipers.
- SelectAire air conditioning.
- Deluxe seat belts — seat and shoulder harness belts are color-keyed to the interior. A small, round seat belt warning light mounts in the lower instrument panel to the left of the headlight switch. The light is marked "belt".

TRUNK

LUGGAGE COMPARTMENT MAT: In 1971, luggage compartment mats are deleted from the convertible and SportsRoof models. Instead, a spatter type paint is used to cover the luggage compartment floor and inner fenderwells. A grey burtex mat is used in hardtop luggage compartments.

SPARE TIRE: On hardtops and convertibles, the standard spare tire mounts in the conventional position on the passenger side of the luggage compartment. SportsRoof spare tires mount in a new position to the upper right of the luggage compartment center due to a lack of space in the '71's right-hand corner. However, a bracket exists in the corner for securing the optional space saver spare and air cannister.

WHEELS

STANDARD TIRE AND WHEEL: Standard Mustang wheels are stamped steel with a ventilated disc welded to a safety type rim. In 1971, all Mustang wheels, regardless of six or eight cylinder engine, attach with 5 lugs.

Standard tire is an E78x14 black sidewall on all models except Boss 351.

WHEELCOVER: The standard 1971 Mustang wheelcover is a 10½ inch chrome hub cap with "FORD MOTOR COMPANY" imprinted around the center. However, most 1971 Mustangs are equipped with a base wheelcover — a flat brushed aluminum type with 15 black-painted depressions around the outside perimeter.

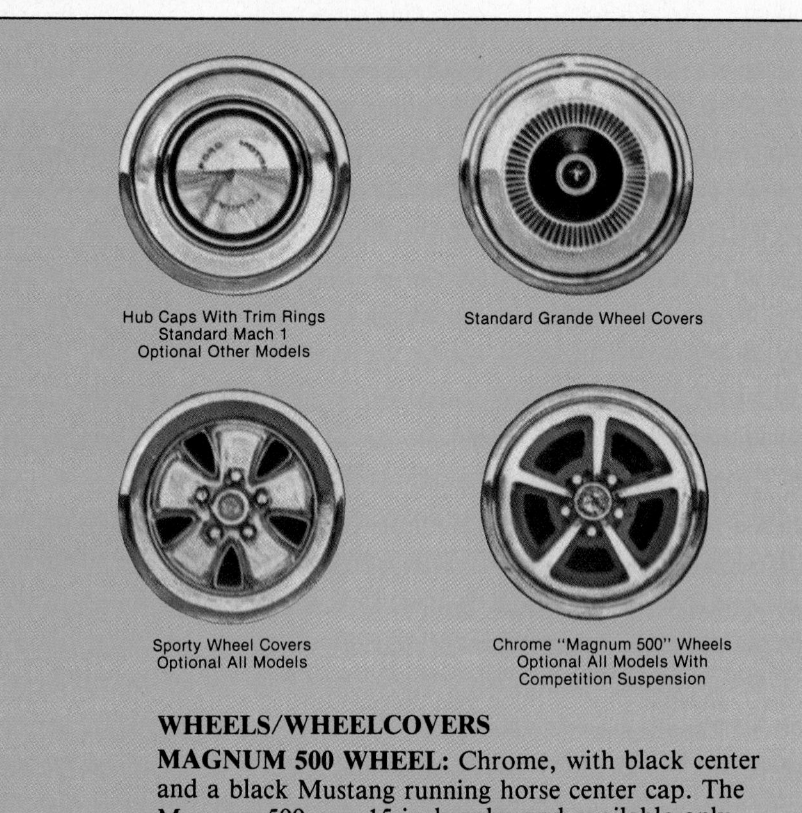

Hub Caps With Trim Rings
Standard Mach 1
Optional Other Models

Standard Grande Wheel Covers

Sporty Wheel Covers
Optional All Models

Chrome "Magnum 500" Wheels
Optional All Models With
Competition Suspension

WHEELS/WHEELCOVERS

MAGNUM 500 WHEEL: Chrome, with black center and a black Mustang running horse center cap. The Magnum 500s are 15 inch only, and available only with the Competition Suspension and F60x15 tires. The space saver spare tire is also mandatory.

HUB CAPS WITH TRIM RINGS: A dish-type flat hub cap, brushed aluminum, with bright trim rings, was available for all 1971 Mustang models, standard with the Mach 1 (14 inch) and Boss 351 (15 inch).

SPORTS WHEELCOVERS: The Sporty wheelcover is identical to the Sport wheelcovers that were standard on the 1970 Mach 1, optional on other 1970 models. They feature 5 triangular-shaped slots and 5 mylar simulated lug nuts. The '71 covers, however, have a lighter colored web and dark gray background.

POWER ASSISTS

- Power front disc brakes.
- Power steering — includes variable ratio steering gear on models equipped with the Competition Suspension.

SHIFTERS WITH OPTIONAL TRANSMISSIONS

FOUR-SPEED: In 1971, the Mustang 4-speed shifter continues as a Hurst unit with an aluminum T-handle.

AUTOMATIC: The automatic transmission shifter is identical to the unit used in 1970, including the shifter indicator plate.

PERFORMANCE EQUIPMENT

- Traction-Lok differential.
- Heavy-duty battery — 70 amp.
- Optional ratio axle.
- Drag-Pack axle — for 429 engines only. Includes the Traction-Lok differential with 3.91 gears, or the "Detroit Locker" differential with 4.11 axle ratio. The Drag-Pack option also includes special 429 engine modifications — cap screw connecting rods, four-bolt main bearing block, and forged pistons. The engine is also balanced differently with a modified crankshaft, flywheel, and damper.
- Competition Suspension — includes extra heavy-duty front and rear springs, extra heavy-duty front and rear shock absorbers, heavier front stabilizer bar, and rear stabilizer bar (351 4-barrel or larger only). Staggered rear shocks are also included with 351 4-barrel, Boss 351, and 429 engines.

POWERTEAMS

ENGINE: The 250 cubic inch 6 cylinder engine replaced the 200 as standard equipment in 1971 (except Mach 1 and Boss 351). The 351 Windsor 2-barrel engine was dropped and replaced by the 351 Cleveland 2-barrel, a smaller-valved offspring of the 351 Cleveland 4-barrel. Another version of the 351 Cleveland, the Boss 351 4-barrel, debuted in 1971 as the replacement for the 1970 Boss 302. The Boss 351 was available only in a Boss 351 SportsRoof package with 4-speed transmission and Competition Suspension.

In May of 1971, still another 351 Cleveland 4-barrel was introduced. This version was called the 351 CJ, for Cobra Jet, and featured a lower compression ratio (8.6:1 compared to the regular 351 4-barrel's 10.7).

SUSPENSION

The 1971 Mustang suspension system is the same type used in the previous 1969-70 Mustangs.

COOLING SYSTEM: Radiator capacities in 1971 are dependent upon engine size.

FUEL TANK: Fuel tank capacity is reduced in 1971, from 22 gallons in 1970 to 20 for all models.

MUSTANG POWER TEAM SELECTIONS

Engine	TRANSMISSION			REAR AXLE RATIOS								
				3-Speed			4-Speed Manual			Cruise-O-Matic		
	3-Speed	4-Speed	Cruise-O-Matic	Std.	Opt.	Traction-Lok	Std.	Opt.	Traction-Lok	Std.	Opt.	Traction-Lok
250-c.i.d. 1v Six Std.	Std.	N/A	Opt.	3.00	N/A	3.00	N/A	N/A	N/A	2.79	3.00*	3.00*
302-c.i.d 2v V-8 Opt. (1)	Std.	N/A	Opt.	2.79	3.00*	3.00*	N/A	N/A	N/A	2.79	3.00*	3.00*
351-c.i.d. 2v V-8 Opt.	Std.	N/A	Opt.	2.75	3.00* 3.25	3.00* 3.25	N/A	N/A	N/A	2.75	3.00* 3.25	3.00* 3.25
351-c.i.d. 2v w/Ram Air Opt.	Std.	N/A	Opt.	3.00*	3.25	3.00* 3.25	N/A	N/A	N/A	3.00*	3.25	3.00* 3.25
351-c.i.d. 4v V-8 Opt.	N/A	Opt.	Opt.	N/A	N/A	N/A	3.25*	N/A	3.25* 3.50	3.00*	3.25	3.00* 3.25 3.50
351-c.i.d. 4v w/Ram Air Opt.	N/A	Opt.	Opt.	N/A	N/A	N/A	3.25*	N/A	3.25* 3.50	3.25*	N/A	3.25* 3.50
351-c.i.d. 4v HO V-8 (3)†	N/A	Std.	N/A	N/A	N/A	N/A	N/A	N/A	3.91	N/A	N/A	N/A
429-c.i.d. 4v V-8 CJ Opt.	N/A	Opt.	Opt.	N/A	N/A	N/A	3.25*	3.50	3.25* 3.50	3.25*	3.50	3.25* 3.50
429-c.i.d. 4v V-8 CJ-R Opt.	N/A	Opt.	Opt.	N/A	N/A	N/A	3.50 (2)	N/A	3.50 (2)	3.50 (2)	N/A	3.50 (2)
429-c.i.d. 4v V-8 (Drag Pk.) Opt.	N/A	Opt.	Opt.	N/A	N/A	N/A	N/A	N/A	3.91 4.11	N/A	N/A	3.91 4.11

(1) Standard on Mach 1
(2) 3.25 used when air conditioning ordered
(3) Available on Boss 351 only
(†) Ram Air with 351-4v HO

* Mandatory ratio with air conditioning
N/A Not Available

MACH 1

The 1971 Mach 1 SportsRoof retains much of its prior performance flair, although the standard Mach engine is reduced to the 302 2-barrel V-8. However, the 351s are optional, and, by ordering either of the powerful 429s, the Mach 1 buyer could drive away in one of the fastest Mustangs ever.

The new '71 SportsRoof bodystyle necessitated a newly designed Mach 1. The honeycomb grille and color-keyed urethane front bumper combination are unique to the Mach 1 (except for a late-model year hardtop "Sports" version). The Mach 1's previously luxurious interior is gone for 1971 — the standard interior is base SportsRoof, but a Mach 1 Sports Interior was available optionally.

EXTERIOR:

- Hood — Three different hoods were available for the 1971 Mach 1. Base models with the 302 engine are equipped with the standard SportsRoof hood, without NASA scoops. However, the NASA scooped hood was available, at no extra cost, for the 302 models. With the 351 or larger engines, the NASA hood is standard, but the scoops are not functional unless equipped with the Ram-Air option.
- Color-keyed front hood and fender moldings.
- Urethane front bumper — color-keyed to the exterior color.
- Honeycomb grille — The black honeycomb grille is unique to the Mach 1 and Boss 351 models (and the late '71 "Sports" Mustangs). The grille includes a small Mustang running horse/tri-color bar fastened to the center and a pair of rectangular sportslamps mounted inboard of the headlights.
- Bright lower body side moldings.
- Black or argent lower body side paint — depending upon the exterior color. The paint extends to the front and rear valance panels.
- "MACH 1 MUSTANG" decal on front fenders.
- Color-keyed dual racing mirrors.

- Black honeycomb rear panel applique - with bright metal moldings.
- Pop-open gas cap — The 1971 pop-open gas cap is a new design. It is round, with a series of simulated rivets around the outside base perimeter. A vertical bar extends the length of the cap in the center.
- "MACH 1" decal on rear deck lid.
- Deck lid tape stripes — extends across the rear of the car from quarter panel to quarter panel.
- Flat hub caps with trim rings — with E70x14 white sidewall tires on 302 and 351 models; F70x14 white sidewalls with 429; and F70x14 black sidewalls with raised white letters with 429 Cobra Jet.
- Bright dual exhaust extensions — with 351 4-barrel and 429 engines. The '71 dual exhaust extensions are round, and fit beneath a specially cut-out rear valance panel.

INTERIOR:

Unless optionally ordered with the Mach 1 Sports Interior, Mach 1s are standardly equipped with the base SportsRoof interior. A Mach 1 identification plaque replaces the "MUSTANG" plaque on the instrument panel center.

SUSPENSION:

The standard Mach 1 suspension is the heavy-duty Competition Suspension.

TAPE STRIPE

A Boss 351-type body side tape stripe was available optionally for the 1971 Mach 1 Mustang. The triple stripe begins at the blacked-out front valance panel, extends upward over the side marker light, then sweeps back toward the rear of the car, becoming thinner until terminated at the rear edge of the rear quarter panel.

SPORTS HARDTOP

In an attempt to bolster spring Mustang sales, Ford added a sporty version of the Mustang hardtop to the line-up in April 1971. The coupe was dressed-up with the Mach 1 honeycomb grille and color-keyed urethane bumper, non-functional NASA scooped hood, Boss 351 side stripes, and the lower body side paint treatment.

GRANDE

The 1971 Mustang Grande hardtop was, again, the luxury Mustang, with standard vinyl roof and special interior treatments.

EXTERIOR:

- Vinyl roof — full, either white, blue, green, or brown with bright bead moldings.
- Bright "Grande" script lettering on "C" pillar.
- Dual accent paint strip on body side — the paint stripe extends from the leading edge of the front fender, along the body line, before tapering off just aft of the door. The stripe color depends upon the exterior color of the car. The accent stripe is deleted from cars with the Protection Package.
- Color-keyed dual racing mirrors.
- Bright wheel lip and rocker panel moldings.
- Chrome-plated wheelcovers — The standard Grande wheelcovers feature a large, black center, with the Mustang running horse/tri-color bar. A series of thin, rectangular simulated slots encircle the black center. Other Mustang wheelcovers were available optionally.

INTERIOR:

- Deluxe 2-spoke steering wheel.
- Deluxe instrument panel applique — black, included on both the driver's and passenger side instrument panels. The center panel is covered with a simulated wood-grain applique.
- Molded door panel.
- Deluxe Lambeth cloth seat inserts.
- Electric clock.
- Ash tray in right rear quarter panel.
- Bright metal trim on pedal pads.
- Interior identification plaque — "GRANDE" in place of the "MUSTANG" plaque on the instrument panel center.

1971 Boss 351 prototype with non-production rear panel and deck lid paint treatment.

BOSS 351

At its introduction in November of 1970, the Boss 351 Mustang SportsRoof had the distinction of replacing both the 1970 Boss 302 and Boss 429. Its mandatory engine is the Boss version of the 351 Cleveland 4-barrel, with solid lifters, aluminum intake manifold, and 4 bolt main bearing block.

The exterior of the Boss 351 contained a unique blacked-out NASA scooped hood, chrome bumper (with Mach 1-type color-keyed hood and fender extensions) and standard side stripes.

EXTERIOR:
- Front spoiler — either black or argent.
- Honeycomb grille — identical to the Mach 1.
- NASA hood — with functional scoops. The Boss 351 hood is almost fully covered with low-gloss black or argent paint (depending upon body color). Twist-type hood locks are incorporated, and "RAM-AIR" decals are placed on the outboard sides of each scoop.
- Color-keyed front hood and fender moldings.
- Lower body side paint treatment.
- Body side tape stripe — identical to the optional Mach 1 stripe, either black or argent.
- "BOSS 351 MUSTANG" front fender and rear deck lid decals.
- Dual color-keyed racing mirrors.
- Black or argent lower back panel.
- Flat hub cap/trim rings — with F60x15 black sidewall tires with raised white letters.

INTERIOR:

The Boss 351's interior is standard SportsRoof, although all Mustang interiors were available optionally. The Instrumentation Group, with tachometer and tri-pod gauge (oil pressure, alternator, and temperature in the center instrument panel) are standard with the Boss 351. The Hurst 4-speed shifter is also included.

PERFORMANCE EQUIPMENT:
- Competition Suspension with staggered shocks.
- Four-speed transmission (mandatory).
- Power front disc brakes.
- Special cooling package — includes extra-capacity radiator, radiator shroud, and flex fan.
- Dual exhaust — rear tail pipes are turned down ahead of rear valance panel.
- 3.91 Traction-Lok differential.
- 80 ampere battery

REV LIMITER:

All Boss 351s were originally equipped with an Autolite engine governer that limited rpms to 6,150. The limiter is attached to the passenger side spring tower.

1972

Inside and out, the 1972 Mustangs look virtually identical to the 1971 cars. Of course, after a major restyling in 1971, the Mustang was ready for a year of styling refinements. But in 1972, these traditional changes were held to a minimum as Ford invested engineering time and other developmental money into meeting more stringent government controls — especially on emissions. Sales were still down dramatically from the peak ponycar years, and the Mustang was not the big money-maker of the mid to late 1960's. Automotive writers even speculated that the Mustang might soon share bodies and running gear with the intermediate-sized Torino. But ultimately Ford went with the "Mustang II" program, to ready a totally new car for 1974, hopefully to return the Mustang to a smaller package, and then regain the high volume sales of the originals.

Under the hood, the big 429 was gone, even though it had been a major reason why Ford went to the larger cars in 1971. What remained were a group of de-tuned, low compression engines that burned regular fuel. The high lead, premium-burners were gone. Even the transmission/rear axle combinations were fewer in number, simply because each variation had to be driven 50,000 miles for certification.

The Boss 351 SportsRoof was also dropped. So the Boss 351 engine was gone too, although early in the model year Ford sold a 351 "HO", which was the successor to the 351 Boss V-8. Other specialty models included the Mach 1 SportsRoof, the luxury Grande hardtop, plus a mid-year introduced Mustang Sprint available in two different packages.

BODYSTYLES

The three Mustang bodystyles — hardtop, convertible, and SportsRoof — remained for 1972, but optional model availability decreased to only two with the deletion of the high performance Boss 351, leaving only the luxury Grande and the performance-oriented Mach 1. All body dimensions remained the same as 1971.

Of all Mustangs, the 1972 models are the most difficult to distinguish from their previous year counterparts. For the first time in Mustang history, the front grille did not change at the beginning of the model year, thus the 1972 frontal appearance is identical to the '71. All 1972 Mustangs, except Mach 1s, can be readily identified from the rear by the MUSTANG script lettering above the right taillight; '71 models used M-U-S-T-A-N-G block letters across the rear of the deck lid.

Since the 1972 Mustang is virtually unchanged from the 1971, this chapter will deal only with the differences between the two model years. All other 1972 information can be referenced in the previous 1971 chapter.

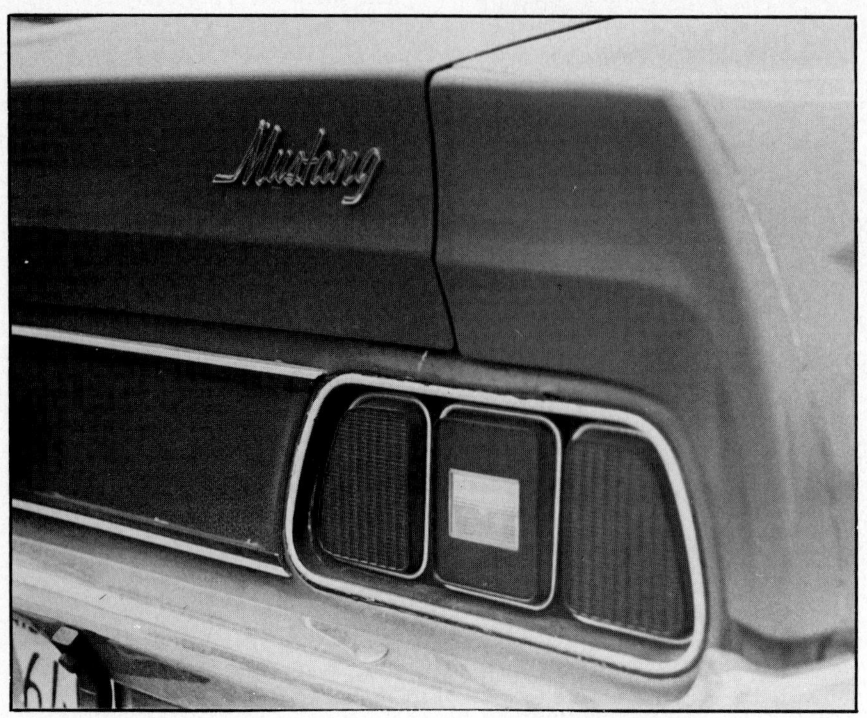

EXTERIOR

STANDARD MOLDINGS: For 1972, chrome wheel lip and rocker panel moldings are standard on all Mustang models except the Mach 1. In 1971, the moldings were an extra cost option on base Mustangs, standard only with the Grande.

OUTSIDE MIRRORS: At the beginning of the 1972 model year, dual color-keyed outside rear-view mirrors were standard equipment on all Mustangs. However, at mid-year, Ford reverted back to the single chrome rectangular mirror, mounted on the driver's door, on standard hardtops, convertibles, and SportsRoofs.

SCRIPT LETTERING: The rear appearance of the 1972 Mustang changed slightly. A small, MUSTANG script emblem attached to the deck lid above the right taillight, replacing the 1971-style M-U-S-T-A-N-G block letters that stretched across the rear of the deck lid.

INTERIOR

STANDARD STEERING WHEEL: The Deluxe 2-spoke steering wheel is standard equipment in the 1972 Mustang. It was offered as an extra cost option in 1971.

SEAT BELT CHANGES: All Mustangs built after January 1st, 1972 received a new seat belt reminder system and rear seat belt retractors.

The 1972 seat belt reminder system includes a reminder light mounted on the passenger side instrument panel and a buzzer located under the panel. Both the light and buzzer operate when the ignition switch is in the "On" position, the transmission is in any forward or reverse position and the driver's seat belt is not extended the distance normally used for fastening. If the passenger seat is occupied, a switch in the seat also activates the system until the passenger seat belt is pulled out a specified distance.

The rear seat belt retractors are hidden below the seat, and a belt guide is located between the seat and trim panel.

CONVERTIBLE INTERIOR UPGRADED: The 1972 Mustang convertible interior is upgraded with knitted vinyl seats, molded door panels with woodgrain inserts, and Deluxe left- and right-hand black instrument panel appliques.

POWERTEAMS

The most significant 1972 Mustang changes came in the engine compartment. The large 429 engines — the very reason that the Mustang was enlarged in 1971 — were deleted entirely, making the 351 the largest available Mustang powerplant in 1972. Compression ratios for all Mustang engines were lowered, and horsepower ratings were measured SAE net — at the rear of the transmission with all

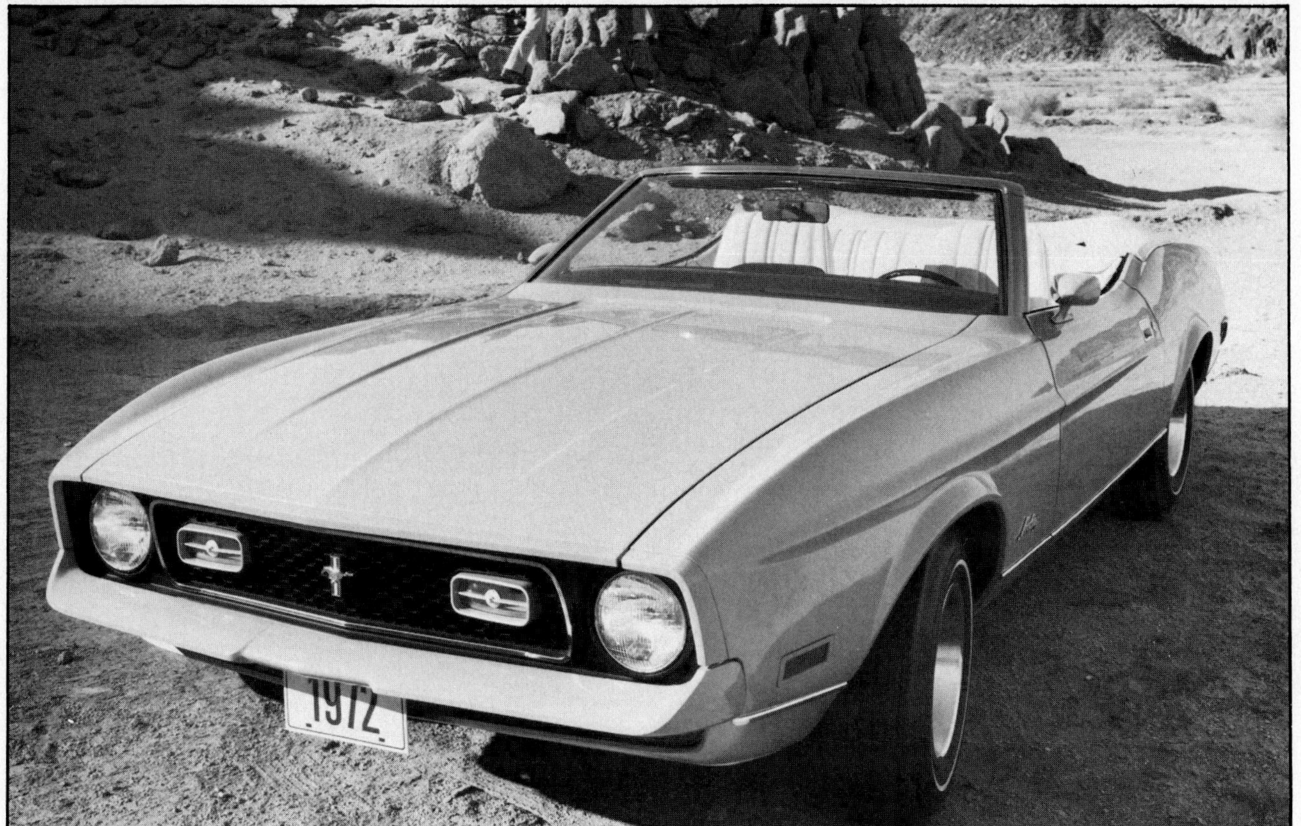

NEW EXTERIOR DECOR GROUP

The Exterior Decor Group replaces the Interior Decor Group from 1971, which is discontinued.

- Lower body side paint treatment — with chrome molding.
- Honeycomb grille and sportslamps.
- Color-keyed front bumper.
- Color-keyed hood and fender moldings.
- Flat brushed aluminum hub caps with trim rings.

The Exterior Decor Group was available for base hardtops and convertibles only.

BODY SIDE TAPE STRIPE

The Mach 1-type body side tape stripe was optional for the Mach 1 and hardtops and convertibles equipped with the Exterior Decor Group.

COLOR-GLOW PAINT

Special Ivy Glow and Gold Glow metallic paints were available for the 1972 Mustangs.

VINYL ROOF

Hardtops equipped with the full vinyl roof (standard on Grande) received a Mustang running horse/tri-color bar on the "C" pillar.

PROTECTION PACKAGE

The 1972 Mustang Protection Package was upgraded to include front and rear bumper guards.

OPTIONAL AXLE RATIO

Optional axle ratios were not available with the 351 HO engine or 302s in combination with the Cruise-O-Matic transmission. Also, the Detroit Locker differential option was dropped in 1972.

DUAL RAM INDUCTION

During the first half of 1972 Mustang production, the functional Ram-Air hood was available for all V-8 models. At mid-year, however, the option was restricted to 351 2-barrel models only.

351 4-BARREL

- NASA hood (non-functional).
- 55 ampere alternator and battery.
- Special intake manifold, valve springs, and Autolite 4300-D carburetor.
- 2½ diameter exhaust outlets.
- 4-bolt main bearing caps and modified camshaft.
- Competition Suspension (at extra cost).
- Cruise-O-Matic (3.25 ratio axle) or wide ratio 4-speed (3.50 ratio axle) transmission.

351 4-BARREL HIGH-OUTPUT

- 4-speed transmission.
- Power front disc brakes.
- Space saver spare.
- F60x15 black sidewall tires with raised white letters.
- Dual exhaust.
- Competition Suspension with staggered shocks.
- Special cooling package.
- 3.91 Traction-Lok rear axle.
- Electronic rpm limiter.
- 90 ampere battery.

HURST SHIFTER

All 4-speed equipped 1972 Mustangs, like '71, were fitted with the Hurst shifter. However, the shifter knob in '72 is round and black, in place of the previous aluminum T-handle.

MUSTANG POWER TEAM SELECTIONS

Engine	TRANSMISSION			REAR AXLE RATIOS								
				3-Speed Manual			4-Speed Manual			Cruise-O-Matic		
	3-Speed	4-Speed	Cruise-O-Matic	Std.	Opt.	Traction-Lok	Std.	Opt.	Traction-Lok	Std.	Opt.	Traction-Lok
250 CID 1v (2) Six Std.	Std.	N/A	Opt.	3.00	N/A	3.00	N/A	N/A	N/A	2.79	3.00*	3.00* 2.79
302 CID 2v (2) V-8 Opt. (1)	Std.	N/A	Opt.	3.00*	N/A	3.00*	N/A	N/A	N/A	2.79 3.00**	3.00*	3.00* 2.79
351 CID 2v (2) V-8 Opt.	Std.	N/A	Opt.	2.75*	3.25*	2.75* 3.25*	N/A	N/A	N/A	2.75	3.25*	2.75 3.25*
351 CID 2v (2) w/Ram Air Opt.	Std.	N/A	Opt.	3.25*	N/A	3.25*	N/A	N/A	N/A	3.25*	N/A	3.25*
351 CID 4v V-8 Opt.	N/A	Opt.	Opt.	N/A	N/A	N/A	3.50	3.25*	3.50 3.25*	3.25*	3.50	3.50 3.25*
351 CID 4v HO V-8 Opt.	N/A	Std.	N/A	N/A	N/A	N/A	N/A	N/A	3.91	N/A	N/A	N/A

(1) Standard on Mach 1
(2) 3-speed manual N/A in California
* Mandatory ratio with air conditioning
** Standard Ratio for California
N/A—Not Available

accessories hooked up and operating.

A very limited number of '72s received the 351 4-barrel HO engine, a low compression version of the 1971 Boss 351. The HO utilizes a special high-lift camshaft, mechanical lifters, forged aluminum pistons, shot-peened connecting rods, and a special intake manifold with an Autolite 4300-D 4-barrel carburetor.

MACH 1

The Mach 1 Mustang entered virtually unchanged from '71. At the rear, the pop-open gas cap is deleted, replaced by the standard Mustang version.

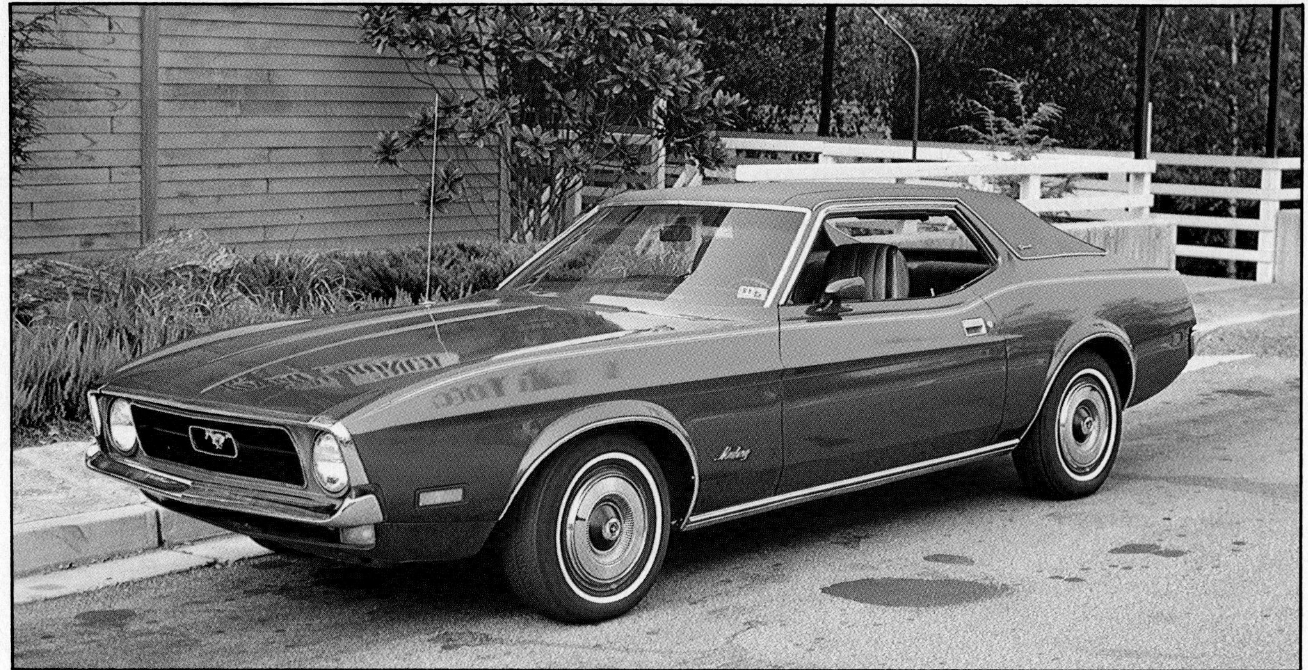

GRANDE

The luxurious Grande version of the 1972 Mustang is little changed from the '71. A new, unique side accent stripe replaces the '71 stripe. The '72 accent stripe is 2-toned, beginning at the edge of the front fender and following the upper body line to the rear of the quarter panel. The stripes were available in 3 different color combinations, depending upon the exterior paint: gold/green, gold/white, and black/orange.

Also, the 1972 Grande includes a trunk mat in the luggage compartment.

SPRINT

During late February, 1972, Ford introduced the Mustang Sprint, a red, white, and blue decorated hardtop or SportsRoof to be sold with similarly-painted Mavericks and Pintos. Two versions were available — Package A and Package B.

Sprint Package A:
- Special white body with dual blue/red stripes on hood, blue/red lower body paint, and blue/red rear panel.
- USA shield emblem on rear quarter panel.
- Exterior Decor Group - with honeycomb grille and color-keyed front bumper, hood and fender moldings.
- Dual color-keyed racing mirrors.
- Flat brushed aluminum hub caps with trim rings.
- E70x14 white sidewall tires.
- Unique interior - with white vinyl bolsters and blue Lambeth cloth inserts, plus white interior trim and color-keyed carpet.

Sprint Package B:
- Includes all items in Package A.
- 15 inch Magnum 500 wheels in place of the hub cap/trim rings.
- F60x15 tires.

1973

For the first time in Mustang history, Ford did not restyle its ponycar after two model years running. Of course, product planners had scheduled a totally new Mustang II for 1974, so a complete restyling for 1973 was definitely out of the question.

However, Ford did make several key exterior changes, making it easy to distinguish the 1973 model from the 1971 and the 1972. For example, the front grille was redesigned, and the rear taillight panel was altered noticeably. Interior changes were barely visible, however, and the engine options were about the same.

You could still buy a Mach 1 SportsRoof (which sported a bold new graphic scheme) and then option it with a high performance 351 Cobra Jet, new this year.

1973 is the final year of the fabulous first generation cars — which are some of the most collectable of the entire post war era. Granted, Ford's ponycar had grown bigger and heavier with each restyling. But the character and excitement of the original Mustang concept was still present.

Buyers could still choose a sporty hardtop, convertible, or fastback, then equip it with a personal group of options and accessories. So the Mustang continued the marketing philosophy of the previous model years. And, as the final models, the 1973's hold a special place in Mustang history, particularly the convertible, which is the last factory-assembled open Ford ever built.

BODYSTYLES

All three 1973 Mustang body styles — hardtop, convertible, and SportsRoof — retain the basic size and styling of the 1971-72 Mustang. However, the '73s can be distinguished easily by their new front grille and bumper, plus bright taillight bezels. Both the Grande and Mach 1 models remain for the last year of first generation Mustang production. The Grande is virtually unchanged, except for the '73 styling updates, but the Mach 1 is revamped with new side and rear deck stripes.

EXTERIOR

GRILLE: The Mustang grille is completely redesigned for 1973. The grille opening is similar to the '71-72 in size and shape, but the plastic grille mesh is a larger egg-crate type, mounted farther

forward in the opening than the recessed '72 grille. A chrome Mustang running horse and corral with short vertical bars at the top and bottom, similar to the 1966 Mustang, is attached to the grille center. New, vertical parking/turn signal lights mount at each end of the grille. The entire grille opening is trimmed with a bright molding.

HEADLIGHTS: The 1973 Mustang headlights fit in the fender extensions, on either side of the grille. In '73, the lamps are surrounded by a new chrome, rectangular bezel.

BUMPER: To meet the Federal Government's 5-mile-per-hour frontal impact standards, the 1973 Mustang is equipped with a new front bumper impact-absorbing system that includes a molded urethane with steel reinforcement bumper, an impact beam, and a pair of absorbers. The bumper and beam reinforcement are mounted to the car by two energy-absorbing devices that attach to the frame. Each energy-absorbing device consists of a steel "I" beam section, or ram, inside a steel outer case. A rectangular rubber block on either side connects the ram to the case. During impact up to 5 m.p.h., the bumper and impact beam deflect and the "I" beam ram is driven rearward, stretching the rubber blocks which soak up the initial impact, preventing damage to other operating components. After impact, the rubber resumes its normal shape and immediately returns the bumper to its original position.

Externally, the new bumper is color-keyed to the exterior of the car. The urethane is shaped much like the Decor bumper from '72, but the '73 version protrudes forward further.

VALANCE PANEL: The 1973 Mustang valance panel, no longer used as a mounting spot for the parking lights, is thinner than before, barely visible behind and below the new bumper.

HOOD: The 1973 hood is unchanged from 1972. However, the front trim is color-keyed to match the exterior.

SIDE EXTERIOR: The side exterior in 1973 is virtually identical to the 1971-72. The front fender is reshaped slightly to provide space for the larger front bumper, and the fender moldings are color-keyed to the exterior. The MUSTANG script lettering behind the front wheelwell remains, and the chrome wheel lip/rocker panel molding continues as standard equipment on base models. A door-mounted, chrome rectangular non-remote mirror is standard on the driver's side.

WINDOWS: The 1973 Mustang windows are unchanged from '72, except for the new tinted windshield requirement for the convertible.

ROOF: Roof styling and design for the '73 Mustang is the same as the '71-72 models.

REAR EXTERIOR: The 1973 Mustang can be distinguished from the rear by its new taillight bezels. Previously, in 1971-72, the bezels were black. In 1973, however, the bezels are bright, although they retain the same shape as the earlier units. The rear panel is covered with a grain black applique with chrome trim. A '71-72 type gas cap is centered in the panel.

REAR BUMPER: The chrome rear bumper in 1973 uses new brackets that position the bumper farther away from the car, allowing the Mustang to meet the Federal Government's 1973 rear bumper impact standard of 2½ miles-per-hour without major damage.

DECK LID: Mustang deck lids in 1973 are identical to the '72 models. The MUSTANG script lettering continues on the passenger side above the right taillight.

REAR VALANCE PANEL: The 1973 rear valance panel is unchanged from 1971-72.

DECOR GROUP

- Lower body side paint - either black or argent, depending upon the body color. Includes a bright molding along the upper edge.
- Honeycomb grille - with small Mustang running horse/tri-color bar and blacked-out headlight bezels.
- Flat brushed aluminum hub caps with bright trim rings.
- Standard rocker panel and wheellip moldings are deleted - available only on standard hardtops and convertibles - not available with Appearance Protection Group or special paint.

TAPE STRIPE

With the Decor Group, a special black or argent tape stripe (depending upon the body color) was available. The stripe is identical to the 1971 Boss 351 stripe.

DELUXE BUMPER GROUP

The new-for-'73 Deluxe Bumper Group includes rear bumper guards with rubber inserts and a horizontal rubber strip along the bumper edge.

METALLIC GLOW PAINT

In 1973, a third Glow Paint was added to the Mustang color selection. In addition to the already available Ivy Glow and Gold Glow, a new Blue Glow became optional on the paint list.

TU-TONE HOOD

The Tu-Tone hood option includes the NASA scooped hood, black or argent (depending upon the body color) hood paint, and twist-type hood locks.

APPEARANCE PROTECTION GROUP

- Body side molding - with vinyl insert.
- Spare tire lock.
- Door edge guards.
- Body side stripe on Grande deleted with the Appearance Protection Group option - not available with Mach 1 or Decor Group.

OTHER EXTERIOR OPTIONS

- Rear bumper guards - with rubber inserts.
- Door edge guards.
- Vinyl Roof - includes a Mustang running horse/tri-color bar on the "C" pillar. The full vinyl roof was available only on hardtop models.
- 3/4 vinyl roof - for SportsRoofs only.
- Dual color-keyed racing mirrors - not available with special paint.
- Rear deck spoiler - SportsRoof and Mach 1 only.

INTERIOR

The basic Mustang interior design and layout was unchanged for 1973. Hardtops (except Grande) and SportsRoofs kept their standard interior trim, but the convertible model received an exclusive interior with knitted vinyl seat trim, molded door panels, and other Deluxe appointments.

INSTRUMENT PANEL: The 1973 Mustang instrument panel, gauges, and gauge arrangement is identical to the 1971-72 Mustang. Two large pods straddle the steering column — the left-hand pod contains oil pressure, temperature, brakes, and alternator warning lights; the right-hand pod houses the speedometer, odometer, and running horse-shaped high beam headlight indicator. A smaller, center-mounted pod contains the fuel gauge. Arrow-shaped turn signal indicators are positioned at each side of the fuel gauge.

In 1973, the convertible interior is upgraded to include Deluxe black instrument panel appliques.

INSTRUMENT CONTROLS: The 1973 instrument controls are also unchanged. The headlight switch mounts on the instrument panel to the left of the steering column, and the windshield wiper/washer switch and cigarette lighter mount to the right of the column.

A foot-operated emergency brake lever, with its accompanying release handle, attach below the instrument panel above the floor-board-mounted headlight high beam switch. Push/pull air vent knobs below both the driver and passenger instrument panels operate the DirectAire ventilation system.

The center instrument panel continues to house the small

Standard seats and door trim panel.

Grande Interior.

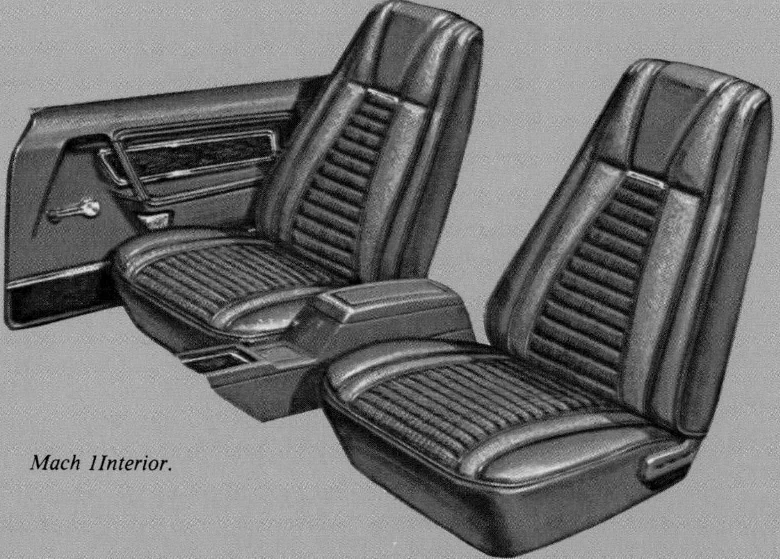

Mach 1Interior.

storage compartment, rectangular Mustang running horse emblem, optional radio, and heater/defroster controls.

STEERING WHEEL: The standard 1973 steering wheel is the Deluxe 2-spoke with wood-grain insert.

SHIFTER: A chrome 3-speed shifter is supplied with the base 250 and 302 models. The 351 2-barrel, however, was not available with a manual transmission , so it was equipped with the Cruise-O-Matic automatic transmission and T-handled shifter. All 1973 Mustangs are equipped with a mini-console, unless optioned with the full length console.

BUCKET SEATS: The 1973 hardtop and SportsRoof high back bucket seats are identical to the seats used during 1971-72. Convertible seats, however, are upgraded with deluxe knitted vinyl inserts.

REAR SEAT: A bench seat, with pleats and material to match the front buckets, is supplied with all 1973 Mustangs.

DOOR PANEL: Standard door panels, identical to the ones used in 1972, are supplied with the 1973 Mustang hardtops and SportsRoof. Molded panels, like those used with earlier Decor interiors, are added to the convertible in 1973.

INTERIOR LIGHTS: Overhead dome interior lights are standard with the hardtop and SportsRoof models. Convertible courtesy lights are located under the instrument panel.

CONVENIENCE GROUP

- Trunk, under hood, glove compartment and map lights.
- Front "lights-on" warning buzzer.
- Automatic seat back release.
- Under instrument panel courtesy lights (standard on convertible).
- Parking brake warning light.
- Glove compartment lock.

OTHER INTERIOR OPTIONS

- SelectAire air conditioning.
- Electric rear window defroster.
- Tinted glass.
- Deluxe seat belts - seat belts are color-keyed to the interior.
- Sport deck rear seat - fold-down rear seat for SportsRoofs only. Includes an F78x14 space saver spare tire.
- Console - includes a rectangular electric clock positioned in front of the shifter. On models with the instrument panel clock, a blanking plate is fitted in the console's clock slot.
- Floor mats - front, color-keyed to the interior.
- Interval windshield wipers.

MACH 1 SPORTS INTERIOR

The optional Mach 1 Sports Interior was available for all 1973 Mustang Mach 1s and SportsRoofs with V-8 engine.

- Knitted vinyl high back bucket seats with accent stripes - identical to the '71-72 Mach 1 Sports Interior seats.
- Instrumentation Group - with oil pressure, temperature, and alternator gauges in a tri-pod set-up in the center instrument panel.
- Molded door panels - with wood-grain insert.
- Unique carpet - with color-keyed rubber floor mats.
- Deluxe instrument panel appliques - black on the driver and passenger side, wood-grained in the center panel.
- Bright pedal pads.
- Rear seat ash tray - mounted in the right quarter panel trim.

INSTRUMENTATION GROUP

The Instrumentation Group that debuted with the 1971 Mustang continues unchanged into 1973. A special tri-pod panel in the center instrument panel includes oil pressure, temperature, and alternator gauges, as well as an instrument panel tachometer (in the large left-hand instrument pod) and trip odometer. Available only with 8 cylinder engines.

RADIOS

- AM - includes a speaker mounted under the crash pad.
- AM-FM - includes a speaker mounted in each door. An AM-FM selector bar is included under the radio face.
- AM-8-TRACK TAPE - includes a speaker in each door.

BASIC EQUIPMENT GROUPS

To simplify the ordering of basic options, Ford offered a pair of Basic Equipment Groups to the 1973 Mustang buyer.

BASIC EQUIPMENT GROUP "A":

- Cruise-O-Matic automatic transmission.
- Power steering.
- Power front disc brakes.
- AM radio.
- White sidewall tires.

BASIC EQUIPMENT GROUP "B":

- Includes all items in Group "A" plus:
- Air conditioning.
- Tinted glass.
- Full length console.

STEERING WHEELS

LEATHER WRAPPED: A new-for-'73 option is the leather wrapped Deluxe 2-spoke steering wheel (not available with the 3-spoke Rim-Blow).

RIM-BLOW: The 1973 3-spoke Rim-Blow steering wheel features a color-keyed pad with oblong slots in each spoke. A black, round emblem fits in the center with a Mustang running horse/tri-color bar. The wheel itself is simulated wood-grain, with an inner rubber strip that sounds the horns when depressed.

TILT-WHEEL: The 1973 Mustang tilt-steering column features 5 different positions. Power steering is a required option.

HUB CAPS WITH TRIM RINGS
Standard Mach 1
Optional Other Models

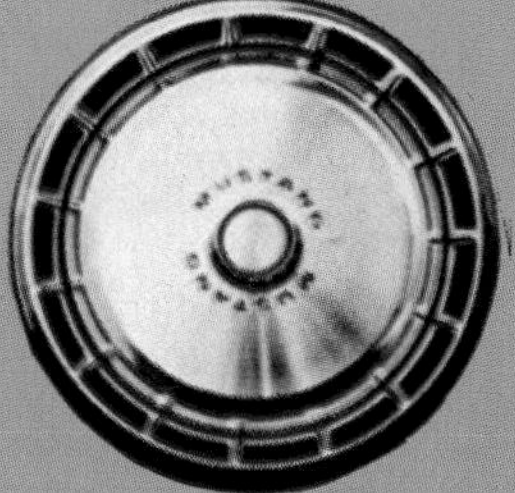

BASE WHEELCOVER
Not Available Mach 1

FORGED ALUMINUM WHEEL
Optional All Models

SPORTS WHEELCOVER
Optional All Models

WHEELS/WHEELCOVERS

Four optional wheels were available for the 1973 Mustang. The hub cap/trim ring and Sports wheelcovers are identical to the covers used in 1972. The Magnum 500 was discontinued in '73, replaced by a dish-type forged aluminum wheel with 5 slots. Most '73 Mustangs were equipped with the Base wheelcover and Grandes received a unique Deluxe cover (page 217).

RADIAL TIRES

Steel-belted radial ply tires were offered as optional Mustang equipment for the first time in 1973.

4-SPEED SHIFTER

Mustangs with the 351 4-barrel's optional 4-speed shifter are equipped with a Hurst shifter. The '73 style Hurst features a round, chrome shaft with a flattened area on either side for the inscribed HURST lettering. A round, black shifter knob with an inscribed shift pattern tops the shifter.

TRUNK

LUGGAGE COMPARTMENT

LUGGAGE COMPARTMENT FINISH: The luggage compartment floor in 1973 is covered with a gray spatter-type paint (except Grande).

SPARE TIRE: On hardtops and convertibles, the spare tire mounts in the standard position on the right side of the luggage compartment. SportsRoof spare tires mount to the upper right of the luggage compartment.

WHEELS

STANDARD WHEEL AND TIRE: The standard 1973 Mustang wheel, like all previous Mustang wheels, is stamped steel with ventilated disc welded to a safety type rim. All wheels are 5 lug.

WHEELCOVER: The standard 1973 Mustang wheelcover is a 10½" chrome hub cap with color-keyed wheels. However, most 1973 Mustangs are equipped with a full wheelcover — a flat brushed aluminum type, identical to the '72 wheelcover, with 15 black-painted depressions around the outside perimeter.

POWERTEAMS

ENGINE: The 250 cubic inch 6 cylinder engine remained as the standard Mustang powerplant in 1973 (except Mach 1).

POWER TEAM SELECTIONS

Engine	TRANSMISSION			REAR AXLE RATIOS								
				3-Speed Manual			4-Speed Manual			Cruise-O-Matic		
	3-Speed	4-Speed	Cruise-O-Matic	Std.	Opt.	Traction-Lok	Std.	Opt.	Traction-Lok	Std.	Opt.	Traction-Lok
250 CID 1V Six Std.	Std.	N/A	Opt.	3.00	N/A	3.00	N/A	N/A	N/A	2.79	3.00*	2.79 3.00*
302 CID 2V (1) V-8 Opt.	Std.	N/A	Opt.	3.00*	N/A	3.00*	N/A	N/A	N/A	2.79	3.00*	2.79 3.00*
351 CID 2V V-8 Opt.	N/A	N/A	Opt. (2)	N/A	N/A	N/A	N/A	N/A	N/A	2.75*	3.25*	2.75* 3.25*
351 CID 2V w/Ram Air Opt.	N/A	N/A	Opt. (2)	N/A	N/A	N/A	N/A	N/A	N/A	3.25*	N/A	3.25*
351 CID 4V V-8 Opt.	N/A	Opt.	Opt.	N/A	N/A	N/A	3.50	3.25*	3.50 3.25*	3.25*	3.50	3.25* 3.50

(1) Standard on Mach 1
(2) Required option
*Mandatory ratio with air conditioning
N/A—Not Available

SUSPENSION: The 1973 Mustang suspension system is basically identical to the 1971-72 suspension. However, the '73 front suspension is improved by providing an additional ¼ inch in travel and longer shock absorbers for a smoother ride.

OTHER MECHANICAL COMPONENTS

BRAKES: The Mustang braking system was improved in 1973. Larger front and rear drums are incorporated on standard hardtops and SportsRoofs, and power front disc brakes are standard equipment with the convertible.

FUEL TANK: Fuel capacity was lowered in 1973, from 20 gallons to 19.5.

MACH 1

The 1973 Mach 1 SportsRoof features a new look with restyled tape stripes on the body side and rear deck. The 302 2-barrel engine remains as the standard powerplant, and both 351s, 2-barrel and 4-barrel, are extra cost options.

EXTERIOR:

- Hood - The 302-equipped Mach 1 hood is the standard Mustang version, but the non-functional NASA scoop hood was available at no extra cost. With either 351 engine, the NASA hood is standard equipment.
- Honeycomb grille - with small Mustang running horse/tri-color bar and blacked-out headlight bezels.
- Side stripes - New-for-'73 Mach 1 side stripes extend from the forward edge of the front fender to the rear quarter panel wheelwell. A concentric pin stripe encircles the wide stripe. "MACH 1" is cut out of the stripe on the rear quarter panel, and the MUSTANG script lettering continues on the front fender, within the stripe.
- Flat brushed aluminum hub caps with bright trim rings.
- Black honeycomb rear panel

RAM INDUCTION

The dual Ram Induction NASA scooped hood was available only with the 351 2-barrel engine. The option includes functional scoops (with a special under-hood chamber that directs cold outside air into the carburetor air cleaner - a valve in each scoop is operated by engine vacuum; at low speeds when engine vacuum is high, the valve remains shut; at full throttle, the engine vacuum drops and the valve opens, allowing cooler air to enter the carburetor), black or argent tu-tone hood paint, twist-type hood locks, and "351 Ram Air" decal on the outboard side of each scoop.

POWER ASSISTS

- Power front disc brakes - required at extra cost with 351 engines; standard on convertibles.
- Power side windows - includes new-for-'73 wood-grained control panels mounted on the door panels and rear quarter trim. The driver's master control panel contains 5 switches - one for each window and a window lock. A single switch is supplied for the other window locations. SportsRoofs rear quarter windows become retractible with the power window option.
- Power steering.

SPECIAL/HEAVY DUTY OPTIONAL EQUIPMENT

- Optional axle ratio.
- Traction-Lok differential.
- Extra cooling package - standard with air conditioning, not available with the 250 6-cylinder.
- Heavy-Duty battery - 70 ampere.

COMPETITION SUSPENSION

- Extra heavy duty front and rear springs.
- Extra heavy duty front and rear shock absorbers.
- Staggered rear shock and rear stabilizer bar - 351 4-barrel engine only.

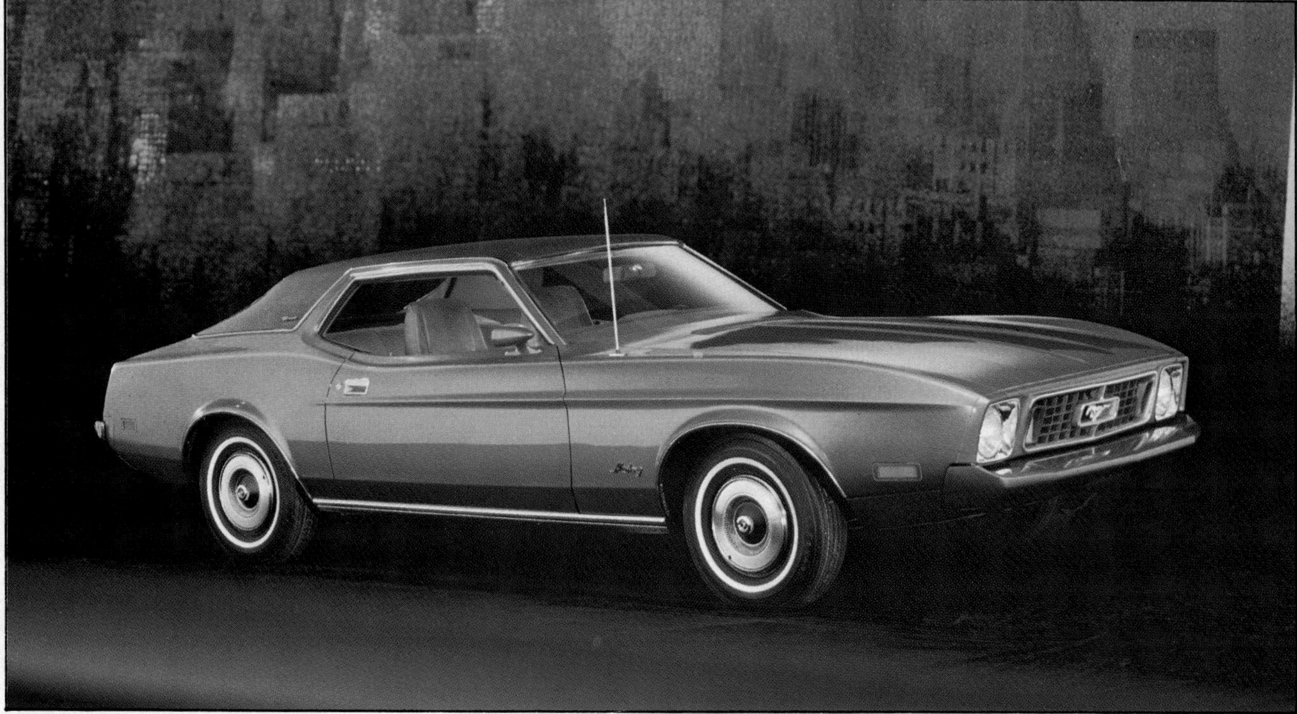

appliques - with bright trim.
- Rear deck lid stripe - with "MACH 1" positioned at the right side of the deck lid.
- Color-keyed dual racing mirrors.
- Chrome exhaust extensions - round exhaust pipes that fit below cut outs in the rear valance panel (351 4-barrel only).

INTERIOR:

Unless optionally ordered with the Mach 1 Sports Interior, the 1973 Mach 1 is standardly equipped with the base Mustang interior trim. A "MACH 1" identification plaque replaces the "MUSTANG" emblem on the center instrument panel.

The Competition Suspension is standard equipment with the Mach 1 package.

GRANDE

The 1973 Grande continues as the luxury model of the Mustang hardtop. It features all of the standard hardtop components, plus extras like vinyl roof, molded door panels, and Deluxe wheel covers.

EXTERIOR:

- Full vinyl roof - either black, white, blue, avocado, ginger, or brown with bright moldings and "GRANDE" script lettering on the "C" pillar.
- Color-keyed dual racing mirrors.
- Deluxe wheel covers.
- Dual-tone accent stripe on bodyside - identical to the 1972 Grande.

INTERIOR:

- Deluxe interior panel appliques - black on the driver and passenger side panels; wood-grained on the center instrument panel.
- Molded door panels - with wood-grain insert.
- Deluxe cloth seat inserts - front and rear.
- Electric clock - mounted in the large left-hand instrument panel pod.
- Rear ash tray - in the right rear quarter trim.
- Bright metal trim on pedal pads.
- "GRANDE" identification emblem on the center instrument panel.
- Trunk mat.

VEHICLE IDENTIFICATION

1964½-1973 MUSTANG IDENTIFICATION, WARRANTY PLATES, CERTIFICATION LABELS, AND SHELBY SERIAL NUMBERS

Mustangs have an eleven character identification number stamped in several locations on the car's chassis and body platform. For official vehicle identification, including title and registration purposes, the number is in one specific location each year. For the 1964½ through 1967 model years, the VIN (vehicle identification number) is stamped on the top upper flange of the left front fender apron. In 1968 only, it is stamped on an aluminum tab riveted to the instrument panel close to the windshield on the passenger side of the car, visible through the windshield, from the outside. In 1969 and subsequent years, the aluminum tab was logically relocated to the driver's side — still riveted to the instrument panel — and visible from the outside, through the windshield.

For the years 1964½-1969, a reverse-stamped Warranty Plate is riveted to the rear face of the driver's side door. At the point of original sale, a similar plate affixed to an owner's card was issued to the purchaser. In 1970 and subsequent years, the Warranty Plate was discontinued and a Vehicle Certification Label is used. This is a reverse printed, opaqued, clear vinyl label instead of the former metal plate.

The VIN also appears on the Warranty Plate, as well as the Vehicle Certification Label, but clearly states "Not For Title or Registration". The VIN is a composite alpha-numeric code for the model year, assembly plant, body serial or sales code #, engine, and consecutive unit number.
Additional coded information contained on the plate or label — depending on model year — includes body type, exterior color, interior trim, manufacture date, district code, axle and transmission codes.

1965 through 1967 Shelbys were manufactured at Ford's San Jose, California plant, with final assembly at Shelby American factory in Los Angeles. 1968 Shelbys were manufactured in Metuchen, New Jersey, with final assembly in Ionia, Michigan, by the A.O. Smith Company. Complete manufacture and assembly of 1969 Shelbys was at Ford's Dearborn, Michigan assembly plant. 1970 Shelbys are simply left over '69 models which received minor cosmetic changes and had the first digit of their VIN changed from "9" to "0".

1965 through 1967 Shelby Mustangs have a serial number tag riveted atop the Ford VIN on the driver's side inner fender panel. In 1968 the Shelby serial number was a combination Ford VIN/Shelby serial number. The Shelby number is again riveted into the cutout area in the inner fender panel on a metal plate. The Ford VIN appears in the normal windshield position.

1965 through 1967 Shelby Mustangs did not receive warranty plates, but do have two holes punched in the rear of the driver's door, although never utilized by Shelby. The '68 Shelby got a regular warranty plate affixed to it's door for vehicle equipment data, but included "SPECIAL PERFORMANCE VEHICLE" stamped onto it, indicating a limited warranty was in effect. In 1969, the special Shelby serial plate no longer appears on the car's inner left fender and the cars are identified in the same method as other Mustangs. A special plate, however, was pop riveted just beneath the warranty plate, which read, "SHELBY AUTOMOTIVE".

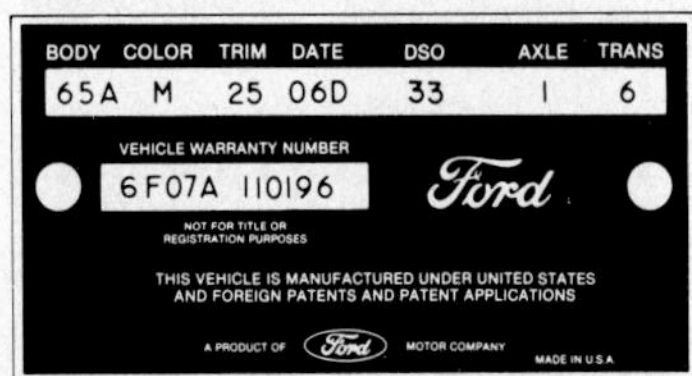

Typical Mustang warranty or patent plate.

Typical Shelby serial number plate.

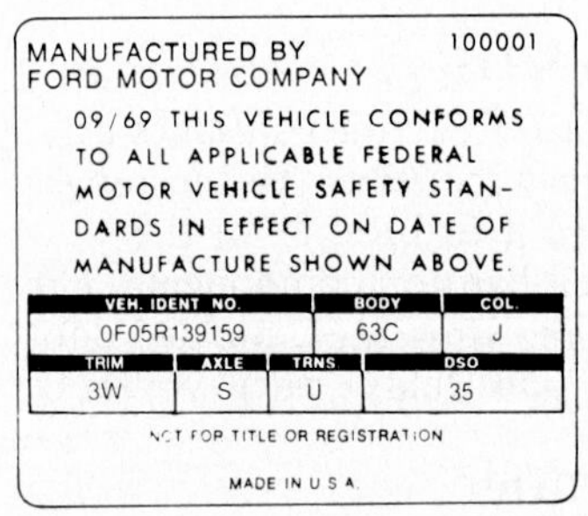

Typical Mustang certification label.

FORD VIN BREAKDOWN

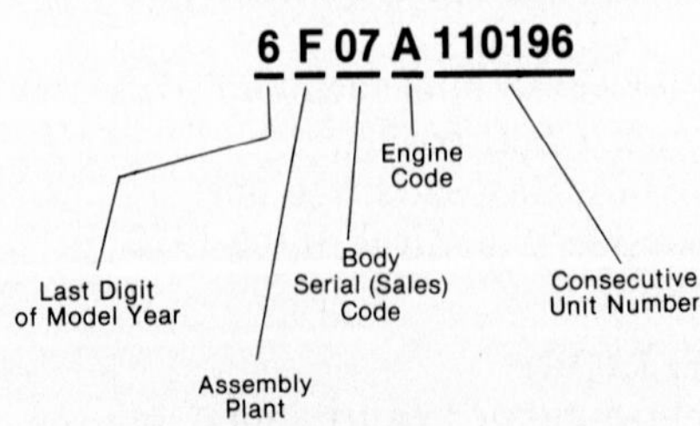

ASSEMBLY PLANT CODES (Mustang and Shelby)

F	Dearborn, Mich.
R	San Jose, Ca.
T	Metuchen, N.J.

BODY SERIAL OR SALES CODE BY BODY TYPE

CODE	1964½ —1966	1967 —1968	1969 —1973
01		Hardtop	Hardtop
02		Fastback	SportsRoof
03		Convertible	Convertible
04			Grande
05			Mach 1
07	Hardtop		
08	Convertible		
09	Fastback		

1964½-1973 ENGINE CODES, INCLUDING SHELBY

CODE	1964½	1965	1966	1967	1968	1969	1970	1971	1972	1973
A		289-4V	289-4V	289-4V						
C		289-2V	289-2V	289-2V	289-2V			429-4V[5]		
D	289-4V low comp.									
F	260-2V				302-2V	302-2V	302-2V	302-2V	302-2V	302-2V
G						302-4V Boss[4]	302-4V Boss[4]			
H						351-2V	351-2V	351-2V	351-2V Ram Air	351-2V Ram Air
J					302-4V			429-4V[5] Ram Air		
K	289-4V[3] Hi-Perf.	289-4V[3] Hi-Perf.	289-4V[3] Hi-Perf.	289-4V[3] Hi-Perf.						
L						250-1V	250-1V	250-1V	250-1V	250-1V
M						351-4V	351-4V	351-4V		
Q						428-4V	428-4V	351-4V Ram Air	351-4V	351-4V
R					428-4V[1] Ram-Air	428-4V Ram Air	428-4V Ram Air	351-4V Boss[4]	351-4V HO[6]	
S				390-4V	390-4V 428-4V[2]	390-4V				
T		200-1V	200-1V	200-1V	200-1V	200-1V	200-1V			
U	170-1V									
X										
Y										
Z						429-4V Boss[4]	429-4V Boss[4]			
2				289-4V GT350						
4				428-8V GT500						
W					427-4V[4]					

[1] 1968 "R" Engine is used in '68½ Cobra Jet and GT500KR.
[2] 1968 "S" Engine is 390 in Mustang and 428 in Shelby.
[3] 1964½—1967 "K" Engine has mechanical lifters.
[4] All "BOSS" and "HO" Engines have mechanical lifters.
[5] 1971, 429CJ has hydraulic lifters, SCJ has mechanical lifters.
[6] 1972, 351 HO is like BOSS 351, but has lower compression ratio.

BODYSTYLE CODES BY YEAR

	1965	1966	1967	1968	1969	1970	1971	1972	1973
63A	FB, S/I, Bu/St	FB, S/I, Bu/St	FB, S/I, Bu/St	FB, S/I, Bu/St	SR, S/I, Bu/St	SR, S/I, Bu/St	N/A	N/A	N/A
63B	FB, L/I, Bu/St	FB, L/I, Bu/St	FB, L/I, Bu/St	FB, L/I, Bu/St	SR, L/I, Bu/St	SR, L/I, Bu/St	N/A	N/A	N/A
63C	N/A	N/A	N/A	FB, S/I, Bn/St	Mach 1, * Bu/St	Mach 1, * Bu/St	N/A	N/A	N/A
63D	N/A	N/A	N/A	FB, L/I, Bn/St	N/A	N/A	SR, S/I, Bu/St	SR, S/I, Bu/St	SR, S/I, Bu/St
63R	N/A	N/A	N/A	N/A	N/A	N/A	Mach 1, , Bu/St	Mach 1, , Bu/St	Mach 1, , Bu/St
65A	HT, S/I, Bu/St	HT, S/I, Bu/St	HT, S/I, Bu/St	HT, S/I, Bu/St	HT, S/I, Bu/St	HT, S/I, Bu/St	N/A	N/A	N/A
65B	HT, L/I, Bu/St	HT, L/I, Bu/St	HT, L/I, Bu/St	HT, L/I, Bu/St	HT, L/I, Bu/St	HT, L/I, Bu/St	N/A	N/A	N/A
65C	HT, S/I, Bn/St	HT, S/I, Bn/St	HT, S/I, Bn/St	HT, S/I, Bn/St	H/T, S/I, Bn/St	N/A	N/A	N/A	N/A
65D	N/A	N/A	N/A	HT, L/I, Bn/St	HT, L/I, Bn/St	N/A	HT, S/I, Bu/St	HT, S/I, Bu/St	HT, S/I, Bu/St
65E	N/A	N/A	N/A	N/A	Grande, * Bu/St	Grande, * Bu/St	N/A	N/A	N/A
65F	N/A	N/A	N/A	N/A	N/A	N/A	Grande, *, Bu/St	Grande, * Bu/St	Grande, * Bu/St
76A	CV, S/I, Bu/St	CV, S/I, Bu/St	CV, S/I, Bu/St	CV, S/I, Bu/St	CV, S/I, Bu/St	CV, S/I, Bu/St	N/A	N/A	N/A
76B	CV, L/I, Bu/St	CV, L/I, Bu/St	CV, L/I, Bu/St	CV, L/I, Bu/St	CV, L/I, Bu/St	CV, L/I, Bu/St	N/A	N/A	N/A
76C	CV, S/I, Bn/St	CV, S/I, Bn/St	CV, S/I, Bn/St	N/A	N/A	N/A	N/A	N/A	N/A
76D	N/A	N/A	N/A	N/A	N/A	N/A	CV, S/I, Bu/St	CV, S/I, Bu/St	CV, S/I, Bu/St

Abbreviations: HT = Hardtop
FB = Fastback
CV = Convertible
SR = SportsRoof

S/I = Standard Interior
L/I = Luxury Interior
Bu/St = Bucket Seats
Bn/St = Bench Seat

N/A = Not Available

* Interior unique to this model only

1964½-1973 INTERIOR TRIM CODES

1964½ Interior Trim

CODE	TRIM SCHEMES
42	White Vinyl w/Blue Appt.
45	White Vinyl w/Red Appt.
46	White Vinyl w/Black Appt.
48	White Vinyl w/Ivy Gold Appt.
49	White Vinyl w/Palmino Appt.
56	Black Vinyl & Cloth
82	Blue Vinyl w/Blue Appt.
85	Red Vinyl w/Red Appt.
86	Black Vinyl w/Black Appt.
89	Palomino Vinyl w/Palomino Appt.

1965 Interior Trim

CODE	TRIM SCHEMES
22	Blue Vinyl w/Blue Appt.
25	Red Vinyl w/Red Appt.
26	Black Vinyl w/Black Appt.
26	Ivy Gold w/Gold Appt.
29	Palomino Vinyl w/Palmino Appt.
D2	White w/Blue Appt.
D5	White w/Red Appt.
D6	White w/Black Appt.
D8	White w/Ivy Gold Appt.
D9	White w/Palomino Appt.
62	Blue and White Luxury
65	Red Luxury
66	Black Luxury
67	Aqua and White Luxury
68	Ivy Gold and White Luxury
69	Palomino Luxury
F2	White w/Blue Appt. Luxury
F5	White w/Red Appt. Luxury
F6	White w/Black Appt. Luxury
F7	White w/Aqua Appt. Luxury
F8	White w/Ivy Gold Appt. Luxury
F9	White w/Palomino Appt. Luxury
32	Blue Bench
35	Red Bench
36	Black Bench
39	Palomino Bench
76	Black Fabric and Vinyl
79	Palomino Fabric and Vinyl

1966 Interior Trim

CODE	TRIM SCHEMES
22	Blue w/Blue Appt.
25	Dk. Red w/Red Appt.
26	Black w/Blk. Appt.
27	Aqua w/Aqua Appt.
D2	Parchment w/Blue Appt.
D3	Parchment w/Burgundy Appt.
D4	Parchment w/Emberglo Appt.
D6	Parchment w/Blk. Appt.
D7	Parchment w/Aqua Appt.
D8	Parchment w/Ivy Gold Appt.
D9	Parchment w/Palomino Appt.
62	Blue & White Lux. Int.
64	Emberglo & Parchment Lux. Int.
65	Red Lux. Int.
66	Black Lux. Int.
67	Aqua & White Lux. Int.
68	Ivy Gold & White Lux. Int.
F2	Parchment w/Blue Appt. Lux. Int.
F3	Parchment w/Burgundy Appt. Lux. Int.
F4	Parchment w/Emberglo Appt. Lux. Int.
F6	Parchment w/Blk. Appt. Lux. Int.
F7	Parchment w/Aqua Appt. Lux. Int.
F8	Parchment w/Ivy Gold Appt. Lux. Int.
F9	Parchment w/Palomino Appt. Lux. Int.
32	Blue Bench
35	Red Bench
36	Black Bench
C2	Parchment w/Blue Appt. Bench
C3	Parchment w/Burgundy Appt. Bench
C4	Parchment w/Emberglo Appt. Bench
C6	Parchment w/Black Appt. Bench
C7	Parchment w/Aqua Appt. Bench
C8	Parchment w/Ivy Gold Appt. Bench
C9	Parchment w/Palomino Appt. Bench

1967 Interior Trim Codes

CODE	TRIM SCHEMES
2A	Black, Std. Buckets
2B	Blue, Std. Buckets
2D	Red, Std. Buckets
2F	Saddle Std. Buckets
2G	Ivy Gold, Std. Buckets
2K	Aqua, Std. Buckets
2U	Parchment, Std. Buckets
6A	Black, Luxury Buckets
6B	Blue, Luxury Buckets
6D	Red, Luxury Buckets
6F	Saddle, Luxury Buckets
6G	Ivy Gold, Luxury Buckets
6K	Aqua, Luxury Buckets
6U	Parchment, Luxury Buckets
4A	Black, Bench Seat
4U	Parchment, Bench Seat
7A	Black, Comfortweave Bkt.
7U	Parchment, Comfortweave Bkt.
5A	Black, Luxury Comfortweave
5U	Parchment, Luxury Comfortweave

1968 Interior Trim Codes

CODE	TRIM SCHEMES
2A, 6A*	Black, All Vinyl Buckets
2B, 6B*	Blue, All Vinyl Buckets
2D, 6D*	Dk. Red, All Vinyl Buckets
2F, 6F*	Saddle, All Vinyl Buckets
2G, 6G*	Ivy Gold, All Vinyl Buckets
2K, 6K*	Aqua, All Vinyl Buckets
2U, 6U*	Parchment, All Vinyl Buckets
2Y, 6Y*	Nugget Gold, All Vinyl Buckets
8A, 9A*	Black, Comfortweave Bench
8B, 9B*	Blue, Comfortweave Bench
8D, 9D*	Dk. Red, Comfortweave Bench
8U, 9U*	Parchment, Comfortweave Bench
7A, 5A*	Black, Comfortweave Buckets
7B, 5B*	Blue, Comfortweave Buckets
7D, 5D*	Dk. Red, Comfortweave Buckets
8U, 5U*	Parchment, Comfortweave Buckets

*Used w/Decor Group

1969 Interior Trim Codes

CODE	TRIM SCHEMES
2A	Black, Vinyl Buckets
2B	Blue, Vinyl Buckets
2D	Red, Vinyl Buckets
2G	Ivy Gold, Vinyl Buckets
2Y	Nugget Gold, Vinyl Buckets
4A, DA*	Black, Com'weave Hi-Buckets
4D, DD*	Red, Com'weave Hi-Buckets
DW*	White, Com'weave Hi-Buckets
5A	Black, Com'weave Luxury
5B	Blue, Com'weave Luxury
5D	Red, Com'weave Luxury
5G	Ivy Gold, Com'weave Luxury
5W	White, Com'weave Luxury
5Y	Nugget Gold, Com'weave Luxury
8A, 9A*	Black, Com'weave Bench
8B, 9B*	Blue, Com'weave Bench
8D, 9D*	Red, Com'weave Bench
8Y, 9Y*	Nugget Gold, Com'weave Bench
7A	Black
7B	Blue, Conv. Deluxe Buckets
7D	Red, Conv. Deluxe Buckets
7G	Ivy Gold, Conv. Deluxe Buckets
7W	White, Conv. Deluxe Buckets
7Y	Nugget Gold, Conv. Deluxe Buckets
1A	Black, Luxury Cloth & Vinyl
1B	Blue, Luxury Cloth & Vinyl
1G	Ivy Gold, Luxury Cloth & Vinyl
1Y	Nugget Gold, Luxury Cloth & Vinyl
3A	Black, Mach 1 Knitted Vinyl
3D	Red, Mach 1 Knitted Vinyl
3W	White, Mach 1 Knitted Vinyl

*Interior Decor Group

1970 Interior Trim Codes

CODE	TRIM SCHEMES
BA	Black, All Vinyl
BB	Blue, All Vinyl
BE	Vermillion, All Vinyl
BF	Ginger, All Vinyl
BG	Ivy, All Vinyl
BW	White, All Vinyl
EA	Black, Com'weave Vinyl
EB	Blue, Com'weave Vinyl
EG	Ivy, Com'weave Vinyl
EW	White, Com'weave Vinyl
TA	Black, Com'weave Vinyl
TB	Blue, Com'weave Vinyl
TG	Ivy, Com'weave Vinyl
TW	White, Com'weave Vinyl
UE	Vermillion, Blazer Stripe Cloth
UF	Ginger, Blazer Stripe Cloth
CE	Vermillion, Blazer Stripe Cloth
CF	Ginger, Blazer Stripe Cloth
AA	Black, Houndstooth Cloth & Vinyl
AB	Blue, Houndstooth Cloth & Vinyl
AE	Vermillion, Houndstooth Cloth & Vinyl
AF	Ginger, Houndstooth Cloth & Vinyl
AG	Ivy, Houndstooth Cloth & Vinyl
3A	Black, Mach 1 Knitted Vinyl
3B	Blue, Mach 1 Knitted Vinyl
3G	Ivy, Mach 1 Knitted Vinyl
3W	White, Mach 1 Knitted Vinyl
3E	Vermillion, Mach 1 Knitted Vinyl
3F	Ginger, Mach 1 Knitted Vinyl

1971 Interior Trim Codes

CODE	TRIM SCHEMES
1A	Black, All Vinyl
1B	Med. Blue, All Vinyl
1E	Vermillion, All Vinyl
1F	Med. Ginger, All Vinyl
1R	Med. Green, All Vinyl
1W	White, All Vinyl
3A	Black, Knitted Vinyl
3W	White, Knitted Vinyl
2E	Vermillion, Cloth & Vinyl
2F	Med. Ginger, Cloth & Vinyl
2B	Med. Blue, Cloth & Vinyl
2R	Med. Green, Cloth & Vinyl
5A	Black, Knitted Vinyl
5W	White, Knitted Vinyl
5E	Vermillion, Knitted Vinyl
5B	Med. Blue, Knitted Vinyl
5R	Med. Green, Knitted Vinyl
5F	Med. Ginger, Knitted Vinyl
CA	Black, Knitted Vinyl
CW	White, Knitted Vinyl
CE	Vermillion, Knitted Vinyl
CB	Med. Blue, Knitted Vinyl
CR	Med. Green, Knitted Vinyl
CF	Med. Ginger, Knitted Vinyl
4A	Black, Cloth & Vinyl
4B	Med. Blue, Cloth & Vinyl
4E	Vermillion, Cloth & Vinyl
4F	Med. Ginger, Cloth & Vinyl
4R	Med. Green, Cloth & Vinyl

1972 Interior Trim Codes

CODE	TRIM SCHEMES
4F	Med. Ginger, Cloth & Vinyl
4E	Vermillion, Cloth & Vinyl
4B	Med. Blue, Cloth & Vinyl
4R	Med. Green Cloth & Vinyl
4A	Black, Cloth & Vinyl
5B	Med. Blue, Knitted Vinyl
5A	Black, Knitted Vinyl
5E	Vermillion, Knitted Vinyl
5W	White, Knitted Vinyl
5R	Med. Green, Knitted Vinyl
5F	Med. Ginger, Knitted Vinyl
1E	Vermillion, All Vinyl
1W	White, All Vinyl
1A	Black, All Vinyl
1B	Med. Blue, All Vinyl
1R	Med. Green, All Vinyl
1F	Med. Ginger, All Vinyl
2E	Vermillion, Cloth & Vinyl
2F	Med. Ginger, Cloth & Vinyl
2B	Med. Blue, Cloth & Vinyl
2R	Med. Green, Cloth & Vinyl
CA	Black, Knitted Vinyl
CW	White, Knitted Vinyl
CE	Vermillion, Knitted Vinyl
CB	Med. Blue, Knitted Vinyl
CR	Med. Green, Knitted Vinyl
CF	Med. Ginger, Knitted Vinyl

1973 Interior Trim Codes

CODE	TRIM SCHEME
AA	Black, All Vinyl
AB	Med. Blue, All Vinyl
AF	Med. Ginger, All Vinyl
AG	Avocado, All Vinyl
AW	White, All Vinyl
CA	Black, Knitted Vinyl
CB	Med. Blue, Knitted Vinyl
CF	Med. Ginger, Knitted Vinyl
CG	Avocado, Knitted Vinyl
CW	White, Knitted Vinyl
FA	Black, Cloth & Vinyl
FB	Med. Blue, Cloth & Vinyl
FF	Med. Ginger, Cloth & Vinyl
FG	Avocado, Cloth & Vinyl
GA	Black, Mach 1, Knitted Vinyl
GB	Med. Blue, Mach 1, Knitted Vinyl
GF	Med. Ginger, Mach 1, Knitted Vinyl
GG	Avocado, Mach 1, Knitted Vinyl
GW	White, Mach 1, Knitted Vinyl

MONTH	CODE 1st Year	CODE 2nd Year
January	A	N
February	B	P
March	C	Q
April	D	R
May	E	S
June	F	T
July	G	U
August	H	V
September	J	W
October	K	X
November	L	Y
December	M	Z

DATE CODE: 1st two digits are the day of the month in which car was assembled. Letter denotes month in which car was assembled. For production year over 12 months, refer to 2nd year column. ie: 1964-65.

TRANSMISSION CODES

CODE	1965	1966	1967	1968	1969	1970	1971	1972	1973
1	3-Spd. Man.	3-Spd. Man.	3-Spd. Man.	3-Spd. Man	3-Spd. Man.	3-Spd. Man.	3-Spd. Man.	3-Spd. Man.	3-Spd. Man.
3			3-Spd. Man.						
5	4-Spd. Man.	4-Spd. Man.	4-Spd. Man.	4-Spd. Man.	4-Spd. Man.	4-Spd. Man.	4-Spd. Man.	4-Spd. Man.	4-Spd. Man.
6	C-4 Atm.	C-4 Atm.			4-Spd. Man.*	4-Spd. Man.*	4-Spd. Man.*		
E								4-Spd. Man.	4-Spd. Man.
U			C-6 Atm.	C-6 Atm.	C-6 Atm.	C-6 Atm.	C-6 Atm.	C-6 Atm.	C-6 Atm.
W			C-4 Atm.	C-4 Atm.	C-4 Atm.	C-4 Atm.	C-4 Atm.	C-4 Atm.	C-4 Atm.
X					FMX Atm.	FMX Atm.	FMX Atm.	FMX Atm.	FMX Atm.

* Denotes close-ratio

REAR AXLE RATIO CODE

CODE	1965	1966	1967	1968	1969	1970	1971	1972	1973
1	3.00:1	3.00:1	3.00:1	2.75:1	2.50:1				
2		2.83:1	2.83:1	2.79:1	2.75:1	2.75:1	2.75:1	2.75:1	2.75:1
3	3.20:1	3.20:1	3.20:1		2.79:1	2.79:1	2.79:1	2.79:1	2.79:1
4	3.25:1	3.25:1	3.25:1	2.83:1	2.80:1	2.80:1	2.80:1	2.80:1	
5	3.50:1	3.50:1	3.50:1	3.00:1	2.83:1	2.83:1			
6	2.80:1	2.80:1	2.80:1	3.20:1	3.00:1	3.00:1	3.00:1	3.00:1	3.00:1
7	3.80:1			3.25:1	3.10:1	3.10:1			3.40:1
8	3.89:1	3.89:1		3.50:1	3.20:1	3.20:1		3.18:1	
9	4.11:1			3.10:1	3.25:1	3.25:1	3.25:1	3.25:1	3.25:1
A	3.00:1*	3.00:1*	3.00:1*		3.50:1	3.50:1	3.50:1	3.50:1	3.50:1
B					3.07:1	3.07:1	3.07:1	3.07:1	
C	3.20:1*	3.20:1*	3.20:1*		3.08:1	3.08:1		3.55:1	
D	3.25:1*	3.25:1*	3.25:1*		3.91:1				
E	3.50:1*	3.50:1*	3.50:1*	3.00:1*	4.30:1				
F	2.80:1*	2.80:1*		3.20:1*		2.33:1			
G	3.80:1*			3.25:1*					3.55:1
H	3.89:1*	3.89:1*		3.50:1*				3.78:1	
I	4.11:1*								
J					2.50:1*				
K					2.75:1*	2.75:1*	2.75:1*	2.75:1*	2.75:1*
L		2.83:1*			2.79:1*				2.79:1*
M					2.80:1*	2.80:1*	2.80:1*	2.80:1*	
N					2.83:1*				
O or Ø					3.00:1*	3.00:1*	3.00:1*	3.00:1*	3.00:1*
P					3.10:1*				
Q					3.20:1*				
R					3.25:1*	3.25:1*	3.25:1*	3.25:1*	3.25:1*
S					3.50:1*	3.50:1*	3.50:1*	3.50:1*	3.50:1*
T					3.07:1*				
U					3.08:1*				
V					3.91:1*	3.91:1*	3.91:1*	3.91:1*	3.91:1*
W					4.30:1*	4.30:1*			
X						2.33:1*			
Y							4.11:1*		

*Denotes locking differential

CONSECUTIVE UNIT NUMBER

Each model year, each assembly plant began production with the number 100,001 for the models listed at right. Consecutive numbering continued for models listed in these categories, regardless of model or type, throughout the production.

MODELS CONSECUTIVELY NUMBERED TOGETHER:

1965-1968	1969	1970	1971	1972-1973
Falcon	Ford	Ford	Ford	Ford
Fairlane	Fairlane	Falcon	Torino	Torino
Mustang	Falcon	Fairlane	Maverick	Maverick
	Mustang	Mustang	Mustang	Mustang
	T-Bird	T-Bird	T-Bird	T-Bird
		Maverick		Pinto

1964½-1973 MUSTANG EXTERIOR PAINT CODES

	1964½	1965	1966	1967	1968	1969	1970	1971	1972	1973
A or 9A	Raven Black	Raven Black	Raven Black	Raven Black	Raven Black	Raven Black	Raven Black	Raven Black	Wimbledon White	Wimbledon White
B or 2B	Pagoda Green	Midnight Turquoise	——	Frost Turquoise	Royal Maroon	Royal Maroon	——	Maroon Metallic	Bright Red	Bright Red
C or 6C	——	Honey Gold	——	——	——	Black Jade	Dk. Ivy Green Met.	Dk. Ivy Green Met.	Med. Yellow Gold	Medium Yellow Gold
D or 3D	Dynasty Green	Dynasty Green	——	Acapulco Blue	Acapulco Blue	Acapulco Blue	Yellow	Grabber Yellow	——	Med. Blue Metallic
E or 4E	——	——	——	——	——	Aztec Aqua	——	Yellow Gold	Bright Lime	——
F or 3F	Guardsman Blue	——	Light Blue	Arcadian Blue	Gulfstream Aqua	Gulfstream Aqua	——	——	Grabber Blue	——
G	——	——	——	——	——	——	Med. Lime Metallic	——	——	——
H or 5H	Caspian Blue	Caspian Blue	Sahara Beige	Diamond Green	——	——	——	——	Med. Brown Metallic	Med. Brown Metallic
I	——	Champagne Beige	——	Lime Gold	Lime Gold	Lime Gold	——	Grabber Lime	——	——
J, 3J, J9	Rangoon Red	Rangoon Red	——	——	——	——	Grabber Blue	Grabber Blue	Brt. Blue Metallic	——
K or 3K	Silversmoke Gray	Silversmoke Gray	Nightmist Blue	Nightmist Blue	——	——	Bright Gold Metallic	——	——	Blue Glow
L	——	——	——	——	——	——	——	——	——	——
M or 5M	Wimbledon White	Wimbledon White	Wimbledon White	Wimbledon White	Wimbledon White	Wimbledon White	Wimbledon White	Wimbledon White	——	Medium Copper Met.
N or 4N	——	——	——	Diamond Blue	Diamond Blue	——	Pastel Blue	Pastel Blue	——	Medium Aqua
O	——	Tropical Turquoise	——	——	Seafoam Green	——	——	——	——	——
P or 4P	Prairie Bronze	Prairie Bronze	Antique Bronze	——	——	Winter Blue	——	Med. Green Metallic	Med. Green Metallic	Med. Green Metallic
Q or 4Q	——	——	Brittany Blue	Brittany Blue	Brittany Blue	——	Med. Blue Metallic	——	Dark Green Metallic	Dark Green Metallic
R	——	Ivy Green	Dark Green Metallic	——	Highland Green	——	——	——	——	——
S	Cascade Green	——	——	Dusk Rose	——	Champagne Gold	Med. Gold Metallic	——	——	——
T or 5T	——	——	Candyapple Red	Candyapple Red	Candyapple Red	Candyapple Red	Red	——	——	Saddle Bronze Met.
U or U9	——	——	Tahoe Turquoise	——	Tahoe Turquoise	——	Grabber Orange	——	——	——
V	Sunlight Yellow	Sunlight Yellow	Emberglo	Burnt Amber	——	——	——	Light Pewter Met.	——	——
W	——	——	——	Clearwater Aqua	Meadowlark Yellow	Meadowlark Yellow	——	——	——	——
X	Vintage Burgundy	Vintage Burgundy	Vintage Burgundy	Vintage Burgundy	Presidential Blue	——	——	——	——	——
Y	Skylight Blue	Silver Blue	Silver Blue	Dark Moss Green	Sunlit Gold	Indian Fire	——	——	——	——
Z or Z9	Chantilly Beige	——	Med. Sage Metallic	Sauterne Gold	——	——	Grabber Green	Grabber Green	——	——
1	——	——	——	——	——	——	Calypso Coral	——	——	——
2 or 2J	——	——	——	——	——	Lime	Light Ivy Yellow	——	Maroon	——
3 or 3B	Poppy Red	Poppy Red	——	——	——	Calypso Coral	——	Bright Red	Light Blue	Light Blue
4 or 4F	——	——	Silver Frost	Silver Frost	——	Silver Jade	——	——	Med. Lime Metallic	——
5 or 5A	Twilight Turquoise	——	Signalflare Red	——	——	——	——	Medium Brown Met.	Lt. Pewter Metallic	——
6 or 6E	——	——	——	Pebble Beige	Pebble Beige	Pastel Gray	Silver Blue Metallic	Silver Blue Metallic	Med. Bright Yellow	Med. Bright Yellow
7	Phoenician Yellow	——	——	——	——	——	——	——	——	——
8	——	Springtime Yellow	Springtime Yellow	Springtime Yellow	——	——	——	Light Gold	——	——
SPECIAL	——	——	Med. Palomino Metallic	Playboy Pink	——	——	——	Gold Metallic	6F Gold Glow	4C Ivy Glow
SPECIAL	——	——	Med. Silver Metallic	Anniversary Gold	——	——	——	Gold Glamour	4C Ivy Glow	Brt. Green Gold Met. 4B
SPECIAL	——	——	Ivy Green Metallic	Columbine Blue	——	——	——	——	——	6F Gold Glow
SPECIAL	——	——	Tahoe Turq. Metallic	Aspen Gold	——	——	——	——	——	——
SPECIAL	——	——	Maroon Metallic	Blue Bonnet	——	——	——	——	——	——
SPECIAL	——	——	Silver Blue Metallic	Timberline Green	——	——	——	——	——	——
SPECIAL	——	——	Sauterne Gold Met.	Lavender	——	——	——	——	——	——
SPECIAL	——	——	Light Beige	Bright Red	——	——	——	——	——	——

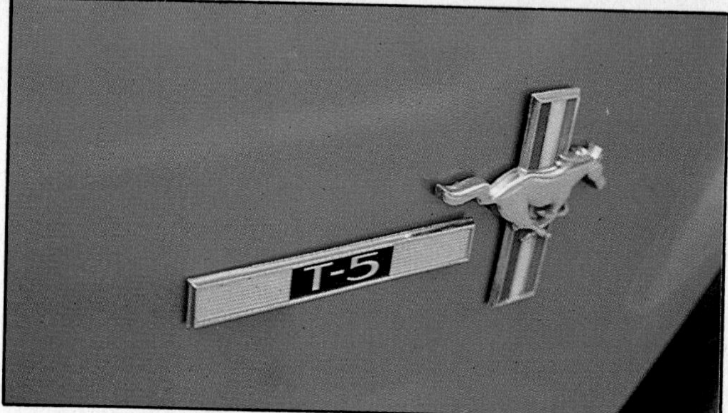

1966 T-5. Mustangs destined for export to Germany were given a T-5 designation because the word "Mustang" was already copyrighted in that country. The "Mustang" nomenclature is eliminated completely, and T-5 emblems placed on the fenders. All T-5s received the DSO number 95.

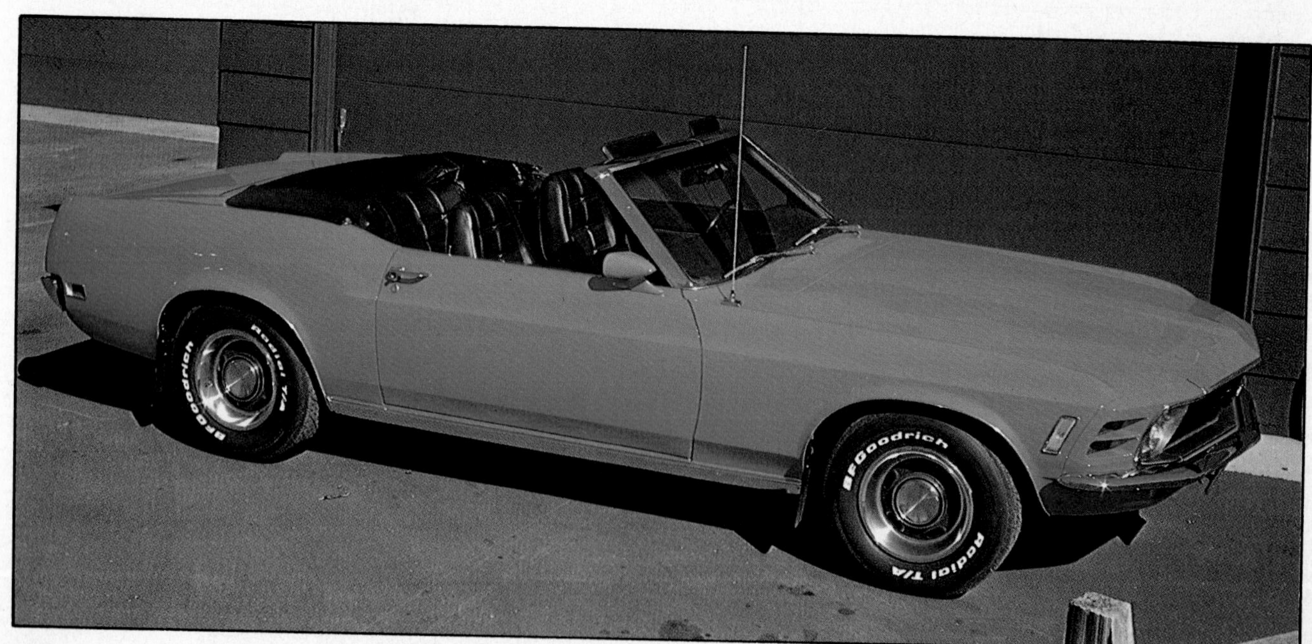

1970 Mustang Convertible

(DSO) DISTRICT CODE

A two digit code number for the district which ordered the car. Foreign Special Orders will have a complete order number in this space.

DISTRICT	1964 thru 1966	1967 thru 1968	1969 thru 1971	1972	1973
Boston	11	→	→	→	→
Buffalo	12	37	→	→	12
New York	13	→	→	→	→
Pittsburgh	14	38	→	→	14
Newark	15	→	→	→	→
Atlanta	21	→	→	→	→
Charlotte	22	→	→	→	→
Philadelphia	23	16	→	→	→
Jacksonville	24	→	→	→	→
Richmond	25	→	→	→	→
Washington	26	17	→	→	→
Cincinnati	31	27	47	→	→
Cleveland	32	→	→	42	→
Detroit	33	→	→	48	→
Indianapolis	34	→	46	→	→
Lansing	35	→	→	45	→
Louisville	36	28	→	→	→
Chicago	41	→	→	→	→
Fargo	42	→	→	→	→
Rockford	43	→	→	→	→
Twin Cities	44	→	→	58	→
Davenport	45	→	56	→	→
Denver	51	→	→	76	→
Des Moines	52	→	→	→	→
Kansas City	53	→	→	→	→
Omaha	54	→	→	→	→
St. Louis	55	→	→	→	→
Dallas	61	→	→	52	→
Houston	62	→	→	57	→
Memphis	63	→	→	23	→
New Orleans	64	→	→	26	→
Oklahoma City	65	→	→	→	→
Los Angeles	71	→	→	→	→
San Jose	72	→	→	→	→
Salt Lake City	73	→	→	→	→
Seattle	74	→	→	→	→
Milwaukee	––	43	→	→	→
Phoenix	––	75	→	→	→
Body Company	––	––	87	→	→
Ford Of Canada	81	→	→	→	→
Government	83	→	→	→	→
Home Office Reserve	84	→	→	→	→
American Red Cross	85	→	→	→	→
Transportation Services	89	→	→	→	→
Export	90-99	→	→	→	→

1965-1970 SHELBY SERIAL # VIN BREAKDOWN*

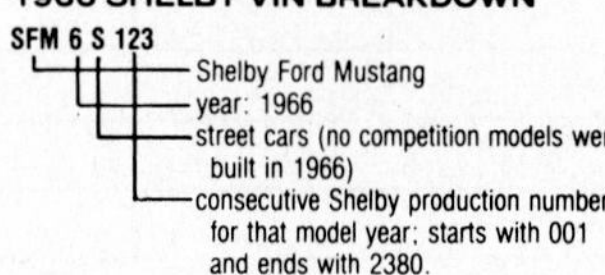

1966 SHELBY VIN BREAKDOWN

SFM 6 S 123
- Shelby Ford Mustang
- year: 1966
- street cars (no competition models were built in 1966)
- consecutive Shelby production number for that model year; starts with 001 and ends with 2380.

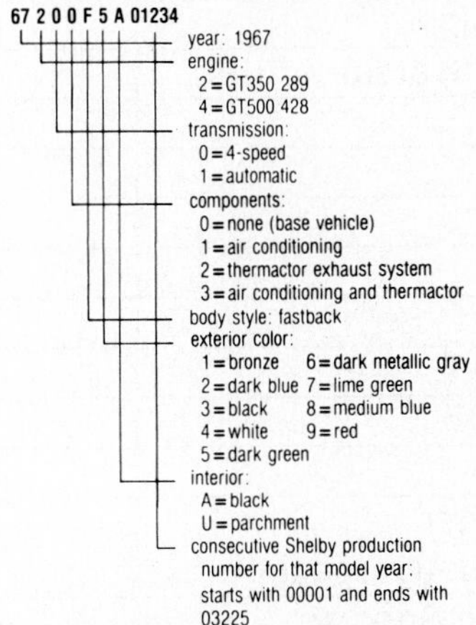

1968 SHELBY VIN BREAKDOWN

8 T 02 J 123456-00001
- same as Ford VIN
- consecutive number of Shelby production; begins with 00001 and ends with 04450.

1969-1970 FORD/SHELBY VIN BREAKDOWN

9 F 02 R 48 0123
- year: 1969
- Ford assembly plant: F=Dearborn, Michigan (all 1969 Shelbys were built in Dearborn)
- body style: 02=fastback; 03=convertible
- engine: M=351 (GT350)
  R=428 CJ (GT500)
- 48=Shelby code (all '69-'70 Shelbys carried this "48" and no other Mustangs did; a car must have this number to be a Shelby)
- consecutive production number; begins with 0001; last car produced has not been established at this time, is currently thought to be around 3300.

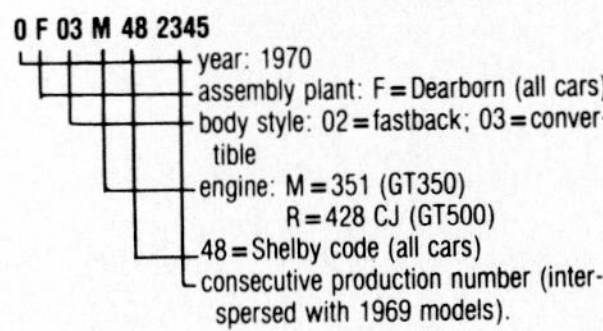

*All above VIN information taken from the "SHELBY BUYER'S GUIDE" written by Richard J. Kopec.

INDEX TO CATEGORIES BY MODEL YEAR

	CATEGORY BEGINS ON PAGE NUMBER LISTED BELOW FOR MODEL YEAR INDICATED								
CATEGORY	**'64½ '65**	**'66**	**'67**	**'68**	**'69**	**'70**	**'71**	**'72**	**'73**
Introduction	14	62	88	110	134	162	184	202	208
Bodystyles	20	63	89	111	135	163	185	203	209
Exterior	22	65	90	112	136	164	186	204	209
Interior	31	71	96	118	141	167	191	204	212
Trunk	29	70	103	124	149	172	196		215
Wheels	46	78	103	126	150	172	196		215
Tires	46	78	103	126	150	172	196		215
Wheel Covers	46	78	103	126	150	173	196		215
Powerteams	50	80	104	127	151	173	197	204	215
Suspension	47	79	104	127	152	175	197		216
Cooling System	48	79	105	128	152	175	197		
Exhaust	48	79	106	128	152	175			
Brakes	49	82	105	128	152	175			216
GT	54	82	94	116	140				
Shelby	60	84	107	131	159	183			
T-5		83							
Mustang E					158				
Sprint 200		83							
Pace Car	18								
Pace Setter			106						
High Country Special				131					
California Special				129					
Mustang Sprint				129				207	
Mach 1					154	176	198	206	216
Grande					153	178	200	207	217
Cobra Jet				128					
Boss 302					156	180			
Boss 429					157	182			
Boss 351							201		
Grabber						183			
Sports Hardtop							199		

Mustang 1 - the first Ford to ever carry the Mustang name. Although only a styling prototype, the Mustang 1's acceptance by the American motoring public secured Ford Motor Company's interest in producing what has become "the most recognized car of the post war era".